STRENGTH

FOR EACH DAY

365 Devotions to Make *Every* Day a *Great* Day

JOYCE MEYER

New York • Nashville

FaithWords

Hachette Book Group

1290 Avenue of the Americas, New York, NY 10104

faithwords.com

twitter.com/faithwords

First Edition: October 2021

FaithWords is a division of Hachette Book Group, Inc.

The FaithWords name and logo are trademarks of Hachette Book Group, Inc.

The publisher is not responsible for websites (or their content) that are not owned by the publisher.

The Hachette Speakers Bureau provides a wide range of authors for speaking events. To find out more, go to www.hachettespeakersbureau.com or call (866) 376-6591.

Unless otherwise noted, Scripture quotations marked NIV are taken from the Holy Bible, New International Version®, NIV®. Copyright ©1973, 1978, 1984, 2011 by Biblica, Inc.™ Used by permission of Zondervan. All rights reserved worldwide. www.zondervan.com The "NIV" and "New International Version" are trademarks registered in the United States Patent and Trademark Office by Biblica, Inc.™ | Scripture quotations are taken from the Amplified® Bible, Copyright © 2015 by The Lockman Foundation. Used by permission. www.Lockman.org. | Scripture quotations marked AMPC are taken from the Amplified® Bible, Copyright © 1954, 1958, 1962, 1964, 1965, 1987 by The Lockman Foundation. Used by permission. www.Lockman.org. | Scripture quotations marked NKJV are taken from the New King James Version®. Copyright © 1982 by Thomas Nelson. Used by permission. All rights reserved.

ISBNs: 978-1-5460-2645-7 (paper over board), 978-1-5460-0065-5 (large print), 978-1-5460-2644-0 (ebook)

Printed in the United States of America

LSC

Printing 2, 2022

INTRODUCTION

We need strength for each day in many different areas of our lives. We need physical strength, emotional and mental strength, and, most importantly, spiritual strength. Jesus is our strength, and we can receive as much of His strength as we need each day by spending time with Him, studying His Word, and asking Him to give us what we need.

I look at the devotions in this book like little bursts of energy. They are not long, but they are powerful because they are filled with God's Word. Read and meditate on one each morning and keep the book handy so you can read one anytime you want or need to be strengthened and encouraged.

Read them slowly, really think about what you read, and consider how you can apply it to your life. You will reap a harvest of spiritual growth and understanding as you sow thought and study into the truth you read (Mark 4:24 AMPC).

No matter how young or how strong we are, we are still limited in what we can do or handle, but God is unlimited. As we wait on Him, we renew our strength, and He enables us to do anything we need to do.

WHEN YOU NEED STRENGTH

But they who wait for the Lord shall renew their strength; they shall mount up with wings like eagles; they shall run and not be weary; they shall walk and not faint. —ISAIAH 40:31 ESV

If you drove your car daily and never stopped to refill the gas tank, you would soon be stranded on the highway with a problem you could have avoided. You might even end up needing to push your car to the side of the road. We can consider this example in deciding how to run our lives. Isaiah says, "Even youths shall faint and be weary" (Isaiah 40:30 ESV). At times, we all grow tired and feel that we can't go on. The weariness may be mental, emotional, or physical, but we can avoid it by learning to spend regular time with God and allowing Him to refuel and refresh us. I recommend spending this kind of time with Him daily, and I believe that even more than once a day is advisable.

Don't wait until you are out of fuel and stranded on the highway of life before you go to God for help. He is always available and always happy to spend time with you. Many people ask what they should do when they spend time with God, but I think that simply setting aside time to be with Him is more important than how you spend the time. You may pray (talk to God and listen to Him). You might also study the Bible, listen to music that builds you up spiritually, read a book written by a good Bible teacher, or simply sit in God's presence and enjoy Him. When you do any of these things, He will strengthen you.

Just as you pay attention to the gas gauge in your car and are careful to get gas before the tank is empty, pay attention to the signs that you are growing weary. Do something before you feel completely drained instead of pushing yourself too hard day in and day out, trying to meet life's demands. Be wise and refuel regularly!

"Father, I am sorry for those times when I try to do things on my own without coming to You to obtain Your strength. Help me to always put You first. In Jesus' name, I ask this. Amen."

PRIORITIES

He also is the Head of [His] body, the church; seeing He is the Beginning, the Firstborn from among the dead, so that He alone in everything and in every respect might occupy the chief place [stand first and be preeminent]. —COLOSSIANS 1:18 AMPC

The beginning of a new year is always a good time to examine our priorities and make sure that Jesus is first in our lives. We may need to reevaluate our priorities several times throughout the year, but we can begin by making sure today that unimportant things have not crept into our lives and pushed Jesus out of first place.

Sometimes we feel weak instead of strong because we are unhappy and frustrated, and we don't even know why. We often feel this way because our priorities are out of order. Anyone can make this mistake, so there is no need to feel condemned about it if it has happened in your life, but there is a need to make a change. Ask God to show you anything you need to see in this area and, with His help, make any adjustments that you need to make.

"Lord, I want You to be first in my life. Please show me any area in which my priorities are out of order. Show me anything that needs to be eliminated or relegated to a place of lesser importance so You and You alone can occupy first place in my life. Amen."

POSITIVE PEOPLE FEEL STRONG

Be transformed (changed) by the [entire] renewal of your mind [by its new ideals and its new attitude]. –ROMANS 12:2 AMPC

Have you noticed that the more positive you are, the stronger you feel? Think about it. When you are negative, you feel gloomy and weak. This is why the enemy puts negative thoughts into our minds. He wants us weak, not strong. If he sees that we agree with the thoughts he whispers to us and that we allow them to influence our emotions, he continues his lies. The more we believe them, the weaker we become.

You can choose today to resist negative thoughts and to think positively instead through renewing your mind according to God's Word. The more positive your attitude is, the stronger you feel. As a follower of Jesus Christ, you have every reason to be positive today. You can be sure that God loves you, that He fights your battles for you, that He has a good plan for your life, and that He is with you in everything you do (Exodus 14:14; Deuteronomy 20:4; Jeremiah 29:11; 31:3; Ephesians 1:7–9).

"Father, help me to resist the enemy's attempts to reinforce negative thinking in my mind. I want to be transformed by the renewal of my mind, according to Your Word, and walk in the strength that comes from being positive. In Jesus' name. Amen."

LIVE WELL

If we live, we live to the Lord, and if we die, we die to the Lord. So then, whether we live or we die, we belong to the Lord.

—ROMANS 14:8 AMPC

My aunt died recently at the age of ninety. Situations such as this always remind me of how transitory life is and of the profound reality that each of us has only one life to live. My aunt lived a long life, but the length of our lives is not nearly as important as how well we live. Each day that goes by is one we can never get back, so we should live it with purpose, making sure that whatever we spend our time on is worth it.

Let me ask you: Are you leaving a legacy that you can be proud of? I urge you to enjoy your life, to live for God's honor and glory, and to make sure that, during your earthly journey, you live in such a way that you feel good about the way you have lived and that you will be missed when your life is complete.

"Lord, thank You for the life You have given me. I recognize that it is a precious gift and should not be wasted. Help me live well for Your glory. Each day that I live, let me be a benefit to others. Thank You. In Jesus' name. Amen."

INCREASE

For whatever a man sows, that and that only is what he will reap.

—GALATIANS 6:7 AMPC

Most of us get excited about the thought of increase in our lives, but we would do well to remember that God's Word says that we reap only according to what we have sown. If we want to receive more, we need to give more. Giving is the source of true joy. Nothing makes us happier than being a blessing to someone else.

I believe God wants me to challenge you to make a decision to give more this year than ever before. Give to His kingdom work, give to the poor and needy, and give to those who are less fortunate than you are. Even if you can only increase your giving a small amount, I urge you to do so in faith and expect greater increase in your own life. It is impossible to outgive God! He is the very essence of generosity, and He delights in the prosperity (the well-being) of His children (Psalm 35:27). When we give more, we reap more, and then we can continue being a blessing each time we see a need.

I am challenging you to join me in taking every opportunity you can find to be a greater blessing everywhere you go.

"Father, thank You for giving Jesus to us. Let Your Spirit of generosity dwell in me and grant me the grace to give more and more. Thank You. In Jesus' name. Amen."

BEGIN AGAIN

Therefore, if anyone is in Christ, he is a new creation. The old has passed away; behold, the new has come. −2 CORINTHIANS 5:17 ESV

The promise of new beginnings is abundantly clear in Scripture. The good news is not only that this promise provides benefits to new believers in Christ, but that it is available to us as often as we need it. The one requirement for its fulfillment is that we let go of failure and take hold of the new beginning God offers us.

I have needed to apply this promise to my own life recently. I believe God has asked me to do something, and although I agree with Him and get started well, I seem to eventually fail, and then I need to start over again. My two choices are to feel guilty because of my failure or to begin again. I choose to begin again, and if you need a new beginning, I pray that you will do likewise.

No matter how you need a new beginning in some area of your life, Jesus has His arms outstretched and is waiting for you to let Him help you begin again.

"Father, thank You for new beginnings. Help me let go of the old and start fresh without feelings of guilt and failure. In Jesus' name. Amen."

CONFIDENCE THAT SETS YOU APART

Hezekiah trusted in, leaned on, and was confident in the Lord, the God of Israel; so that neither after him nor before him was any one of all the kings of Judah like him. —2 KINGS 18:5 AMPC

According to today's scripture, Hezekiah "trusted in, leaned on, and was confident in the Lord." The verse goes on to say that this is what set Hezekiah apart from all the other kings of Judah. Let me ask you today: What sets you apart from the people around you? When they think of you, do they immediately understand that you trust in, lean on, and are confident in the Lord?

I don't think we can overemphasize how important our confidence in the Lord is. To be confident in Him is to place the full weight of our belief in Him, never doubting that He will come through for us.

Our confidence in the Lord is what enables us to trust in and lean on Him. It's interesting to me that the Amplified Bible, Classic Edition version of this verse says that Hezekiah "leaned on" the Lord. The only reason we would lean on something would be because we believe it will support us. We wouldn't lean on it if we thought it would collapse under our weight. We will only lean on something we trust. And we will only trust something or someone in whom we have confidence.

The Lord will never fail you or forsake you if you place your trust in Him (Deuteronomy 31:8).

"Father, I choose today to trust in, lean on, and place all my confidence in You alone. In Jesus' name. Amen."

THE STORMS OF LIFE

I can do all this through him who gives me strength.

—PHILIPPIANS 4:13

Not all storms are in the weather forecast. Some storms of life surprise us when we don't expect them. When this happens, our first thought may be, *Oh no, not another problem. I don't think I can deal with this.* However, we should be careful not to allow our wrong thinking to defeat us. God's Word teaches us that we can do all things through Jesus, who is our strength (Philippians 4:13).

Paul experienced times of plenty and times of lack, but he learned to be content, regardless of his circumstances (Philippians 4:11–12). His contentment came from trusting God completely in all situations.

You are stronger than you think you are, and you can deal with more than you think you can handle. If you take life one day at a time and continue drawing strength from Jesus, you really can do anything you need to do.

None of us knows what a day may hold, but we can be confident that because God helps us, we will be strong and victorious.

"Father, I want to be content in every circumstance, and I want to have the confidence that I can do all things through Christ, who is my strength. Help me realize that You are greater than any problem I may have. In Jesus' name. Amen."

FOR SUCH A TIME AS THIS

Yet who knows whether you have come to the kingdom for such a time as this? —ESTHER 4:14 NKJV

I doubt that Queen Esther, as a young orphan girl, had any idea that she would eventually become the wife of a king and that God would use her to save an entire nation. She probably never dreamed she would one day be considered one of the strongest women in biblical history. What was the source of Esther's strength? Her faith in God.

When an evil man threatened to annihilate the Jewish people, Esther intervened, asking her husband, the king, to spare them. Approaching the king without an invitation was very brave of Esther, and it went against the custom of her day. Her risk came with a great reward, as the king received her warmly and granted her request.

We see from today's scripture that Esther understood that saving her people was part of the reason she had become the king's wife. When you find yourself in an unlikely or challenging situation, remember Esther and realize that being there may be part of God's plan for your life. The source of your strength, like Esther's, is in your faith in God.

"Father, I am available to You, and I want to serve You with all my heart. Use me today. In Jesus' name. Amen."

PLEASING GOD

That you may walk (live and conduct yourselves) in a manner worthy of the Lord, fully pleasing to Him and desiring to please Him in all things. —COLOSSIANS 1:10 AMPC

Let's ask ourselves today if we desire to please God or if we desire for God to please us. I think most of us would say that we would like to have both, but what if that is not possible? What if the things that would please me do not please God? Am I willing to give up something in order to please Him? Jesus said it best in the Garden of Gethsemane when He asked the cup of suffering to be taken from Him, but quickly added, "Nevertheless not My will, but Yours, be done." (Luke 22:42 NKJV).

I recommend asking God for anything you want, because He invites us to come boldly to His throne of grace (Hebrews 4:16). But in addition to making those bold requests, I also recommend that you ask the Lord not to give you anything you ask for unless it pleases Him. The truth is that no matter what we have, it is impossible to be satisfied and content unless having it is within God's will for our lives.

"Father, I want to please You in all things. I ask You to guide me in such a way that I will do that. Pleasing You is my main desire, and should I drift away from that goal, I ask that You always bring me back to it. In Jesus' name. Amen."

EXAMINE YOURSELF

Why do you stare from without at the very small particle that is in your brother's eye but do not become aware of and consider the beam of timber that is in your own eye? –MATTHEW 7:3 AMPC

If the devil can keep us occupied finding fault with others, he will be successful in preventing us from seeing and dealing with our own faults. The Bible never tells us to examine others, but it does tell us to examine ourselves (Lamentations 3:40). We should not examine ourselves to the point of condemnation, nor should we be excessively introspective, but properly examining ourselves does help us not to be too quick to find fault with others.

Let us be merciful to those around us, because when we sow mercy, we will reap mercy. I think mercy is something we all need in great measure. God is merciful, and in representing Him, we should strive to be the same way.

Is there someone in your life to whom you need to extend mercy today? If so, why not do it now? If you do, I can promise you that a burden will lift off of your heart.

"Father, please help me be merciful at all times and to always remember that when I observe a speck in my brother's eye, I probably have a beam of timber in my own."

CONSISTENT JOY

Go and enjoy choice food and sweet drinks, and send some to those who have nothing prepared. This day is holy to our Lord. Do not grieve, for the joy of the Lord is your strength. –NEHEMIAH 8:10

I recently spoke with a neurosurgeon who specializes in the spine and brain. He conducts many studies on the brain and how different factors affect it. He said that researchers have learned that when we give to others, the area of the brain that releases joy lights up during a scan or an imaging procedure. I know from experience that giving makes me happy and being selfish makes me unhappy.

In our scripture for today, Nehemiah and his people were told to celebrate because they had just successfully completed the task that God had given them to do—rebuilding the walls of Jerusalem. Not only were they to celebrate with good food and drink, but they were also instructed to send provisions to people who had none. I think part of celebrating our victories should always include giving to those in need. It is truly more blessed to give than to receive (Acts 20:35).

Nehemiah told the people not to grieve, because the joy of the Lord was their strength. We can all find reasons to be sad and unhappy when we look at what we don't have or when we focus on seemingly negative things that happen to us. We can also find reasons to rejoice by looking at what God has already done for us and celebrating the victories we have enjoyed in the past, while expecting more victory in the future. Don't let the devil steal your joy, because it is more important to you than you may think. Joy keeps you strong, and we all need strength.

"Father, I ask that You help me choose joy in every situation. In Jesus' name. Amen."

YOU ARE NOT YOUR OWN

Do you not know that your body is the temple (the very sanctuary) of the Holy Spirit Who lives within you, Whom you have received [as a Gift] from God? You are not your own.

—1 CORINTHIANS 6:19 AMPC

Most of us wake up each day assuming that our lives belong to us and therefore we can do as we please, but the truth is the exact opposite. We are not our own, for Jesus purchased us with His own blood and made us His own. We should seek daily to do God's will and to glorify Him in the practical aspects of our lives.

Let each decision you make today be made with the thought that you are not your own and that you need to consider what God would have you do in every situation. Being obedient to God's will is the pathway to an amazing life—a life filled with joy, peace, and every good thing. Make a habit of asking, "What would Jesus do in this situation?" and then follow Him.

"Father, thank You for living in me. Speak clearly to me at all times and show me Your will. Grant me the grace to always follow You and to glorify You in all my ways. Amen."

MAKING PROGRESS

But the path of the [uncompromisingly] just and righteous is like the light of dawn, that shines more and more (brighter and clearer) until [it reaches its full strength and glory in] the perfect day [to be prepared]. —PROVERBS 4:18 AMPC

Wanting to make progress, no matter what we are doing, is built into our nature. This includes wanting to make spiritual progress in becoming progressively more like Jesus. I want to assure you today that if you are studying God's Word and spending time with Him, you are growing. Sometimes growth is imperceptible because it occurs a little bit at a time, but it is definitely taking place.

Satan wants to discourage you by having you look at how far you have to go, but God wants to encourage you today by letting you know that you are changing a little bit at a time. As you continue to be diligent, you will reach a point in the future when you will be amazed at what God has done in you. Enjoy where you are today!

"Father, thank You for changing me daily, little by little, into Your image. My desire is to get as close to You as I can, and I trust that You are working in me. Thank You. In Jesus' name. Amen."

GOD IS FAITHFUL

But the Lord is faithful, and he will strengthen you and protect you from the evil one. –2 THESSALONIANS 3:3

We have an enemy who continually seeks to steal, kill, and destroy us (John 10:10), and his name is Satan. But God has promised to protect us from the enemy if we put our trust in Him. We can only overcome fear with faith, so I remind you today to put your faith in God, claiming today's scripture for yourself, and believing that God will always strengthen you and protect you from Satan.

God is faithful, and He always does what He promises to do. He cannot lie, and He cannot fail us. All He needs in order to work mightily in our lives is our faith. He wants us to believe Him and enter His rest while He fights our battles for us.

What battle are you fighting right now? Don't make the mistake of trying to fight it alone. God is with you, and He will help you by giving you the strength you need to stand strong while He works in your life and in your situation.

"Father, I know that You are faithful. I repent for doubting You and choose to trust You in every situation in my life. In Jesus' name. Amen."

KEEP YOUR EYES ON GOD

We do not know what to do, but our eyes are on you.

—2 CHRONICLES 20:12

How many times a week do you think, *I just don't know what to do.* At times we find ourselves not knowing what to do in minor situations—such as having a meeting canceled and getting an unexpected afternoon of free time. At other times, we agonize over not knowing what to do regarding an important decision, such as whether or not to make a long-distance move, whether or not to enter into a marriage or start a family, or whether or not to take a big risk by investing all of our money to start a new business.

Jesus says in John 15:5 that apart from Him, we can do nothing. He wants to be involved in every area of our lives, and He is eager to help us in every circumstance. He has every answer we need—even answers we could never think of on our own—and He will give it to us if we ask Him for it.

Today, whether you are facing a significant, weighty situation or something more minor, if you don't know what to do, my advice is the same: Tell God you don't know what to do, but that you will keep your eyes on Him because you know He does have the answer and will guide you.

"Father, when I do not know what to do, help me keep my eyes on You. In Jesus' name. Amen."

ENJOY THE JOURNEY

The thief comes only in order to steal and kill and destroy. I came that they may have and enjoy life, and have it in abundance (to the full, till it overflows). —JOHN 10:10 AMPC

Jesus came to earth so we could enjoy our lives, but it will never happen unless we realize that life is a journey that involves many different ingredients, including a lot of waiting. Most of us just want to get to our desired destination or reach our goal, but actually, the joy is in the journey. When we do reach our destination, the journey is over, and before long we want another challenge.

Everything in the earthly realm operates according to the law of gradual growth. Most things grow so slowly that the natural eye cannot even see it happening. Think of a tree. It is growing all the time, but we cannot see it grow.

God could have arranged for everything to happen very fast, but He didn't. I think this is because we can only appreciate what we have to wait for. The anticipation of the good things to come is part of what makes them exciting. I urge you today to make a decision to stop being in such a hurry and simply enjoy your journey.

"Father, help me realize that my times are in Your hands, and to trust that Your timing is perfect. I ask this in Jesus' name. Amen."

GOD HEARS AND ANSWERS PRAYER

Ask and it will be given to you; seek and you will find; knock and the door will be opened to you. –MATTHEW 7:7

The devil wants us to believe that God neither hears nor answers our prayers, but this is not true. You may think He hears and answers other people but not you, because you have too many faults. However, God's Word reminds us of Elijah, who sinned just as we do, calling him "a human being with a nature such as we have…and he prayed earnestly for it not to rain, and no rain fell on the earth for three years and six months" (James 5:17 AMPC).

God has especially designed prayer for people who need His help. But if we do not believe that He hears and answers us, and if we do not ask Him for what we need in faith, we will not have it (James 1:6–8). We are invited to pray on every occasion, with all kinds of prayers and requests (Philippians 4:6).

You can never pray too often or ask God for too much. God delights in our dependence upon Him. When we pray, if we believe we will receive, we will have what God has planned for us (Mark 11:24). We may not get it immediately, because there is typically a waiting period between our asking and receiving. This is a time when our faith is being tested, but let me encourage you not to give up during those times, because your answer is on its way. Come boldly to the throne of God and receive the help you need anytime you need it (Hebrews 4:16).

"Father, I want to have a powerful prayer life. I ask You to help me trade worry and anxiety for faith and trust in You, that You're working on my behalf. In Jesus' name. Amen."

HOLD ON!

A stone was brought and placed over the mouth of the den, and the king sealed it with his own signet ring and with the rings of his nobles, so that Daniel's situation might not be changed. –DANIEL 6:17

Harriet Beecher Stowe said, "When you get into a tight place and everything goes against you until it seems that you cannot hold on for a minute longer, never give up then, for that is just the place and time when the tide will turn."

Are you in that kind of place today, a place that feels tight to you, where you think everything is going against you? Some days are like that, and they are times when you simply need to stand firm in faith and hold on just a minute longer.

Several people in the Bible found themselves up against very difficult circumstances that tried their faith. One of those people was Daniel. To say that he felt everything was against him in the lions' den would be a huge understatement. He found himself all alone in a dark pit full of hungry lions. Without a miracle (which did happen), he knew he would be killed in a very painful way.

God knows exactly how much pressure you can take and how much struggle you can bear. In a difficult situation, He is always with you. He will eventually deliver you, but until He does, you can be confident that He will not leave you alone in your circumstances. Use your difficulty to your advantage, and ask God to strengthen you as you wait for Him to move mightily on your behalf.

"Father, when I am in a tight place, give me grace and strength to hold on a minute longer and not to give up. Amen."

SEEING THE EXTRAORDINARY
IN THE ORDINARY

For You are great and work wonders! You alone are God.

—PSALM 86:10 AMPC

To a small child, everything is amazing. But as we grow older, we lose sight of the wonder all around us. I would like to suggest that we recapture the wonder of everyday life. Life is never merely ordinary when we live it with God. He is always doing amazing things, and we simply need to take the time to look for them.

The sun comes up every day, and it is amazingly beautiful, but few of us pay any attention to it. I have four grown children who are all healthy and serving God, and that is amazing. I have been married to Dave for fifty-four years, and—wow—is that ever amazing! We tend to look for things that are extraordinary, but the truth is that amazing wonder is all around us in the things we see and experience each day. Let's learn to see the extraordinary in ordinary, everyday life. I can promise you it is there if you will simply look for it.

"Father, You are truly amazing, and there is nothing mundane or ordinary about living life with You. Help me see all the extraordinary things that fill my life each day and to appreciate them. Thank You. In Jesus' name. Amen."

LIVING LIFE ON PURPOSE

Look carefully then how you walk! Live purposefully and worthily and accurately, not as the unwise and witless, but as wise (sensible, intelligent people). —EPHESIANS 5:15 AMPC

Living life on purpose rather than merely drifting aimlessly through one day after another is very important. We only get one life, and we should make it count. I encourage you to do something each day that adds value to someone else, and your day will be well spent.

We cannot live according to our feelings and behave wisely at the same time. Good choices often have nothing to do with emotions, so we need to learn to live beyond them. Enjoy the good feelings when they are present, but don't let not having them control you. Live life on purpose.

Begin each day thinking about what you believe would be good choices to make, and don't let yourself be distracted by useless things that steal your time and produce no good fruit.

"Father, I am sorry for the time I have wasted in my life. Beginning today I want to live my life on purpose, according to Your will. Help me. Thank You. In Jesus' name. Amen."

WHERE DO WE FIND STRENGTH?

God is our refuge and strength, an ever-present help in trouble.

—PSALM 46:1

I love that God is ever-present. There is never a time when He is not with us, but we may miss out on the help He is ready to give us by forgetting about Him and trying to do things in our own strength. He wants us to lean and rely on Him. Leaning on God for absolutely everything is not an indication of weakness; it's actually a sign of wisdom.

Jesus says that apart from Him we can do nothing (John 15:5). We may do things, but we will struggle and be frustrated because nothing works with ease unless we invite Jesus to be involved in it. What are you trying to do on your own that is frustrating you? Whatever it is, stop. Then tell the Lord you are sorry for leaving Him out of it, and ask Him to take the lead in your situation and give you the grace to follow Him.

I have tried many things on my own, such as changing myself, changing my husband, and changing my children. I saw their flaws and wanted to correct them, but only God can change a human heart. I also tried in my own strength to make my ministry grow, but that ended in misery too. I have learned to ask God for what I need and lean on Him to bring it to pass. Anytime I forget about this, before long

I find myself struggling again trying to do it myself. Let go and let God show His strength through you.

"Father, I am grateful for Your strength. I need You in everything I do, and I'm sorry for the times I have left You out and tried to do things on my own. My strength is not enough. I need Yours. In Jesus' name. Amen."

ARE YOU USABLE?

But we have this treasure in jars of clay to show that this all-surpassing power is from God and not from us. –2 CORINTHIANS 4:7

Have you ever dropped a clay flowerpot, or kicked one on your patio accidentally and cracked it? If so, you know that clay pots are very fragile. When Paul writes that we have a treasure "in jars of clay," he is pointing out the fact that human beings have weaknesses and flaws. We are like cracked pots. God created us this way on purpose, so that people will see His power in our lives. They know there are certain things we could never do in our own strength, and when God does them, they realize He is working. God works through our weaknesses and shows His strength.

If you were to put a lamp inside of a clay pot and then cover the pot with a lid, no one would even know the light was in the pot. But if the pot had cracks in it, slivers of light would shine through them. The imperfections draw attention to the light. The same principle applies to your life. Whatever your shortcomings may be, realize that God can use them to show others His power and glory.

"Father, help me to realize that although I have imperfections, they are simply opportunities for others to see Your power. In Jesus' name. Amen."

TIME

Making the very most of your time [on earth, recognizing and taking advantage of each opportunity and using it with wisdom and diligence], because the days are [filled with] evil.

—EPHESIANS 5:16 AMP

Our time is very valuable. Once we use it for something, it is gone, and we cannot get it back. Investing our time in worthy pursuits—things we will be satisfied with later in life—is very important. Time is too valuable to waste! If you don't feel that you are using your time in the best way possible, you are the only one who can change that. It helped me a lot when I realized that my time is a gift to me from God and if I don't like what I am doing with it, I need to make changes.

Don't complain about something that only you have the power to change. Never put off until tomorrow what needs to be changed today. Let the Holy Spirit guide you, and take action.

"Father, I want to use wisdom with my time, and I ask You to help me make changes where they are needed. I ask this in Jesus' name. Amen."

MERCY

So be merciful (sympathetic, tender, responsive, and compassionate) even as your Father is [all these]. –LUKE 6:36 AMPC

I have recently been thinking about mercy and how important it is in our lives. God is merciful, and without His mercy, our sins would consume us. Jeremiah writes in Lamentations 3:22–23 that God's mercies are new every morning. If you need mercy, take a moment and receive it right now by faith as a gift from God.

We are to be merciful toward others, just as our Father is merciful toward us. Is there anyone in your life to whom you need to extend mercy? If so, I urge you not to put it off. Anger is a useless emotion that is not the will of God. Its effect on us is not beneficial. In contrast, when we give mercy to others in their failures, we not only help them, but we also help ourselves.

"Father, Your mercy is beautiful, and I am grateful for it. Help me be a merciful person at all times. Thank You. In Jesus' name. Amen."

WHAT YOU SAY MATTERS

Let the weak say, "I am strong." –JOEL 3:10 NKJV

There are two words we need to eliminate from our conversation when talking about our ability: *I can't.* Don't talk yourself into failure before you even try something. Many things look daunting to us, and indeed they would be if we tried to do them without God. But with Him, all things are possible (Matthew 19:26). He gives strength to the weak and weary, and in today's scripture we see that the prophet Joel said, "Let the weak say, 'I am strong.'"

What we say matters, because we can talk ourselves into believing we can do something or believing we can't. Admitting that you can't do something is all right, as long as you add "But God can do it through me." You are not a natural, normal human being; you are filled with God's Spirit. This means you have supernatural ability to do anything God wants you to do.

When you face a challenge and you feel inadequate and weak, instead of verbalizing over and over that you are too weak, say that you are strong by declaring, "I can do all things through Christ who strengthens me" (Philippians 4:13 NKJV). We want to say what God says about us, and He says we are strong.

"Father, I repent for saying that I am weak when You have told me in Your Word that I am strong in You. Therefore, I say in faith, 'I am strong in Christ Jesus!' In Jesus' name. Amen."

DOING THE RIGHT THING
AT THE RIGHT TIME

But be doers of the word, and not hearers only, deceiving your-selves. —JAMES 1:22 ESV

In listening to people tell me of their troubles and miseries, I find that they don't lack knowledge of what to do about their struggles; the problem is that they don't do what they know they need to do. Learning something is always easier than doing it, but knowledge does us no practical good if we do not take action.

The lessons God has taught us always have to be applied, especially when applying them is not easy to do. But when we do the right thing when it is difficult, that's when we mature and grow in our faith. If you have a problem right now, ask yourself what you would tell someone else to do if that person had your same problem. Then take your own advice, and do it yourself. You'll be well on your way to victory.

"Father, thank You for this reminder that I need to be a doer of Your Word, not a hearer only. Help me always be obedient to You. In Jesus' name. Amen."

WALK WITH GOD HABITUALLY

Enoch walked [in habitual fellowship] with God three hundred years after the birth of Methuselah and had other sons and daughters.

—GENESIS 5:22 AMP

The name Enoch may not be as familiar to you as the names of other great men and women of God mentioned in the Old Testament, such as Abraham, Moses, Joseph, Deborah, and Esther. But Enoch had something in common with everyone who has ever accomplished great things for Him. According to the amplification of today's scripture, Genesis 5:22, he had developed the habit of fellowship with God. Genesis 5:24 notes that "[in reverent fear and obedience] Enoch walked with God" (AMP).

At the end of Enoch's life, he did not die a natural death. God transferred him directly to heaven in a supernatural way. This man developed such an intimate relationship with God that this world could no longer hold him.

I cannot overemphasize the importance of living in habitual fellowship (or relationship) with God, spending time in His presence every day. No matter what is on your calendar or your to-do list today, nothing is more important than your personal time with God. If you will make a habit of fellowshipping with Him, as Enoch did, you will be amazed at how wonderful your life will be and how much you will enjoy it.

"Father, I love Your presence. Help me to walk in habitual fellowship with You. In Jesus' name. Amen."

LITTLE BY LITTLE

But if we hope for what is still unseen by us, we wait for it with patience and composure. —ROMANS 8:25 AMPC

As I am writing this, I am healing from a surgery, and the recovery seems very slow. It is challenging because I want to feel great *right now*. But oftentimes, God delivers us little by little, and our job is to learn to wait well and stay positive while we wait. What are you waiting for? Whatever it is, I am sure you would like to see more progress than you are seeing.

I want to encourage you—and myself—that more is happening than we realize. The best way to see our progress is to look at it over a period of time, rather than daily. I am much better than I was four weeks ago, but I can barely tell if I am any better than I was yesterday. God is working in me and in you, and He is faithful, so don't be discouraged. Just keep believing and saying, "God is working."

"Father, thank You for working in me and in my life. Although I cannot always see what You are doing, I know that You are working and that things will turn out well. Thank You. In Jesus' name. Amen."

REMEMBERING

They forgot God their Savior, Who had done such great things in Egypt. —PSALM 106:21 AMPC

The Israelites invited much trouble into their lives by simply forgetting God when their circumstances were prosperous. Calling upon God when we are in need is one thing, while it is quite another to realize that we need Him at all times, whether we are struggling or at ease. One of the best things we can do is take time to remember and thank God for all the great things He has done in our lives.

We often remember what we should forget and forget what we should remember. For example, we should forget the offenses of other people toward us, but we often rehearse them daily and allow them to become etched in our memory. Let us forget those negative situations we have endured and focus on remembering how great our God is—and let's rehearse all of His goodness to us.

"Father, I ask You to forgive me for the times I have forgotten You. You are good, and I give thanks today for Your extreme generosity toward me. In Jesus' name. Amen."

STAYING CALM PROMOTES GOOD HEALTH

A calm and undisturbed mind and heart are the life and health of the body, but envy, jealousy, and wrath are like rottenness of the bones. —PROVERBS 14:30 AMPC

Staying healthy and feeling well physically should be a goal that we not only desire but work toward each day of our lives. We only have one life to live, and living it with energy and strength is very important.

We put tremendous stress on ourselves by allowing negative emotions to drain us of needed energy. I encourage you today to set your mind to stay calm and think about things that add energy rather than diminishing it. If you have anything against anyone, forgive that person and let the offense go. When we forgive, it's like letting someone out of prison, and we quickly find that we are the ones who have been set free.

Don't worry about tomorrow, but instead enjoy today. When tomorrow dawns, you will find the grace to deal with anything that comes with it.

"Father, thank You for reminding me how important it is to stay calm. I put my trust in You, and I ask that You help me not to be upset about anything. I ask this in Jesus' name. Amen."

GRATITUDE IS THE FUEL FOR JOY

Be happy [in your faith] and rejoice and be glad-hearted continually (always); be unceasing in prayer [praying perseveringly]; thank [God] in everything [no matter what the circumstances may be, be thankful and give thanks]. —1 THESSALONIANS 5:16–18 AMPC

Just as the food we eat turns into energy for our bodies, gratitude is the fuel for joy. Ungrateful people only see and focus on what they do not have. Therefore, they are never able to be joyful in what they do have. One of the best habits you can develop is to begin each day with true gratitude. Be specific and thank God and people (when appropriate) for the blessings they provide. What are you thankful for? God tells us to "be thankful and say so" (Psalm 100:4 AMPC).

It is easy to find fault with your place of employment, but why not thank God and your employer for giving you a job instead? It is also easy to find fault with the people in our lives, and most of us are quite willing to voice our feelings. But I have found that my joy increases when I purpose to find the things I appreciate and love about the people in my life and consider the blessings I would miss if those people were not part of my life.

Do you desire greater joy? If so, I encourage you to increase your gratitude, and it will turn into joy.

"Father, I have so much to be thankful for. Help me remember to be grateful and say so to You every single day. In Jesus' name. Amen."

A STRONG TOWER

The name of the Lord is a strong tower; the righteous run to it and are safe. —PROVERBS 18:10 NKJV

Have you ever seen the Leaning Tower of Pisa? It's one of the seven wonders of the medieval world. For centuries, it has leaned to the point that it looks like it will fall over any minute. I can't imagine it would be a place where people would take refuge during times of trouble, because it does not look safe.

If you have ever seen the Tower of London, you know that it appears sturdy and impregnable. In fact, it's not only a strong tower; it's also located within a fortress. The idea that people would flee to that tower for safety seems reasonable.

As believers, we don't need to rely on earthly structures for safety or security. Today's scripture says, "The name of the Lord is a strong tower." When I teach on the name of Jesus, I say that His name represents all that He is. This means that everything God is—all of His attributes, His character, and His power—is a secure place for us. If you are facing trouble or difficulty today, run into His presence. It's the safest place you'll ever find.

"Father, I don't look to anything on earth for safety or security. I look to You alone. In Jesus' name. Amen."

THINKING GODLY THOUGHTS

We lead every thought and purpose away captive into the obedience of Christ (the Messiah, the Anointed one).

—2 CORINTHIANS 10:5 AMPC

Thinking in ways that please God and are acceptable to Him is easier on some days than on others. I remember when I went on a mission trip to Thailand, and the flight from the United States took twenty-three and a half hours. Needless to say, I was tired when we arrived, and I also experienced jet lag for a few days after arriving. The first few hours of the morning seemed to be the most difficult because I woke up at two or three a.m. and was dealing with a lot of negative thoughts during those hours.

When I am tired or I feel bad physically, thinking the way I know God wants me to think is much more difficult for me than when I am rested and feeling strong. During those early-morning hours in Thailand, I thought I never wanted to go on a mission trip again. Thankfully, I changed my mind and went on other trips after this one.

I encourage you to do all you can do to help yourself feel well and strong. Get plenty of rest, and don't try to make difficult decisions when you are really tired. Resting our bodies properly helps us hear from God and be more sensitive to His leading in our thoughts and our behavior.

"Father, I want to think in a way that pleases You at all times, but I need Your help in order to do it. Grant me wisdom to rest properly and keep me in good health. In Jesus' name. Amen."

MAKE AND MAINTAIN PEACE

Blessed [spiritually calm with life-joy in God's favor] are the makers and maintainers of peace, for they will [express His character and] be called the sons of God. —MATTHEW 5:9 AMP

Have you ever known anyone who seems to stir up trouble everywhere they go? A gathering of people can be fairly calm and enjoyable, but when that person arrives, it becomes tense and unpleasant. In contrast, have you ever known someone who can be in the midst of conflict and seem to de-escalate it with just a few words of wisdom, a look, or a steady, quiet demeanor? This is the kind of person today's scripture describes.

Everywhere we look today, we seem to see a lack of peace. In some cases and some places in the world, there is all-out war. In other places, there is unrest. In others, there are disagreements and differences of opinion that make living together or working together uncomfortable. People of peace can go into these circumstances and calm the people involved. They know just how to pray and just what to say to defuse anger. Let me encourage you today: Next time you find yourself in a tense situation, choose not to join in and make it worse. Choose instead to ask God to help you bring and keep peace.

"Father, help me to be a maker and a maintainer of peace everywhere I go. In Jesus' name. Amen."

MENTAL DECEPTION

But [now] I am fearful, lest that even as the serpent beguiled Eve by his cunning, so your minds may be corrupted and seduced from wholehearted and sincere and pure devotion to Christ.

—2 CORINTHIANS 11:3 AMPC

Our thoughts determine our attitudes, words, and actions. Because of that, Satan frequently and relentlessly tries to deceive us by placing ungodly thoughts in our minds. Thinking about Jesus and godly principles as often as possible is wise because that helps us continue the process of renewing our minds. We need to learn to think the way God thinks, which means we think according to His Word.

Constantly refusing wrong thoughts and choosing right ones may seem like a battle, but the reward is well worth it. We all want the blessings of joy and peace of mind, but we will miss out on them if we meditate on every thought that comes to us without examining its source. Be sure you are diligent to do your own thinking, and don't let Satan deceive you with his lies.

"Father, I ask You to help me to resist all wrong thoughts and instead choose to think on the good things that You want me to think about. Thank You. In Jesus' name. Amen."

SIMPLE OBEDIENCE

Now therefore listen to me, O you sons; for blessed (happy, fortunate, to be envied) are those who keep my ways.

—PROVERBS 8:32 AMPC

We could avoid many problems in our lives if we would simply obey God. We may be guilty of blaming people or circumstances for trials and tribulations that are actually rooted in our own disobedience. Certainly, everyone experiences difficulty in life, even people who are very obedient to God. If pursuing a greater lifestyle of obedience would prevent some of our problems, why would we not be wise enough to do so?

We should seek to obey God primarily because we love and honor Him, not merely to avoid trouble. But I think we can enjoy a double benefit by letting His Word guide us in all of our actions. Let's follow Mary's advice to the servants at the wedding at Cana: "Whatever He says to you, do it" (John 2:5 AMPC).

"Father, I am sorry for any disobedience in my life. I repent for it, and I receive Your forgiveness. I also ask that You help me and grant me the wisdom to promptly obey all that You want me to do. In Jesus' name. Amen."

THE LORD IS MY STRENGTH

The Sovereign Lord is my strength; he makes my feet like the feet of a deer, he enables me to tread on the heights. –HABAKKUK 3:19

Deer have the ability to bound over rocky, rugged mountain terrain as though it is flat pastureland. Because of this ability that God has placed in them, they can easily maneuver through what looks to be very dangerous territory. The prophet Habakkuk said that he had that same ability, and so do we.

The example of the deer bounding over dangerous heights is intended to help us understand that in Christ, we too can easily navigate places that would seem insurmountable and dangerous. With God's help, we can handle difficult situations while remaining peaceful.

I encourage you not to fear new experiences or situations that look difficult. Ask for and receive by faith God's strength, believing that you too have the spiritual feet of a deer and can leap over difficult terrain in the circumstances of your life.

"Father, I love You, and I resist fear in Your name. Because of Your Word, I believe I can do difficult things with ease. I ask for Your help, and I rely on You at all times. Thank You. In Jesus' name. Amen."

DON'T LET GO OF GOD

He held fast to the Lord and did not stop following him; he kept the commands the Lord had given Moses. –2 KINGS 18:6

In the Old Testament, a twenty-five-year-old man named Hezekiah became king of Judah. Interestingly, his name means "God has strengthened." He was known as a righteous ruler who followed God faithfully and experienced God's favor. Today's scripture says he "held fast to the Lord." This means that no matter what happened, he refused to let go of God. Nothing could cause him to loosen his grip on God.

God never changes (Hebrews 13:8) or moves away from us. Anytime we feel spiritually dry or distant from the Lord, He is not to blame. We are the ones who have changed. We may have slacked off in our Bible study or our prayer. We may have allowed life's pressures and busyness to cause us to turn our hearts and minds from God onto the situations that compete for our attention.

Remember today that God is always near. To stay spiritually strong, follow Hezekiah's example and hold fast to God, not allowing anyone or anything to cause you to loosen your grip on Him or to stray from His presence.

"Father, I pray that I will be like Hezekiah and hold fast to You. May I follow You in all my ways, all the time. In Jesus' name. Amen."

GAINING WISDOM

Happy (blessed, fortunate, enviable) is the man who finds skillful and godly Wisdom, and the man who gets understanding [drawing it forth from God's Word and life's experiences].

—PROVERBS 3:13 AMPC

God's Word and our experience in life both teach us wisdom. Most of us can look back and readily admit that we have learned a lot about how to live simply by going through various situations and gaining experience. I once believed that what people thought of me was very important, but I now know that it is much more important for God to be pleased with me than for people to be pleased.

You may be going through something right now that is difficult. You may not understand why it is happening to you, but it may be teaching you a valuable lesson and giving you experience for something that will help you in the future. Even though we don't enjoy all of our experiences, we can let them teach us valuable lessons. The Bible says that Jesus gained experience through the things that He suffered and they equipped Him to be the source of our salvation (Hebrews 5:8–9). Let the things you go through in life equip you and give you wisdom for the future.

"Father, in Jesus' name I ask You to help me learn valuable lessons from everything I go through in life, as well as from Your Word. Thank You. In Jesus' name. Amen."

THE SOURCE OF YOUR STRENGTH

So he told her everything. "No razor has ever been used on my head," he said, "because I have been a Nazirite dedicated to God from my mother's womb. If my head were shaved, my strength would leave me, and I would become as weak as any other man."

—JUDGES 16:17

You may remember the Old Testament story of Samson, the Nazirite man who did not cut his hair. Not cutting his hair was part of his Nazirite vow, but it was also the secret of his tremendous physical strength.

Samson led the nation of Israel for twenty years, and his enemies, the Philistines, were curious about the source of his strength. When he fell in love with Delilah, the Philistine leaders said to her, "See if you can lure him into showing you the secret of his great strength and how we can overpower him so we may tie him up and subdue him" (Judges 16:5). Samson refused to tell her his secret many times when she asked him about it, but he ultimately gave in to her. After he told her, she shaved his head, and his strength disappeared.

You also have a source of strength. It's not in your hair or in any earthly belonging or physical or mental trait. It's in Christ alone. When you need strength, don't seek it in any worldly source. Ask God to empower you to do whatever you need to do. He will always come through for you.

"Father, may I always look to You for the strength I need, knowing that I will find everything I need in You. In Jesus' name. Amen."

ENJOY SIMPLE THINGS

This is the day which the Lord has brought about; we will rejoice and be glad in it. –PSALM 118:24 AMPC

Each day that God gives us is precious and should be enjoyed. Jesus came to earth so that we might have life and enjoy our lives (John 10:10 AMPC). Most of life is routine and doesn't consist of especially exciting activities. We go to work, we fulfill our duties at home, we take care of our responsibilities, and we do those things over and over, day in and day out. We don't have to let them become boring and make the mistake of thinking we will enjoy ourselves when we get to do something exciting, such as take a vacation or have a birthday party.

Life can be enjoyed if we learn to enjoy the simple things—the sunrise, taking a walk, eating lunch with a friend, or watching children play. A simple attitude adjustment on our part helps us enjoy each day the Lord gives us, rather than wasting it by wishing we were doing something else. As you go through your day today, purpose to enjoy each thing you do, and live the day in gratitude for all that God has given you.

"Father, I want to enjoy each moment You give me here on earth, and I especially want to learn to enjoy simple, everyday things. Remind me daily of how precious life is, and let me see the value in every little thing I do. In Jesus' name. Amen."

REST YOUR MIND

Lean on, trust in, and be confident in the Lord with all your heart and mind and do not rely on your own insight or understanding.

—PROVERBS 3:5 AMPC

Do you know that you can feel tired and worn-out from thinking too much? Mental tiredness is just as real as physical fatigue. Our minds need to rest, just as our bodies do. God's Word encourages us not to be excessive in reasoning. Thinking about things is good and valuable, but moving into worry, anxiety, or merely relying on our own reasoning will exhaust us.

When I return from a conference where I have been studying and teaching for two or three days, I am tired not only physically but mentally and emotionally as well. I have learned to let my mind rest after working hard and not to try to make important decisions or engage in discussions that require deep thought.

The things that you need to think about will still be around tomorrow, so don't hesitate to take a mental rest when you need one. Instead of trying to solve a problem today, why not have some fun and find something humorous that will give you a good laugh? Giving your mind a break may refresh you more than you think.

"Father, help me get the rest I need in all areas of my life, especially in my mind. I love and appreciate You, Lord. Thank You for all that You do for me. In Jesus' name. Amen."

HOW TO AVOID BEING
DISAPPOINTED BY PEOPLE

But Jesus would not entrust himself to them, for he knew all people. He did not need any testimony about mankind, for he knew what was in each person. —JOHN 2:24-25

I remember a time when I was hurt and disappointed by someone I love, but it was my own fault. It took me a while to realize that, but now I am actually glad I had the experience because it reminded me of something that is important for each of us.

Jesus trusted His disciples, but He did not totally depend on them, nor did He expect them never to let Him down or disappoint Him. He knew they had weaknesses and that it was impossible for them to always be what He needed them to be. Anytime we totally depend on another human being, we put ourselves in a position to be hurt.

Only God can be totally depended on. He alone deserves all of our trust, reliance, and dependence. I love my husband and my children very much, and they are all very good to me, but each of them does disappoint me at times, just as I am sure that I disappoint them.

Let me ask you: What are you expecting from your family and friends? Today is a good day to make sure that God is the only One you lean on, rely on, and trust completely.

Trust people, but don't expect them to be perfect. We are all flawed human beings.

"Father, I ask that You would always help me remember to only put all of my trust and confidence in You. You alone are perfect in all of Your ways. In Jesus' name. Amen."

WALKING INTO WALLS

Therefore, since we are surrounded by such a great cloud of witnesses, let us throw off everything that hinders and the sin that so easily entangles. And let us run with perseverance the race marked out for us. —HEBREWS 12:1

One night I got up to go to the bathroom, and the room was dark. I had forgotten that I was in a hotel room, not at home, and I walked right into a wall. Obviously, I couldn't go any farther until I changed direction. We are like that at times in life. We try to do something or to get someplace, and we keep running into walls. We should learn to recognize and remove the hindrances in our lives that keep us from being who God wants us to be and doing what He wants us to do.

Those hindrances could be sin, bitterness, anger, selfishness, greed, or thousands of other things that hinder us as we try to move forward in life. An answer for each of these hindrances is found in God's Word, and if we are willing, He will help us tear down the walls and remove the obstacles in our path. Before we can do anything else, we need to recognize the hindrances. So ask yourself today what is keeping you from running your race with God. Be honest with yourself. Refuse to keep running into walls, but tear them down and start making progress.

"Father, I ask You to show me any hindrances that are keeping me from making progress in my life. Help me to work with You to remove them. Thank You. In Jesus' name. Amen."

NO COMPARISON

I praise you because I am fearfully and wonderfully made; your works are wonderful, I know that full well. –PSALM 139:14

The fact that God created you as a unique individual is amazing. This one truth should cause each of us to rejoice in who He made us to be without comparing ourselves to anyone else.

We can easily look at someone else's abilities, appearance, accomplishments, or personality and think they are better than us. A primary reason for this is that the enemy tries to sabotage our self-image. He whispers to us, "You are not as pretty as she is." Or, "You can't do what he can do."

When thoughts such as these enter our minds and we choose to believe them, we fall into the trap of comparison. In addition to the enemy's negative influence in our minds, the world tries to set standards of beauty or achievement for us, telling us what we should aspire to and what is good. These two forces—the enemy and the world—are against us, so we must make a conscious decision to resist them.

God is for you, not against you (Romans 8:31). He created you to be an original, not to compare yourself with someone else and copy them. Enjoy the unique people God has placed in your life, while giving them the chance to enjoy the unique you.

"Father, thank You for creating me as a unique individual. Forgive me for comparing myself to anyone else and help me see myself as You see me. In Jesus' name. Amen."

BE STRONG

Finally, be strong in the Lord and in his mighty power.

—EPHESIANS 6:10

We live in Christ and He lives in us. The victory that He has won is available to us. Don't talk yourself into being weak and powerless. Confess today's scripture aloud several times each day by saying, "I am strong in the Lord and in His mighty power." As you do, you will begin to feel stronger and more powerful.

God's Word says, "According to your faith let it be done to you" (Matthew 9:29). If you believe nobody likes you, there is a good chance that nobody will. Because of what you believe, you will behave in ways that will cause people to avoid being around you. On the other hand, if you believe you are the kind of person people love to be around, you will have many friends because your behavior will reflect what you believe about yourself.

Satan is the great deceiver, and he delights in telling us lies about ourselves, hoping we will believe them. If we do, then his lies become our reality simply because we have believed them. Be sure that what you believe is backed up by God's Word, because that will help you stay strong on the narrow path that leads to life (Matthew 7:14).

"Father, help me believe that I am strong and that I have Your power inside of me. Help me recognize and resist the lies of the devil. I want to be all You want me to be, and I need Your strength and power in order to do that. In Jesus' name. Amen."

SERVE GOD, NOT OTHER PEOPLE

Whatever may be your task, work at it heartily (from the soul), as [something done] for the Lord and not for men.

—COLOSSIANS 3:23 AMPC

If we do what we do hoping to get a reward of gratitude or appreciation from people, we may often be disappointed. Many people have a tendency to take for granted the things that others do to serve or bless them. This is part of human nature. If we become frustrated or angry because people don't tend to appreciate what we do for them, we waste our time. The flesh (human nature without God) will always disappoint us in some way or another. But there is one person—Jesus—we should serve with all of our efforts. He never disappoints us, and our true reward comes from Him alone.

If and when you find yourself becoming angry or bitter because you have not received the appreciation you feel you deserve, take it as a sign that you need to adjust your motive for your service to others. Serve them only for God and to please Him alone. Trust Him to bring whatever reward He has for you and to do it at the right time. Until then, be content to serve God because of your love for Him and in gratitude for what He has done for you.

"Father, I do appreciate all that You have done for me in and through Jesus. It is my pleasure to serve You. You owe me nothing, but I owe You everything; therefore, whatever reward I receive is a gift from You, not something I deserve. In Jesus' name. Amen."

LIVING IN THE NOW

Now faith is the assurance (the confirmation, the title deed) of the things [we] hope for, being the proof of things [we] do not see and the conviction of their reality. —HEBREWS 11:1 AMPC

Today (now) we have faith that God will take care of any mistakes we made yesterday and that He holds tomorrow in His hand. This alone allows us to enjoy and live fully today. Today is the gift we have from God. To miss the joy and opportunities it holds due to regret over the past or dread of the future is not God's will for us.

True faith must always operate in the "now" season of our lives, and faith alone enables us to be at peace and enjoy the present moment. Everything is in God's hands, and He has a good plan for each of us (Jeremiah 29:11). Rather than dreading or feeling apprehensive about the future, we can live with expectancy regarding it.

Expect something good to happen *to you* and *through you.* As you do, you will find a joy that only God can give coursing through your soul. Let go of what lies behind (Isaiah 43:18–19; Philippians 3:13–14) because God is doing something amazing in you and in your life right now, and you don't want to miss it!

"Father, teach me to live fully in the now season of my life. Help me trust You to work something good out of anything I might regret from my past and to trust that my future holds something wonderful. Thank You. In Jesus' name. Amen."

GREATLY EMBOLDENED

When I called, you answered me; you greatly emboldened me.

—PSALM 138:3

In today's scripture, the psalmist David notes that God "greatly emboldened" him when he called to Him and God answered.

Throughout his life, David encountered situations in which he needed boldness or courage. He needed it as a shepherd when lions and bears attacked his flocks. He needed it when he stood in the shadow of the mighty giant Goliath, intending to kill him with a slingshot. He needed it as king, when he led the armies of Israel in fierce battles against the enemies of God's people.

You may not need courage in the same ways that David needed it, but all of us need boldness in certain ways today. We may need it when someone asks us to cheat in some way at our job. We may need it when we must speak the truth in love to a family member or friend. We may need it when God calls us to take a step of faith, and we cannot possibly imagine the outcome.

Whatever your situation is right now, ask God for the courage you need. Believe that when He answers you, you will be greatly emboldened.

"Father, give me the boldness You want me to have, so I may do what You want me to do. In Jesus' name. Amen."

GUIDED BY PEACE

And let the peace (soul harmony which comes) from Christ rule (act as umpire continually) in your hearts [deciding and settling with finality all questions that arise in your minds].

—COLOSSIANS 3:15 AMPC

We often ask, "How can I know what God's will is?" There are several ways that God speaks to His people, and peace—or the lack thereof—is one of the primary ways. Peace in your soul confirms that your actions or intended actions are within God's will for you; it acts as an umpire, calling the "plays" or choices you're making as right or wrong for you.

We make huge mistakes and put our futures in jeopardy when we move forward with things without having peace in our hearts about them. It is always best to wait to do anything until we are assured that it is pleasing to God.

There is also the principle of what I call "stepping out to find out." We may never know what we are to do unless we begin to move in a certain direction. When we do, we will quickly discover whether peace and grace are with us to continue in that direction or perhaps to go another way. Always let the peace of God rule in your heart, and your life will be fulfilling rather than disappointing.

"Father, thank You for peace. Guide me by peace into Your perfect will for me. Teach me to wait on You until Your peace fills my heart as I make decisions. Thank You. In Jesus' name. Amen."

ONE STEP AT A TIME

The Lord had said to Abram, "Go from your country, your people and your father's household to the land I will show you."

—GENESIS 12:1

When God called Abraham to leave his home and his family, He did not inform him of his final destination or tell him all that would happen to him and through him in the future. He asked him to respond to one instruction: to take just one step.

If you are like many people, you would like for God to give you more than one step at a time. You might like to know steps two, three, and four before you ever venture out. You want to see the entire path before you and to know where it leads and when you will get there.

God didn't give Abraham step two until he had taken his first step by faith. He works the same way with you and me. He unfolds His plan for our lives little by little, and we don't see the next thing until we have done the first thing He asks us to do. With each step we take, our faith increases, and as we take each step by faith, we find ourselves fulfilling God's great purpose for our lives.

"Father, thank You for leading me one step at a time. Give me the faith I need to follow You little by little, every single day. In Jesus' name. Amen."

CONTAGIOUS KINDNESS

But the fruit of the Spirit is love, joy, peace, forbearance, kindness, goodness, faithfulness, gentleness and self-control. Against such things there is no law. –GALATIANS 5:22–23

Kindness is a fruit of the Spirit, one that we should always display in our relationships with other people. The world is often a harsh and unkind place, filled with unkind and unloving people, and if we are not careful, it can make us the same way. Becoming like the world around us is very easy to do if we do not purpose to choose God's ways.

The apostle Paul encourages us to "put on" kindness (Colossians 3:12 NKJV), and to remember that we are representatives of Jesus (2 Corinthians 5:20). One way we can be a witness for Christ is by choosing to be kind to one another. Not only is being kind God's will for us, but it may well be contagious. Others can "catch" kindness from us and then give it to someone else.

Let kindness rule in your home and in all your dealings with others. One of the best ways to release joy in your own life is to give it to others through being kind to them.

"Father, You are always kind to me, even though I don't always deserve it, and I want to treat other people the way You treat me. Grant me the grace and strength to display all the fruit of the Holy Spirit. Thank You. In Jesus' name. Amen."

DEPEND ON JESUS

And whatever you do [no matter what it is] in word or deed, do everything in the name of the Lord Jesus and in [dependence upon] His Person, giving praise to God the Father through Him.

—COLOSSIANS 3:17 AMPC

According to John 15:1–8, Jesus is the vine and we are the branches. He tells us that as we abide in Him we will bear much good fruit, and that apart from Him we can do nothing. We should read and meditate on these verses often because we have a tendency as human beings to be independent and self-reliant.

As you begin any project or task, take a moment to tell Jesus that you are depending entirely on Him for the grace, wisdom, and strength to do it. This ensures that you will do it with His help rather than laboring futilely in your own strength and abilities. Any burden is lighter when it is borne by two instead of one; therefore, I urge you to ask for and receive all the help you can from God, who never grows weary.

After having successfully completed your task, remember to thank God for His help.

"Father, forgive me for all the times I have labored in my own strength. I recognize that I need You at all times, and I want to abide in You so that I may bear good fruit. Help me lean and rely on You. Thank You. In Jesus' name. Amen."

ABIDING IN GOD'S WORD

Then Jesus said to those Jews who believed Him, "If you abide in My word, you are My disciples indeed." –JOHN 8:31 NKJV

Abiding is not something that happens quickly. It is a process. It's not agreeing with certain Scripture passages while rejecting others, and it's not obeying God just one time. It's setting your mind to agree with everything His Word says, whether you like it or not. It's also obeying God time after time after time, in every situation, whether obedience is easy and joyful or difficult and sacrificial. In the Amplified Bible, abiding is described in John 8:31 as "continually obeying" Jesus' teachings and "living in accordance with them."

If abiding in God's Word is not already a habit for you, you can begin the process today. You can be obedient to whatever God is asking you to do. Then tomorrow, you can obey Him again. As you develop the habit of obedience, you will also develop the habit of abiding.

According to John 8:32, abiding in God's Word will help you know the truth that makes you free. It also keeps you aware of God's presence and gives you a sense of closeness to Him. The key to being His disciple, meaning one who follows Him and learns from Him, is to abide in His Word.

"Father, I pray that You would help me to abide in Your Word— continually obeying and living in accordance with Your teachings. In Jesus' name. Amen."

STRENGTH TO FACE FEAR

The Lord is my light and my salvation; whom shall I fear? The Lord is the strength of my life; of whom shall I be afraid?

—PSALM 27:1 NKJV

We live in times when the earth is filled with great fear, but God's children need not be afraid. He is the strength we need to confront fear, move past it, and do all that God wants us to do. If anything in your life is causing you to fear right now, remember that God loves you very much and that His perfect love casts out fear (1 John 4:18).

God doesn't simply give us strength; *He is our strength!* We don't need to fear other people or what they might say about us or do to us. Since God is on our side, we can confidently trust that He will always deal with our enemies as we put our trust in Him.

Refuse to live your life in fear. Fear is from the devil, and it is intended to prevent you from making progress of any kind. The gift of God is faith, and with it, we can overcome all fear.

"Father, thank You for loving me and for being my strength. I will not live in fear because I trust You! In Jesus' name. Amen."

DO NOT REPAY EVIL FOR EVIL

See that none of you repays another with evil for evil, but always aim to show kindness and seek to do good to one another and to everybody. —1 THESSALONIANS 5:15 AMPC

It is impossible to be in this world and deal with people and never be treated unjustly. Evil is present in society, but God has given us a secret weapon against it. When it touches us, we can defeat it with kindness rather than lowering ourselves to return evil for evil. We always overcome evil with good (Romans 12:21).

Always be quick to forgive those who offend you, remembering that your prayers cannot be answered if you hold bitterness in your heart against anyone. When Jesus was dying on the cross at Calvary, one of His last acts on earth was to pray that God would forgive those who crucified Him. Stephen did likewise while he was being stoned to death (Acts 7:59–60). The apostle Paul also forgave his friends who deserted him during his first trial (2 Timothy 4:16).

When people hurt us, we can respond according to our biblical examples. Doing so puts us in a position of power with God and frees us from the agony of anger and hatred.

"Father, I want to always keep my heart clear of anger and resentment, but I need Your grace to do so. Enable me to be kind when others are rude or mean to me, and to trust You to be my vindicator. Thank You. In Jesus' name. Amen."

DEALING WITH DOUBT

Truly I tell you, whoever says to this mountain, Be lifted up and thrown into the sea! and does not doubt at all in his heart but believes that what he says will take place, it will be done for him.

—MARK 11:23 AMPC

Doubt is the enemy of faith, and it is something that we all experience. To doubt means to be between two opinions, or to feel that you are without a way. When doubts arise, we can choose to believe our doubts, or we can doubt our doubts. The devil suggests doubts to us in the form of thoughts, but we don't have to ponder them or allow them to take root in our minds, making us feel confused or lost in our way.

With Jesus, we are never without a way because He is the Way (John 14:6). The only opinion to hang on to is the one about which you have peace in your heart. Feed your faith with the promises of God, and your faith will stay stronger than any doubt you might have.

"Father, help me believe Your Word above anything that I feel or think. I want to trust You at all times and learn to ignore all my doubts. Help me stay strong in faith. Thank You. In Jesus' name. Amen."

THE DECREE OF THE LORD

I will declare the decree of the Lord: He said to me, You are My Son; this day [I declare] I have begotten you. —PSALM 2:7 AMPC

Have you ever seen a movie in which a king issues a royal decree? A royal decree communicates a ruler's desires or commands for his kingdom. Long before the days of television or the Internet, a king would sign a decree and then a group of messengers would take off on horseback to deliver it across the realm, so everyone would know what to do. All citizens, of course, were expected to obey the royal decree.

In today's scripture, the psalmist writes that he will "declare the decree of the Lord." In this particular decree, God declares that Jesus is His only begotten Son. John 3:16 and Hebrews 1:1–5 also affirm this truth.

We can think of the entirety of God's Word as His royal decree. He is our King, and we are the citizens of His kingdom. When we declare His Word with our mouths, believing it in our hearts, our faith-filled words go forth to establish God's desires and commands in our lives. When we believe and speak His royal decree, things in our lives begin to change and line up with His will and His good plan for us.

"Father, thank You for Your Word, Your royal decree. I choose to live my life in obedience to all that You have spoken. In Jesus' name. Amen."

CONVICTION WITHOUT CONDEMNATION

Now when they heard this they were stung (cut) to the heart, and they said to Peter and the rest of the apostles (special messengers), Brethren, what shall we do? –ACTS 2:37 AMPC

The conviction of the Holy Spirit is very valuable to us because it lets us know that we are doing something we should not do and that we need to repent and do God's will instead. It is not an invitation to feel guilty and condemned, because God has revealed the error of our ways.

For many years, I did not know the difference between conviction and condemnation, and anytime I felt convicted, I immediately allowed it to make me feel guilty. God never condemns us, but He does convict us of wrongdoing, and we should thank Him each time He does.

I encourage you not to waste your time feeling guilty, because it is never beneficial in any way. Admit your faults and ask God to forgive you and help you overcome them. Remember that conviction from God is a gift, not something intended to make you feel bad about yourself.

"Father, thank You for each time You convict me of sin. I am glad that You care enough about me to not let me live in darkness and deception. I want Your will in my life. In Jesus' name. Amen."

THE IMPORTANCE OF CONTROLLING OUR EMOTIONS

A man without self-control is like a city broken into and left without walls. —PROVERBS 25:28 ESV

Our emotions are ever changing, and they usually change without notice. We may feel one way one moment and an entirely different way the next. Many factors affect our emotions—the weather, how well we slept the night before, our health, the way people treat us, the projects we need to complete, and many other things. We cannot always prevent this variety of emotions, but we are expected to control our behavior in light of them.

The rise and fall of emotions may well be one of the greatest tests of faith we encounter. We are to live by faith (2 Corinthians 5:7), not by what we see or how we feel. Our decisions are to be based on God's Word and nothing else. If we were to take one week and notice how often our emotions fluctuate, we would have a very interesting project. We would quickly realize how fickle our feelings are and that we cannot allow our emotions to dictate our decisions and behavior.

"Father, I need Your help to live by faith and recognize how often my emotions change. Grant me the strength to do Your will no matter how I feel. Thank You. In Jesus' name. Amen."

WHERE IS GOD?

Then Jacob awoke from his sleep and he said, "Without any doubt the Lord is in this place, and I did not realize it." –GENESIS 28:16 AMP

God is everywhere all the time, but we often fail to realize that He is always near. Learning to recognize and enjoy the presence of God is an important part of our worship of Him, and it is important for us if we want to live with peace, joy, and great courage.

Fear is a huge problem that we must all confront. It not only torments us, but also prevents us from living in the fullness of God's will for us. We often read in Scripture the phrase "Fear not, for I am with you." God has promised to never leave or forsake us, but, like Jacob in today's scripture, we may fail to realize that wherever we are, God is there too.

I recommend that you take a moment several times a day and say, "God is here. He is with me right now." This will not only help you in the present moment, but it will also build in your heart the awareness that you are never alone.

"Father, help me be more aware of Your presence in my life. I believe You are everywhere all the time, and I don't want to ever forget it. In Jesus' name. Amen."

TEMPTATION

When the devil had finished every temptation, he [temporarily] left Him until a more opportune time. —LUKE 4:13 AMP

Are you ever tempted? I am. The Bible tells us that when we are tempted we should pray (Luke 22:40) and submit ourselves to God; resist the devil and he will flee (James 4:7). Thankfully we have the fruit of self-control, and the moment we are tempted to do wrong or even think of doing wrong, we can pray, summon self-control, and remember that God has given us a spirit of power (Galatians 5:22–23; Acts 1:8).

Temptation is not sin as long as we resist it. When we resist temptation properly, sooner or later it will fade away. But the devil will do with us as he did with Jesus: He will wait for a more opportune time to tempt us again.

Temptation to do wrong is a fact of life. Instead of feeling guilty when you are tempted, I urge you to use your faith to resist it and lean on God's grace and power to deliver you. Don't be shocked when you are tempted, but do remember that you are more than a conqueror through Christ (Romans 8:37) and that God is with you to help you in every situation.

"Father, I love You very much and I want to do what is right. Help me resist all temptation to do wrong through the power of Your Holy Spirit. Thank You. In Jesus' name. Amen."

GOD NEEDS OUR FAITH

And whatever you ask in prayer, you will receive, if you have faith.
—MATTHEW 21:22 ESV

Recently I was talking with the Lord, and I told Him something that I needed Him to do for me. Immediately, I heard in my spirit, "I need your faith!" This was quite an eye-opening statement for me. Through these words, I realized that somehow I had weakened in faith and was asking God for help out of need and desperation rather than in faith. We can ask God for many things yet fail to attach our faith to our requests.

I encourage you to ask in faith, believing that God hears you and wants to meet your need. If you know a scripture on which you can base your request, you can remind God that you believe it and that you trust Him to keep His promises. Praying the Word or filling your prayers with Scripture is a good thing to do. When we humbly remind God of His Word, it shows we are putting our trust in it and in Him. It also strengthens our faith while we wait for Him to answer us.

"Father, I am so thankful for the privilege of prayer and I trust You to answer me when I pray in faith, according to Your will. Thank You for helping me. In Jesus' name. Amen."

THE BLESSEDNESS OF POSSESSING NOTHING

For the [whole] earth is the Lord's and everything that is in it.

—1 CORINTHIANS 10:26 AMPC

God is the owner and possessor of all things. When we begin to develop an ownership mentality, we do so out of pride, having forgotten that everything we have is a gift from God and that we are merely stewards of His possessions. The words *me* and *mine* are all too familiar in our thoughts and conversations.

I have come to realize that this ownership mentality is not pleasing to God and that we regularly need to lay everything on the altar of sacrifice and make sure that God alone is on the throne of our hearts. When we possess nothing, we can enjoy everything without the fear of losing it or fear that someone will take it from us.

What do you think you own—your ministry, your business, your family, your money, or your material possessions? Remind yourself today that without God, you are nothing and you have nothing. When God gives you something, be thankful. When He requires it back, release it without self-pity. And always remember that as long as you have Jesus, you have everything you will ever need.

"Father, I confess that things have become too important to me. I want only You to be on the throne of my heart. Let me always be a good steward, and help me avoid an attitude of ownership, for all things belong to You alone. In Jesus' name. Amen."

TAKE RESPONSIBILITY

Then the Lord God said to the woman, "What is this you have done?" The woman said, "The serpent deceived me, and I ate."

—GENESIS 3:13

Have you ever witnessed a scene between two rowdy siblings who don't want to get in trouble for breaking a fragile item while doing something they weren't supposed to be doing? Chances are, each one blames the accident on the other—or on the dog. Rarely does the culprit confess immediately. That's called human nature, and it's been going on since the first man and the first woman were created.

In the Garden of Eden, God knew that Adam and Eve had sinned. Adam blamed Eve, and Eve blamed the serpent, as we see in today's scripture. Both Adam and Eve sinned, but neither accepted responsibility for their actions.

Unwillingness to take responsibility for one's own actions is a major reason some people are unhappy and unsuccessful. Blaming someone else when things go wrong is a sign of immaturity.

To become everything God wants us to be and to enjoy the fullness of His good plan for our lives, we must learn to take personal responsibility whenever it is appropriate to do so. It may not always be comfortable or easy, but it is always the right thing to do.

"Father, help me to take personal responsibility for my actions and mistakes in every situation when I need to do so. Amen."

DELIGHT IN GOD'S WORD

Blessed is the one...whose delight is in the law of the Lord, and who meditates on his law day and night. That person is like a tree planted by streams of water, which yields its fruit in season and whose leaf does not wither—whatever they do prospers.

—PSALM 1:1–3

According to today's passage, those who delight themselves in God's law, meaning His ways and His teachings, will be blessed and fruitful. In addition, verse 3 says that they prosper in what they do. In the Amplified Bible, verse 3 indicates that the word prospers means "comes to maturity." To have a life of blessing, fruitfulness, and maturity in God sounds wonderful to me, and I pray that this is the type of life you long to live. You can expect it if you delight yourself in God's Word.

The only way to delight in something is to let it fill your thoughts. I encourage you to spend time studying and meditating on God's Word, rolling it over and over in your mind. It is full of truth, full of power, full of wisdom, and full of promises for you. Thinking about God's Word will strengthen you, because it will not only enable you to know God's will, but it will also teach you how to do God's will. It will increase your peace and your confidence, and fill you with the faith and hope you need to live the blessed, productive, mature life God has created and called you to live.

"Father, help me to live a life of fruitfulness and maturity as I delight in and meditate on Your Word. In Jesus' name. Amen."

LOVE NOTHING MORE THAN GOD

Therefore, my dearly beloved, shun (keep clear away from, avoid by flight if need be) any sort of idolatry (of loving or venerating anything more than God). –1 CORINTHIANS 10:14 AMPC

One of the best ways to determine whether or not we truly love God more than anything else is to watch how we behave when we lose something. Things in life come and go, and we must learn to enjoy them while we have them, yet not be upset if and when they are gone.

The first command that God gave Moses when He spoke to him after bringing the Israelites out of Egypt was that they were to have no other gods before Him (Exodus 20:3). This command is still in effect today, and remembering it is most important in our lives. Nothing works right for us if God does not come first. As Matthew 6:33 says, we are to seek first the Kingdom of God, and then all other things will be added to us.

Psalm 37:4 promises: "Delight yourself also in the Lord, and He shall give you the desires of your heart" (NKJV).

"Father, I want to keep You first in my life, and I ask You to show me whenever I let something become more important to me than You are. Thank You. In Jesus' name. Amen."

OUR ETERNAL FRIEND

I no longer call you servants, because a servant does not know his master's business. Instead, I have called you friends. —JOHN 15:15

Our God is eternal. He has no beginning and no end. He always has been, and He always will be. He knows everything, He has all power, and He is everywhere all the time. And He is our friend! This is amazing and very comforting.

You can talk to God about anything at any time, and He is always interested. He is not too busy for even the tiniest thing that concerns you. Develop the habit of maintaining a conversation with God in your heart all day long. He delights in you and loves you unconditionally.

Our Lord has a good plan for each of us, and He is daily guiding us into the fullness of that plan. Even when you seem to have lost your way, remember that He knows exactly where you are. He has His eye on you all the time, and your times are in His hands (Psalm 31:15).

"Father, thank You for calling me Your friend and for loving me. In Jesus' name. Amen."

SET YOUR COURSE FOR A GREAT FUTURE

May these words of my mouth and this meditation of my heart be pleasing in your sight, Lord, my Rock and my Redeemer.

—PSALM 19:14

In today's scripture, the psalmist David prays for words and thoughts—the "meditation of my heart"—that are pleasing to the Lord. This is a prayer that all of us should pray often.

The reason it is so important for our words to be pleasing to God is that words have power (Proverbs 18:21). And we will have what we consistently speak. The reason it is so important for our thoughts to be pleasing to God is that our words are rooted in our thoughts, so if we're going to speak pleasing words, we need to think pleasing thoughts. Our thoughts also greatly affect our attitudes, and our attitudes determine in many ways how far we can go in life—in pursuing our dreams and God-given destinies, in our relationships with other people, in our personal relationship with God, in our jobs, in our health and wellness, and in many other areas.

The combination of our thoughts and words sets the course for our future. The enemy will try to get us to agree with his thoughts and words, but if we submit to God and resist him, he will flee (James 4:7).

I encourage you today to position yourself for a great future by choosing thoughts and words that please the Lord.

"Father, may the words of my mouth and the meditation of my heart be pleasing to You. In Jesus' name. Amen."

TURN WORRIES INTO PRAYERS

Do not fret or have any anxiety about anything, but in every circumstance and in everything, by prayer and petition (definite requests), with thanksgiving, continue to make your wants known to God. —PHILIPPIANS 4:6 AMPC

Whatever you might be tempted to worry about today, I encourage you to turn that worry into prayer. Worrying produces nothing but anxiety and tension in our souls. That never brings an answer to our problems, but prayer opens the door for God to work marvelous wonders.

One sincere prayer offered in faith can produce more good than a lifetime of worry and anxiety. When you pray, be sure to give thanks along with your requests, expressing gratitude for the amazing things that God has already done in your life. Thanksgiving opens the windows of heaven, but complaining opens a door for the enemy. We can all find things to complain and murmur about, but grumbling is as useless as worrying. Prayer is your opportunity to receive God's help, so take advantage of that opportunity today and every day of your life.

"Father, thank You for inviting me to pray instead of worry. What a wonderful privilege it is! In Jesus' name, I ask that You teach me to turn all my worries into prayer. Amen."

GOD'S REWARD

After these things, the word of the Lord came to Abram in a vision, saying, Fear not, Abram, I am your Shield, your abundant compensation, and your reward shall be exceedingly great.

—GENESIS 15:1 AMPC

God asked Abram to do some very difficult things, but He also promised him that his reward would be very great. Has God asked you to do something that you find difficult? If so, I want to encourage you to receive His grace (ability) and be obedient and do all that He asks of you. Your reward will come, and when it does, you will be very glad.

God requires that we walk with Him by faith, always doing what He asks us to do, even if it requires a sacrifice. Everything God asks of us will eventually make our lives better because He always has our best interests at heart. Believe in the goodness of God and do not "grow weary of doing good," for you will reap "in due season" if you "do not give up" (Galatians 6:9 ESV).

"Father, help me do all that You ask me to do, and to always walk in faith, trusting that my reward from You will be exceedingly great. In Jesus' name. Amen."

FORGETTING WHAT LIES BEHIND

But one thing I do [it is my one aspiration]: forgetting what lies behind and straining forward to what lies ahead.

—PHILIPPIANS 3:13 AMPC

Are you feeling guilty today about mistakes you have made in the past? If so, I encourage you to repent, receive God's forgiveness, and stop worrying about things you can do nothing about. The apostle Paul, who wrote today's scripture, made many mistakes, yet he was determined to let go of them and press toward the future that God had for him. Although Paul was imperfect in many ways, God used him mightily, and He wants to use you too.

Guilt accomplishes nothing except to make us miserable and keep us from doing the good we could do today. This day is an opportunity for you, so don't ruin it by mourning over the past. God loves you. He not only forgives all your sins; He doesn't even remember them. By faith, receive His love and mercy, and enjoy your day.

"Father, I am very sorry for my past sins and failures. I ask for and receive Your forgiveness and mercy. By Your grace, let me enjoy this day and accomplish great things for Your glory. In Jesus' name. Amen."

HOW CAN I CHANGE?

Are you so foolish and so senseless and so silly? Having begun [your new life spiritually] with the [Holy] Spirit, are you now reaching perfection [by dependence] on the flesh?

—GALATIANS 3:3 AMPC

Our love for Jesus makes us want to be everything He wants us to be. Because of that, we often fall into the trap of trying to change ourselves rather than trusting God to change us. I spent many frustrating years, striving in my flesh (my own strength, ability, energy, and effort without God), to do what only He could do in me.

No doubt, all of us need to change and become more and more like Jesus. This will happen little by little as we study His Word and fellowship with Him.

God has called you to Himself, and only He can complete by His Spirit what He begins in the Spirit. He is the Author and the Finisher of your faith and of all the work that needs to be done in you (Hebrews 12:2).

Tell Jesus your desire, and then lean on Him to bring it to pass. Don't be frustrated with yourself because you are not all that you want to be. God will meet you where you are and help you get to where you need to be.

"Father, I desire to change and be more and more like Jesus, but I can't change myself. I ask You to change me, and I wait on You to do what only You can do. In Jesus' name. Amen."

SEASONS OF TESTING

Consider it wholly joyful, my brethren, whenever you are enveloped in or encounter trials of any sort or fall into various temptations.

—JAMES 1:2 AMPC

We all experience seasons of testing, times when our difficulties last longer than we feel we can endure or when we face multiple challenges at the same time. I have been dealing with sciatica for a while now. If you have ever had it, you know that it hurts! I trust that God will take care of it, but while I am waiting, it is testing my faith.

Paul had a thorn in his flesh, and he wanted God to remove it. But God told him that His strength showed itself most effective through Paul's weakness (2 Corinthians 12:9). In other words, even though Paul was dealing with a challenge, God promised to give him the strength to do what he needed to do. If you are in the midst of trials of any sort right now, I encourage you to receive God's strength while you wait on your total deliverance. He is standing by ready to help.

"Father, thank You that Your strength makes up for all my weaknesses. Help me be patient until my full deliverance comes. In Jesus' name. Amen."

STRENGTH IN MEEKNESS

Now the man Moses was very meek (gentle, kind, and humble) or above all the men on the face of the earth. –NUMBERS 12:3 AMPC

Meekness often gets mistaken for weakness, but they are not the same. I believe that a meek person is one who can maintain balance between emotional extremes and manage emotions appropriately. This requires strength, not weakness. Meekness is not weakness; it is strength under control.

Today's scripture says that Moses was the meekest man on earth, yet people do not think of him as weak. He was a strong person and a strong leader. When we think of him, we think of a man who personally encountered God in the burning bush and of a man who led the Israelites through the Red Sea on dry land. He certainly wasn't perfect, and the Bible clearly shows his imperfections.

At times, anger got the best of him—such as when he killed an Egyptian and when he smashed the tablets with the Ten Commandments written on them because the people were worshipping an idol (Exodus 2:11–12; 32:19). He did make mistakes, but not habitually.

If Moses, in spite of his mistakes, can be known as meek, you and I can become meek too. God created all of us with emotions, and we can use them in healthy ways or in unhealthy ways. Meekness manages emotions wisely.

"Father, help me to manage my emotions wisely, understanding that meekness is not a sign of weakness but of strength. Amen."

LET YOUR LIGHT SHINE

Let your light so shine before men that they may see your moral excellence and your praiseworthy, noble, and good deeds and recognize and honor and praise and glorify your Father Who is in heaven. —MATTHEW 5:16 AMPC

The world is filled with darkness, but light absorbs darkness and puts it out. Jesus is the light of the world, and we are called to let Him shine through us. One way we can do this is to be committed to excellence. Excellent people always go the extra mile and do whatever they do with all their might. They are not average or mediocre; they always do their best.

We see very little excellence in the world today, but we can be an example for others to follow. God's Word teaches us a great deal about excellence. We are exhorted to maintain excellent speech (Proverbs 8:6) and to think about things that are excellent (Philippians 4:8). We are told to prize the things that are excellent and always choose the best (Philippians 1:9–10). Daniel was an excellent servant of God, and his commitment to excellence gained him a promotion above all the other leaders (Daniel 6:3).

Let us strive for excellence because we serve an excellent God.

"Father, You are most excellent, and I want to let You shine through my life. Help me always choose to be excellent in every way. Thank You. In Jesus' name. Amen."

OUR ENEMIES WILL NOT PREVAIL

And they shall fight against you, but they shall not [finally] prevail against you, for I am with you, says the Lord, to deliver you.

—JEREMIAH 1:19 AMPC

We all have enemies of some sort or another, but God is fighting for us. You may be going through something difficult at this time, but be encouraged that God is with you and that His plan is to deliver you. Be steadfast, continuing to do what you know to do, and God will always do what you cannot do.

Whether your enemy is pain in your body, financial lack, friends or family who have deserted you, or anything else, it will not prevail against you. You may need to stand firm for a period of time, and your faith will be tested, but God is faithful, and He will not ultimately let your enemies win. Live with hopeful expectation that your breakthrough is coming very soon.

"Father, thank You very much that I can trust You to fight against my enemies and cause me to be victorious. Help me be patient until my breakthrough comes. In Jesus' name. Amen."

PEACE AND LOVE

Finally, all [of you] should be of one and the same mind (united in spirit), sympathizing [with one another], loving [each other] as brethren [of one household], compassionate and courteous (tenderhearted and humble). —1 PETER 3:8 AMPC

God wants us to get along with one another because there is great power in unity. Satan works hard to keep us in strife and disagreement with one another because he knows it will cause us to be weak and ineffective as God's representatives.

Living in agreement with people is difficult unless we are willing to humble ourselves.

Humility is a beautiful virtue and possibly the most difficult to develop. Jesus is our example in humility, and only He can help us cultivate it in our lives. If you are at odds with anyone at this time in your life, I urge you to forgive any offenses today and make peace with that person in obedience to God.

"Father, help me forgive quickly and humble myself to do whatever I need to do to walk in peace and love. In Jesus' name. Amen."

THE RIGHT TIME TO BE THANKFUL

But as for me, I will sacrifice to You with the voice of thanksgiving; I will pay that which I have vowed. Salvation and deliverance belong to the Lord! —JONAH 2:9 AMPC

Jonah had disobeyed God and was swallowed by a huge fish. But while he was still suffering greatly in the fish's belly, he began to give thanks to God. Soon, he was delivered. It is significant to me that he didn't wait to give thanks until after he had his victory, but he offered a sacrifice of thanksgiving and praise in the midst of his difficulty.

Anytime—and all the time—is the right time to give thanks to God, but it is especially important that we don't forget to do so while we are in the wilderness times of our lives. It is easy to be thankful when our circumstances are joyful and exciting, but it is a sacrifice to do so when there appears to be nothing for which we can thank God.

Thank God today for His presence in your life, and know that your deliverance will come at the right time.

"Father, forgive me for murmuring and complaining when I should be offering You a sacrifice of thanksgiving. I trust You to deliver me at the right time, and I give You thanks while I am waiting. In Jesus' name. Amen."

TALK BACK

Jesus answered, "It is written: 'Man shall not live on bread alone, but on every word that comes from the mouth of God.'"

—MATTHEW 4:4

At some point in your life, someone may have said to you, "Don't you talk back to me!" Or perhaps you have said these words to your children. Talking back is generally considered disrespectful, but there is an instance in which I believe it is both appropriate and necessary. It's always okay to talk back to our enemy, the devil.

When the devil led Jesus into the wilderness to tempt Him, Jesus answered every temptation by saying, "It is written," and then He went on to counter the enemy's claims with Scripture. He fought—and defeated—the enemy with the Word of God (Matthew 4:1–11).

I encourage you to follow Jesus' example. The enemy will come against you with lies, and you can talk back to him using God's Word. For example, he may tell you that God doesn't really love you, and you can say, "God loves me with an everlasting love. He loves me enough to send His Son to die so that I can be in right relationship with Him" (see Jeremiah 31:3; John 3:16). He may say your life will never amount to anything, and you can respond with, "God has great plans for my life, plans to give me a future filled with hope" (see Jeremiah 29:11). One of the best pieces of advice that I could ever give you is to prioritize studying and learning God's Word. This will help you in many ways, especially as you talk back to the enemy and defeat his lies.

"Father, help me to prioritize studying and learning Your Word. Your Word gives me victory in every situation. In Jesus' name. Amen."

BECAUSE OF LOVE

O give thanks to the God of heaven, for His mercy and loving-kindness endure forever! —PSALM 136:26 AMPC

The greatest honor we can give God is to live with joy because of His amazing, unconditional love. We may hear the phrase "God loves you" so often that we fail to realize the impact of these astounding words. The God who created and maintains all that we see in our world is concerned for everything that concerns you, and He delights in you.

For some reason, we are prone to thinking that God is usually a little bit disappointed or even angry with us, but His mercy and loving-kindness endure forever. This means they are active at all times without interruption.

Receive God's mercy and love today, and let it remove all fear from your life. Nothing can separate you from God's love, which is found in Christ Jesus (Romans 8:37–39).

"Father, help me realize how amazing Your love is and to be more aware of it in my life. In Jesus' name. Amen."

LET YOUR WORDS BE FEW

In a multitude of words transgression is not lacking, but he who restrains his lips is prudent. —PROVERBS 10:19 AMPC

If you are a talker, as I am, you may need to read today's scripture and similar verses often. It seems that the more we talk, the more we are likely to say things we wish later we had not said. I pray almost daily that God will guard my lips so I don't say foolish things (Psalm 141:3). It is good to remember that no one, in their own power, can tame the tongue (James 3:8) and that we need God's help in this area.

Merely trying to do what is right without asking for God's help is useless. He wants us to lean on Him in all things and is honored when we do. Jesus said that apart from Him we can do nothing (John 15:5). This certainly includes using wisdom with all of our words.

Use your words today to encourage others. Remember that your words have power, so make sure they are positive and beneficial to you and to the people in your life.

"Father, I need Your help in restraining my lips so that I always speak positive and excellent things. Let my words be pleasing in Your ears. Thank You. In Jesus' name. Amen."

REJOICE!

Rejoice in the Lord always [delight, gladden yourselves in Him]; again I say, Rejoice! —PHILIPPIANS 4:4 AMPC

Satan works tirelessly to steal our joy because he knows that God is happy when He sees us happy. Our joy brings delight to His heart. We are God's children, and just as we are glad to see our children happy, He is glad to see us happy. He wants us to enjoy every moment He gives us.

God's Word teaches us that joy brings healing and strength to us (Nehemiah 8:10; Proverbs 17:22). Worry, discouragement, and fear zap our strength and weaken the body, so it is no wonder that the devil does all he can do to prevent us from being joyful.

I encourage you to make a decision to enjoy this day and every day of your life, no matter what difficulties life may bring. Being sad won't make your troubles go away, but being happy will give you strength to deal with them.

"Father, help me truly realize the value of joy. Remind me to make joy a priority in my life and to be watchful against the temptation to be discouraged and sad. Thank You. In Jesus' name. Amen."

THE POWER OF CONTENTMENT

You shall not covet your neighbor's house. You shall not covet your neighbor's wife, or his male or female servant, his ox or donkey, or anything that belongs to your neighbor. —EXODUS 20:17

Many believers are aware of the Ten Commandments and could probably list some of them. We know they tell us not to "covet," but have we stopped to think about that and apply it to our lives personally? To covet is simply to want what someone else has. The opposite of coveting is being content with what God has given us.

Looking up to certain people is certainly not wrong. We can admire them for their faith, their godly character, their walk with God, their discipline or work ethic, their creativity, or the way they treat other people. We can be encouraged by the opportunities God gives them and the way they use their gifts. God does put people in our lives to help us live as He wants us to live, but we should relate to them in a healthy way, letting their lives inspire us rather than being jealous and wanting exactly what they have.

I urge you today to seek God for what He wants you to have, the life He wants you to live, and the person He wants you to be. Resist the temptation to covet anything anyone else has, and trust God to give you everything you need, exactly when you need it.

"Father, help me today to be content with all that You have given me, not wanting what other people have. In Jesus' name. Amen."

JESUS UNDERSTANDS HOW YOU FEEL

For the enemy has pursued and persecuted my soul, he has crushed my life down to the ground; he has made me to dwell in dark places as those who have been long dead. –PSALM 143:3 AMPC

In today's scripture, David gives an accurate description of depression. This characterization makes it clear that our enemy, Satan, not only comes against our mind and body, but especially delights in attacking our emotions.

Later in Psalm 143, David offers a good prescription for overcoming depression and discouragement. He tells us to remember all the good things that God has done in the past and to meditate on all of His mighty, amazing works (v. 5). David lifted his hands and gave praise and openly spoke with God about how he felt.

God understands how you feel, and He cares. Don't feel you must try to hide feelings of depression from Him. Instead, tell Him everything and ask for His help. He is your glory and the lifter of your head (Psalm 3:3).

"Father, I ask You to help me in my times of discouragement and sadness. Help me to have stable, level emotions. Restore my joy and speak a word of comfort to me. I put my trust in You. In Jesus' name. Amen."

BE DECISIVE

A man's mind plans his way, but the Lord directs his steps and makes them sure. —PROVERBS 16:9 AMPC

Some people struggle to make decisions. They let the fear of making a wrong choice paralyze them, and they end up wasting a great deal of time in indecision. But we can be confident that God will direct our steps if we learn to listen to Him.

Having a plan is not wrong, but be sure to keep your plans before God, and be willing to change them if He indicates that you should. Pray about the decisions you need to make, and then do what you feel peace about doing. I believe God guides us by His Word, His peace, and His wisdom. As we trust Him, He can cause our thoughts to become agreeable to His will (Proverbs 16:3).

God knows your heart, and if you truly want His will, He will guide you to the right place, even if you take a few wrong turns on the way to where you need to be.

"Father, I want Your will more than anything else. As I take steps of faith, please guide me. If I am going in the wrong direction, I trust You to redirect my steps. Thank You. In Jesus' name. Amen."

DON'T LET SIN SEPARATE YOU FROM GOD

But the just shall live by faith [My righteous servant shall live by his conviction respecting man's relationship to God and divine things, and holy fervor born of faith and conjoined with it]; and if he draws back and shrinks in fear, My soul has no delight or pleasure in him.

—HEBREWS 10:38 AMPC

Since the time of Adam and Eve in the Garden, people have been hiding from God when they sin, but that is not His will for us. God wants us to run *to Him*—not from Him—in our times of weakness and failure. He already knows everything we try so hard to hide, because nothing is hidden from Him.

Jesus understands our weaknesses and failures, and His arms are always open wide to comfort us. Don't shrink back in fear of your Lord when you know you have failed. We do not please Him or give Him delight when we run from Him. Don't let anything separate you from the love of God. Stay in close relationship with Him, talk to Him about everything, and never throw away your confidence. Repent and know that because of what Jesus has done for you, your sins are forgiven.

"Father, thank You for Your great mercy and amazing love. I am grateful that I never have to hide from You and that Your love is unconditional. In Jesus' name. Amen."

GOD PROVIDES ALL YOU NEED

And God is able to make all grace abound to you, so that having all sufficiency in all things at all times, you may abound in every good work. —2 CORINTHIANS 9:8 ESV

As a child of God, you can live without fear concerning provision and you can have complete confidence that whatever you need today, or at any time in the future, God will provide abundantly.

The promise is that you will have "all sufficiency in all things at all times." This means you never have to worry about anything. Your Father is faithful, and He always keeps His promises. Put your trust in Him above anyone or anything else.

None of us knows exactly what the future holds, but if we believe this promise, we can face the future with confidence and joy, knowing that whether we need strength, wisdom, finances, healing, courage, or anything else, it is ours through Christ.

"Father, thank You for Your amazing generosity and Your promise to always provide anything and everything I need. In Jesus' name. Amen."

NECESSARY PRUNING

But blessed is the one who trusts in the Lord, whose confidence is in him. They will be like a tree planted by the water that sends out its roots by the stream. It does not fear when heat comes; its leaves are always green. It has no worries in a year of drought and never fails to bear fruit. —JEREMIAH 17:7–8

Today's scripture says the person who trusts the Lord "never fails to bear fruit," meaning that they are productive time after time. This reminds me of what God said when He first created mankind: "Be fruitful and increase in number" (Genesis 1:28). Clearly, this idea of fruitfulness is important to Him, and believers are to live fruitful lives. At times, this means we will need to be "pruned."

Think about a tree. For a tree to be most productive or fruitful, it must be pruned appropriately. In other words, some branches need to be cut off or trimmed back at certain points. That's the only way the tree will stay strong, remain healthy, and produce the maximum amount of quality fruit.

As trees need pruning, we need pruning too. Certain things need to be cut off of our lives at strategic times. Pruning may mean quitting a habit that is keeping us from realizing our full potential or deterring us from God's plan for our lives. It may mean discontinuing unhealthy patterns. Or it may mean drawing unhealthy relationships to a close as God leads.

God is the Master Gardener, and He only prunes in order to produce healthy fruit. Allow Him to prune your life according to His wisdom, and you will enjoy a new level of fruitfulness and productivity.

"Father, I ask You to prune from my life everything that needs to be cut off, so I may never fail to bear good fruit. In Jesus' name. Amen."

GOD HEARS YOUR PRAYER

Hear my voice when I call, Lord; be merciful to me and answer me. My heart says of you, "Seek his face!" Your face, Lord, I will seek. —PSALM 27:7-8

In today's scripture, the psalmist David asks God to hear him and to be merciful and answer him. David had experienced many answers to prayer, and we can see this throughout the Psalms. He had a long history with God, and he was confident that God would hear him.

I hope you know today that God always hears you when you call. As you seek Him, you will find Him. He may not answer according to your timetable, but He hears you when you pray, and even if He doesn't answer immediately, you can be confident that your answer is on its way.

Here are three scriptures you can stand on when you need to be assured that God is listening to you: "But God has surely listened and has heard my prayer" (Psalm 66:19). "The eyes of the Lord are on the righteous, and his ears are attentive to their cry" (Psalm 34:15). "This is the confidence we have in approaching God: that if we ask anything according to his will, he hears us" (1 John 5:14).

"Father, thank You for hearing me when I call You. Help me to seek Your face in every situation. In Jesus' name. Amen."

BE DILIGENT

Never lag in zeal and in earnest endeavor; be aglow and burning with the Spirit, serving the Lord. —ROMANS 12:11 AMPC

Diligence is a key to enjoying the life that Jesus died for you to have. Let me encourage you to be diligent in every way. In other words, keep doing what is right, and do it with all your might. Do your best for God, serving Him fervently.

When we are hurting, have been treated unfairly, or perhaps simply feel weary, continuing to be diligent to do what we know is right can become difficult. We may be tempted to be passive, thinking that nothing we do will make any difference in our circumstances. If and when you feel this way, it is the best time to continue being diligent in prayer, Bible study, giving, serving, and fulfilling other activities to which you are committed.

Continue doing what is right, even when you feel you are wasting your time, because that is when you get the greatest benefit from your determination. That is when you grow spiritually.

"Father, help me be faithful in doing what I know to be right, and help me do it diligently. Thank You. In Jesus' name. Amen."

TAKING THOUGHTS CAPTIVE

We demolish arguments and every pretension that sets itself up against the knowledge of God, and we take captive every thought to make it obedient to Christ. –2 CORINTHIANS 10:5

Our thoughts are extremely important because they are the roots of our words, attitudes, and actions. Our enemy, Satan, suggests to us thoughts that go against God's will and nature, but we don't have to take them as our own and meditate on them.

I find that the enemy frequently offers me wrong thoughts early in the morning, because if he can get my day off to a bad start, the rest of it will usually go badly also. Those thoughts may be thoughts of worry, fear, or discontent, or they may be ideas about being unkind toward someone. Thankfully, I don't have to keep them just because he offers them to me, and neither do you.

We can cast down wrong thoughts and replace them with ones that we know are pleasing to God and in accordance with His will. Thoughts of love, gratitude, trust, courage, and joyful expectation can fill our minds. Ask God to help you recognize wrong thoughts and quickly resist the devil. When you submit to God and resist him, he will flee (James 4:7).

"Father, help me recognize and cast down all wrong thoughts. Help me guard my heart diligently and always be prepared to do Your will. In Jesus' name. Amen."

IMMEDIATE FORGIVENESS

I, even I, am He Who blots out and cancels your transgressions, for My own sake, and I will not remember your sins. —ISAIAH 43:25 AMPC

Do you focus excessively on the past, feeling guilty or condemned about mistakes you've made, sins you have committed knowingly or unknowingly, or offenses against God or other people? Do you struggle to believe you can be happy today and have a great future because you feel your past has been too bad?

Many people allow their past sins and failures to weigh on their hearts and minds for too long. Some people reach a very old age and look back on their lives with tremendous regret because they allowed their past to influence them so much that they didn't do the things they really wanted to do.

Sometimes, the past is a problem because of what we have done to ourselves and to other people. Sometimes it is painful because of what has been done to us. When we have been victims of someone else's wrongdoing, we need to ask the Lord to heal us. When we have sinned or failed, we need to repent. Once we repent to the Lord, forgiveness happens right away. We are immediately released from guilt and condemnation.

How wonderful it is to know that God is merciful and ready to forgive when we admit our sins and repent of them. This is something for which we should be thankful each and every day.

"Father, thank You for immediate forgiveness when I sincerely repent and for making a way for me to live free from guilt. In Jesus' name. Amen."

THE OPPOSITION OF SATAN

You were running well. Who hindered you from obeying the truth?
—GALATIANS 5:7 ESV

It is a fact that when we try to do good, evil always comes to oppose us (Romans 7:21). The apostle Paul said that a "wide door of opportunity" opened to him and with it came "many adversaries" (1 Corinthians 16:9 AMPC). Satan works diligently to oppose our spiritual growth. He does not want us to pray, be generous, walk in love toward others, study God's Word, or do anything else that is good, and we need to be on our guard against him constantly.

Have you decided to do something good or to make progress in some area of your life? If so, don't be surprised if you run into all kinds of opposition and many hindrances. The good news is that if you submit yourself to God and resist the devil, he will flee (James 4:7). Stand firm, and don't let Satan keep you from going forward. Keep praying, trust God to strengthen you, and refuse to give up. Satan cannot defeat a child of God who stays focused and continues to do His will.

"Father, help me recognize the deceits and strategies of Satan, and give me grace to keep doing what is right even in the face of opposition. Thank You. In Jesus' name. Amen."

THE DANGER OF GREED

He who is of a greedy spirit stirs up strife, but he who puts his trust in the Lord shall be enriched and blessed. —PROVERBS 28:25 AMPC

Greed is a terrible thing. No matter how much people have, if they allow greed to rule them, they will always want more and more. In addition, they will never be content with—or thankful for—what they have. We always overcome evil with good (Romans 12:21), so I have found that the best way to prevent greed from ruling in my life is to be aggressively generous. I want to encourage you to ask God daily to show you something you can do for someone else.

Focusing our thoughts on others keeps us from being selfish and self-centered. When we ask God to help us do this, He may show us something as simple as sending someone a text message of appreciation or encouragement. He could show us something that will require a donation of time or money. When we give, we never lose anything because our generous deeds always return to bless us (Luke 6:37–38).

God's Word teaches us to be on our guard against greed, because life does not consist of our possessions (Luke 12:15). The more generous we are, the more joy we will have.

"Father, help me not to be a greedy person who always wants more and more, but instead help me be generous to everyone I can, in every way. Thank You. In Jesus' name. Amen."

THE REWARDS OF SERVING GOD

My flesh and my heart fail; but God is the strength of my heart and my portion forever. –PSALM 73:26 NKJV

Having a relationship with God through Jesus Christ is our greatest reward in life. Serving Him is a privilege, not an obligation. Take a moment to ponder how great it is to have Jesus as the center of your life. He is with you all the time.

God promises us rewards, but we should never serve Him in order to get something. We should serve Him because we love and appreciate Him. God hears and answers our prayers and helps us in our difficulties. He forgives our sins and grants us strength when we are weak. He guides us and does many other wonderful things for us. And He is "a rewarder of those who diligently seek Him" (Hebrews 11:6 NKJV).

We can expect rewards when we get to heaven. Although we don't comprehend what they will be, we know that anything the Lord does for us will be wonderful. He says that when He returns for His people, He will bring His rewards with Him to "give to each person according to what they have done" (Revelation 22:12).

Be excited and look for these rewards, but always remember that God is our greatest reward. He is our portion in life and our inheritance. Live for Him and enjoy Him each day.

"Father, You are my greatest reward in life. Thank You for being my friend and Savior. In Jesus' name. Amen."

BE AT PEACE

If possible, as far as it depends on you, live at peace with everyone.
—ROMANS 12:18 AMPC

God's will is for us to live in peace at all times. Peace is His gift to us. Although not everyone is always willing to be at peace with us, we should strive to make peace with them if at all possible. Jesus said the "makers and maintainers of peace" would be called the children of God (Matthew 5:9 AMPC).

The more we stay at peace and dwell in rest, the easier it is for us to be led by God's Spirit and to hear from Him. God has often reminded me to relax, because that is the best way to allow Him to flow through us and do the work He desires to do. Let your mind, your emotions, and even your body be relaxed, and trust God, who lives in you, to flow through you, guiding you into His perfect will for you in every situation.

"Father, thank You for the wonderful gift of peace. Help me live and remain in peace with all people, at all times. In Jesus' name. Amen."

THE POWER OF INTERCESSION

Abraham approached [the Lord] and said, "Will You really sweep away the righteous (those who do right) with the wicked (those who do evil)?" —GENESIS 18:23 AMP

When we think of Abraham, we often think of him as the father of faith because of the way he believed God for the miracle birth of his son, Isaac, and then for his willingness to sacrifice Isaac when God asked him to do so (Genesis 15:1–6; 22:1–18). But we may not always think of Abraham as an intercessor—a man who prayed powerfully for other people.

When God decided to destroy the cities of Sodom and Gomorrah because of their wickedness, He told Abraham. Abraham had such an intimate relationship with God that he began to ask Him if He would spare the city for the sake of righteous people. First, he asked Him to spare it for fifty, then for forty-five, and on down until God agreed to spare the city for the sake of ten righteous people (Genesis 18:24–32).

Abraham prayed a bold prayer, and because of it, righteous people escaped judgment. You can pray bold prayers too, interceding for the people and situations around you and believing God hears you.

"Father, I pray for the people around me and for the situations in their lives that need Your touch. Intervene, Lord, and help them, I pray. In Jesus' name. Amen."

LIVE MOMENT BY MOMENT

So do not worry or be anxious about tomorrow, for tomorrow will have worries and anxieties of its own. Sufficient for each day is its own trouble. —MATTHEW 6:34 AMPC

God gives us the grace we need for each situation we encounter, but He never gives us grace today for things that will happen in the future. Being concerned about any moment other than the one in which we are living only causes us to waste it. This very moment is the only one we are guaranteed, so why would we not enter into and enjoy it fully?

God wants us to trust Him and to prove our trust by not being concerned about things that are out of our control and beyond our wisdom. Only God can take care of the past and prepare us for the future, and He promises to do so if we trust Him.

The Lord is well aware of anything you will need to face in the future, and although it may seem to be too much for you to handle, it is not too much for Him. He has already been where you are going, and He already has completely taken care of everything that concerns you.

"Father, help me leave everything in my past and future in Your gentle, loving hands and to enjoy each moment You give me. I trust You to take care of me. In Jesus' name. Amen."

TRUST GOD

When I am afraid, I will put my trust and faith in You.

—PSALM 56:3 AMP

Talking about trusting God is easy when you are not the one who needs to do it. We all face some times when trusting God is more difficult than at other times. If you have been waiting for God to do what needs to be done for a long, long time, you may be tempted to doubt or be afraid that it will not happen. God understands those feelings, and you don't need to be condemned by them. The psalmist David admitted in today's scripture that he felt afraid, but even then he put his trust in God.

We cannot always control how we feel, but at the same time we do not have to live according to our feelings. When you are waiting for an answer from God and you feel fear or doubt, counter that feeling by thinking and saying, "I believe that God is working, and I will have my answer soon."

Always remember that trusting God is not an obligation; it is a privilege. Anytime we do trust Him, we are honoring Him, and we can enter His rest while He is doing what only He can do.

"Father, I want to trust You at all times, in all things, but there are times when I feel afraid or begin to doubt. Help me trust You even in those times, because I know that You are faithful. In Jesus' name. Amen."

THE GREATEST FREEDOM OF ALL

And He died for all, so that all those who live might live no longer to and for themselves, but to and for Him Who died and was raised again for their sake. −2 CORINTHIANS 5:15 AMPC

To be free from yourself is the greatest freedom of all. According to today's scripture, Jesus died so we would no longer have to live a selfish, self-centered life. Let me encourage you not to think about yourself excessively. Don't dwell too much on what is wrong with you or what is right about you. People who are of the flesh (human nature without God) set their mind on the things of the flesh (including themselves), but "those who live according to the Spirit set their minds on the things of the Spirit" (Romans 8:5 ESV).

God wants to work through us to help and bless others, but if we are focused on ourselves, we hinder His work. Say goodbye to self and live for God's purposes. Don't be concerned about what others think of you or what will happen to you in the future, but trust God to take care of you and all that concerns you. This sets you free to give yourself to God completely.

"Father, I don't want to be selfish and focused on myself. I ask for Your help to keep my mind on the things that please You and for the grace to no longer live to and for myself. Thank You. In Jesus' name. Amen."

FAITH AND PATIENCE

So that you may not be sluggish, but imitators of those who through faith and patience inherit the promises. —HEBREWS 6:12 ESV

Waiting patiently for what we need and desire seems to be difficult for most of us. It is especially challenging if we are in pain physically or emotionally while we wait. I read that God's Word contains more than 5,400 promises, so I think it is safe to say that He offers a promise of help and deliverance for any situation we face. Knowing that help is available gives us hope, but we usually find that, even though we release our faith to inherit the promises, we still have to be patient, because the answer doesn't always come right away.

During times of waiting, our faith is tested, and we may experience doubt or fear that what we need or desire will never come. But I want to encourage you to stand fast and fight the good fight of faith (1 Timothy 6:12), because your breakthrough will come if you stand firm in your mind and refuse to give up. Be assured that God loves you very much and that His timing in your life will be perfect.

"Father, thank You for giving me the grace to not give up while I wait on You for my breakthrough to come. In Jesus' name. Amen."

STRENGTH ON THE INSIDE

I pray that out of his glorious riches he may strengthen you with power through his Spirit in your inner being. –EPHESIANS 3:16

If you are feeling weak or overwhelmed in some way right now, today's Bible verse will be a great encouragement to you. Paul prays for something many people need and often ask God for—to be strengthened with spiritual power. He notes that the strength we need comes from God—from "his glorious riches"—and it is available to us through the Holy Spirit.

We need strength in many ways, but the type of strength for which Paul prays is the most important: strength in our inner self. The "inner self" refers to our inmost being, which includes our thoughts, emotions, will (ability to make choices), and conscience. Inner strength keeps us steady on the inside and carries us through life's difficulties and challenges victoriously.

Many people ask God for physical strength when they feel fatigued or stressed. This is certainly appropriate, but strength in the inner self is even more valuable than natural energy. When we are strong inwardly, we have God's power working through us to complete all that He asks us to do and to overcome any obstacle we may face.

"Lord, I know that being strong on the inside is more important than being strong in any other way. I ask that You would strengthen me in my inmost being by the power of the Holy Spirit today. Thank You! In Jesus' name, Amen."

THE KEY TO GOOD HABITS

I remain confident of this: I will see the goodness of the Lord in the land of the living. —PSALM 27:13

Have you ever known someone who has many bad habits? I'm not talking one bad habit, such as nail-biting or chewing ice. I'm talking about bad habits that are ingrained in that person's lifestyle. People who have lots of bad habits aren't generally considered strong people. To have the strength we need for each day, we have to be people of good habits in every area of our lives. We may always have areas in which we need to improve, but as long as we are working toward good habits, we are building strength.

The key to developing good habits is to focus on the positive, not the negative. For example, if you want to develop the habit of healthy eating, focus on the good foods you should eat, not what you should not eat. If you want to habitually get up earlier each day, focus on what you will accomplish when you have more time awake, not on the fact that you really would like to crawl back into bed after the alarm goes off.

No matter what habit you are trying to form, remember to focus on the good it will do in your life, not on what you may need to change or give up in order to develop it.

"Father, as I work to change my habits, help me to focus on the positive end results that good habits will bring to my life. In Jesus' name. Amen."

LEARN TO LISTEN

Understand [this], my beloved brethren. Let every man be quick to hear [a ready listener], slow to speak, slow to take offense and to get angry. —JAMES 1:19 AMPC

I encourage you to pray daily that God will use you to be a blessing to other people, and then purpose to listen and pay attention to the ways He may want to work through you. I have learned that if I listen carefully, people often tell me what they need. They are not hinting for me to help them, but in simple conversation and by asking the right questions, I discover what would help and bless them.

It is good to pray to be a blessing, but we must be careful not to do it merely because it sounds spiritual and then fail to listen and take action accordingly. We may not always be able to provide what people need, but in many instances we can if we are truly willing to help.

Being a blessing to others is one of the most powerful things we can do, and although we may need to sacrifice in order to do it, we end up being even more blessed than the ones we help.

"Thank You, Father, for all You have done for me. I ask that You help me be quick to hear what people need and always be willing to help. In Jesus' name. Amen."

LET GOD FIGHT YOUR BATTLES

You shall not need to fight in this battle; take your positions, stand still, and see the deliverance of the Lord. –2 CHRONICLES 20:17 AMPC

Too often, we try to fight our battles by ourselves, but God wants to fight for us if we will let Him. Our role is not to reason the answer to our problems in our minds, but to trust God and continue doing what He asks us to do while He solves our problems.

God wants us to enjoy our lives and be at peace while He works on our behalf doing what only He can do. Each time you are tempted to worry, I encourage you to say (aloud if possible), "God is fighting my battles! He is on my side, and no weapon formed against me shall prosper." (See Isaiah 54:17.)

Take time right now to remember a time in your life when you had a problem and God helped you. Let that victory encourage you to trust Him now.

"Father, show Yourself strong in my life. I cannot solve my problems, but I trust that You can. Thank You. In Jesus' name. Amen."

ARE YOU THIRSTY?

On the last and greatest day of the festival, Jesus stood and said in a loud voice, "Let anyone who is thirsty come to me and drink."

–JOHN 7:37

Have you ever spent time working or exercising outside on a hot day? It makes you thirsty! And nothing satisfies that thirst except a nice, cold drink. A tall glass of ice water will quench your thirst like nothing else.

Just as we know that cold water will quench physical thirst, we know how to quench spiritual thirst—those feelings of need or desperation in our hearts. Jesus tells us in today's scripture that anyone who is thirsty can come to Him and be satisfied. Whenever we have any kind of need, we simply go to Him, and He will meet it. Nothing is too difficult for Him (Jeremiah 32:27), and He never runs out of resources to help us (Philippians 4:19). He is like a fountain that never runs dry.

The only requirement for having Jesus meet your need is to have a need. You can be certain He will welcome you when you go to Him. He says in John 6:37: "All that My Father gives Me will come to Me; and the one who comes to Me I will most certainly not cast out [I will never, never reject anyone who follows Me]" (AMP).

Do you have a need today? Jesus will satisfy your thirst.

"Father, thank You for meeting my every need and satisfying even my deepest thirst. In Jesus' name. Amen."

SLOW DOWN

Enthusiasm without knowledge is no good; haste makes mistakes.

—PROVERBS 19:2 NLT

Society has most of us rushing anxiously from one thing to another and expecting everyone and everything to move quickly so that we will never have to wait on anything. When we feel frustrated and impatient because it takes a few seconds longer than normal for the Internet to pull up the answer to a question we have asked, we might take that as a sign that life has become too hurried.

Although the world is moving at a faster pace all the time, God is not in a hurry. He is extremely patient. If we intend to move in step with God throughout our daily life, we will need to slow down. I tend to think that the more we rush, the more we miss what God wants to show us and say to us.

I encourage you to take a break from rushing. Try walking more slowly, taking some deep breaths several times day, and focusing on one thing at a time. Take time to think, and don't make decisions too quickly, because that often leads to regret.

"Father, I want to walk in step with You. I realize that doing so means I need to slow down. Please help me do things at Your pace rather than the world's. In Jesus' name. Amen."

WORRY AND ANXIETY

So do not worry or be anxious about tomorrow, for tomorrow will have worries and anxieties of its own. Sufficient for each day is its own trouble. —MATTHEW 6:34 AMPC

I am sure none of us wants to worry or be anxious. We plan to stay peaceful, but then life happens. I am amazed at how many unexpected things can happen in one week. They are situations we don't plan for and things that we don't want to deal with, but they come, and we have no choice but to deal with them.

God invites us to enter His rest through believing (Hebrews 4:3, 10). Each time a problem arises, we can worry and become anxious, or we can believe that God will help us deal with it. I believe that staying peaceful during life's storms gives great glory to God and gives us an opportunity to grow in our faith. This doesn't mean that I enjoy trouble, nor do I always react perfectly when it comes, but doing so is my goal.

I encourage you to stay in God's rest today and every day. If trouble comes, just remember that it won't last forever and that God is with you to help you deal with it.

"Father, help me stay calm and peaceful today no matter what happens. I am thankful for Your presence in my life. I lean and rely on You. In Jesus' name. Amen."

LOOK AROUND

The Lord said to Abram after Lot had parted from him, "Look around from where you are, to the north and south, to the east and west." –GENESIS 13:14

Abram (later called Abraham) and his nephew Lot reached a point where the land and its resources were not adequate for both of them and all their people and possessions (Genesis 13:6). Abram decided that he and Lot should go their separate ways (Genesis 13:8–9) and let Lot choose the land he wanted. Lot chose the best place for himself.

We might think Abram would be disappointed that he did not get the best land, but God spoke to him about that in today's scripture, telling Abram that He would give him everything he could see in every direction. He even promised the land to Abram's offspring (Genesis 13:15), though at the time Abram had no children.

Abram could have focused on the fact that he lost out on the best land, but God did not want him to think about that. God wanted him to look all around and see a promise far greater than rich land for his flocks and herds. God wanted him to believe for a great and miraculous future.

No matter what you may have lost or whether you feel other people have gotten something better than you have, God has a great future for you. Don't look at what's behind you; look around you and see God's promise.

"Father, help me not to focus on what I have lost. Help me to lift my eyes to You and have vision in my heart of all that You have for me in the future. In Jesus' name. Amen."

FAITH

Now faith is the assurance of things hoped for, the conviction of things not seen. —HEBREWS 11:1 ESV

Our walk with God is a journey of faith. We believe that He exists and that the promises in His Word are true. We put our confidence and our hope in their reality, even though we do not always see or feel them.

I don't know what difficulty you may be dealing with at this time, but I want to assure you that God loves you and that He has a good plan for you. I urge you to believe what God's Word says more than you believe the way your circumstances look right now. Through faith and patience you will receive the manifestation of God's promises.

God will meet your needs, and you will see the result of your faith if you hold fast and don't give up or back down. Take time right now to remember a time when God did something wonderful for you, and let it encourage you to believe that He will do it again. He is working right now, and you will see the result.

"Father, I put my trust in You. I believe that You are faithful, and that You are working on my behalf right now. In Jesus' name. Amen."

EVERY WORD BEGINS WITH
A THOUGHT

The mouth speaks what the heart is full of. —LUKE 6:45

Every word you speak and every action you take begins with a thought. The thought may be fleeting, or even incomplete or not fully developed, but you won't speak or do anything unless you have thought it first.

Certain thoughts become extremely powerful words and actions—for example, the creation of the world was in God's heart. He knew what He wanted and spoke each aspect of creation. When He spoke, His words had power. Whatever left His mouth came into existence. When God said, "Let there be light," there was light (Genesis 1:3). This same process happened with the sky, the seas, vegetation, the sun, the moon, the stars, and the entire natural world (Genesis 1:1–31).

You are created in God's image (Genesis 1:27), and your words also have power (Proverbs 18:21). Your words start with your thoughts, and they have a powerful impact on your life. Use them wisely and in agreement with what God has spoken in His Word.

"Father, help me to use my words wisely, remembering always that they are extremely powerful. In Jesus' name. Amen."

WHEN THINGS DON'T GO
AS PLANNED

"For My thoughts are not your thoughts, nor are your ways My ways," declares the Lord. —ISAIAH 55:8 AMP

We want things to work out in our lives in certain ways, but experience teaches us that we don't always get what we want. We have a plan for the day, and suddenly something unexpected and unwanted happens—and our plan must change. At times like this, we can choose to trust God or to be upset.

Since being upset won't change anything, why waste time doing it? Choose to trust that God can work out the change for your good and do something even better than what you had planned. Ask Him for anything you want to ask Him for, but trust Him to give you what is best.

"Father, thank You for directing my life according to Your plan, not mine. In Jesus' name. Amen."

FORGIVEN

And their sins and their lawless acts I will remember no more [no longer holding their sins against them]. —HEBREWS 10:17 AMP

When you feel guilty and condemned, please remember that if you have repented of your sin, you have God's promise that you are forgiven. Jesus paid for our sins, and He alone bore the penalty for them. He took our punishment and has set us free from the need to agonize over past mistakes.

Satan is the accuser of God's children (Revelation 12:10). He delights in trying to remind us of past mistakes and seeks to make us miserable, but we don't have to believe him. He is a liar. God not only forgives our sins, but He remembers them no more. This is amazingly good news! You can stop remembering what God has forgotten and get on with joyfully living this day that God has given you.

Focus on what lies ahead of you, not on what is behind. Remember this: Your sins are forgiven, and today is a brand-new beginning.

"Father, thank You very much for Your amazing forgiveness and goodness in my life. Help me let go of the past and enjoy this day. In Jesus' name. Amen."

WHEN LIFE HURTS

But resist him, be firm in your faith [against his attack—rooted, established, immovable], knowing that the same experiences of suffering are being experienced by your brothers and sisters throughout the world. [You do not suffer alone.] –1 PETER 5:9 AMP

We experience many blessings in life, but we also go through times that are painful and challenging. We often feel lonely in our pain, but we aren't, because many other people around us are hurting also. We don't always know the silent suffering that people endure, but we can let our own pain teach us to be compassionate toward them.

Listen carefully to what people tell you about what they are going through, and try to imagine how you might feel in their situation. Jesus suffered greatly in His life, but He also had great compassion for those who were hurting in any way. We may not be able to alleviate someone's pain, but we can lighten their load by truly caring about them.

"Father, help me have great compassion for those who are hurting, and help me learn and become a better person each time I go through something difficult. In Jesus' name. Amen."

A RULE TO LIVE BY

So in everything, do to others what you would have them do to you, for this sums up the Law and the Prophets. —MATTHEW 7:12

Today's scripture is also known as the Golden Rule. When the Golden Rule is at work, whatever we offer to others comes back to us. If we extend generosity by giving to others, we find that people are generous to us. If we show kindness, we reap kindness in return. If we demonstrate friendship, we reap friendship. We often have to be proactive about treating other people well before others will treat us well. We also have to choose, at times, to treat people better than they treat us.

Would you like people to respect you more? Then respect other people. Would you like people to communicate better? Then become a better communicator. Would you like someone to offer to babysit your children so you can have a break or a date with your spouse? Then offer to babysit theirs.

When the Golden Rule is in operation, you may sow into one person's life and reap in an entirely different relationship. For example, you may offer to babysit your sister's children, and she may not reciprocate. But your neighbor may offer to keep your children while you have dinner with your spouse. The goodness you extend to others may not come back to you from the people to whom you give it, and it may not come back when you expect it, but it will come back.

"Father, help me to be proactive in treating people the way I want to be treated. In Jesus' name. Amen."

GRATITUDE INSTEAD OF COMPLAINING

And do not murmur [in unwarranted discontent], as some of them did—and were destroyed by the destroyer. —1 CORINTHIANS 10:10 AMP

If we don't follow the guidance of the Holy Spirit, we may murmur and complain about many things. Complaining weakens us and steals our God-ordained strength. But when we give thanks and are grateful for the many benefits that God bestows upon us, we increase our strength.

The Israelites murmured, and their enemies destroyed them. They were weakened to such a degree that they were unable to fight the good fight of faith. They dealt with struggles, as we all do, but they also had many blessings. However, they chose to focus on the struggles, and their discontent revealed itself in words of complaint.

You might say that complaining opens a door for the devil to attack us, but gratitude builds a wall of protection around us, protection that comes from God. When we experience circumstances that we do not like, we usually don't have to try to complain, but we may have to give thanks on purpose.

"Father, I am sorry for any complaining I have done. I repent, and I receive Your forgiveness. Grant me the grace to speak only words of gratitude for Your goodness in my life. Thank You. In Jesus' name. Amen."

FAITH TO INHERIT
GOD'S PROMISES

So that you may not be sluggish, but imitators of those who through faith and patience inherit the promises. —HEBREWS 6:12 ESV

Living by faith often requires patience. We put our faith in God, and He is faithful to keep His promises, but He never gives us the exact timing of when we will see our circumstances change. If we asked God for something and received it immediately, we would have no need for real faith. It is in the waiting that our faith is tested and tried.

While we wait, the devil will tell us many lies. He may suggest that God doesn't love us or that He is angry with us for something we have done wrong—and that is the reason nothing is changing. He tries to plant seeds of doubt in our mind by suggesting that God's promises to us are not true. These are the times in which we must hold firm to our faith in God.

At the appointed time, God's answers to our prayers and the manifestation of our faith will be seen. God is not always early, but He will never be late, at least not according to His timing.

"Father, grant me the grace to wait patiently on You and trust that Your timing is always perfect. Thank You. In Jesus' name. Amen."

YOUR THOUGHTS CAN STRENGTHEN YOU

Finally, brothers and sisters, whatever is true, whatever is noble, whatever is right, whatever is pure, whatever is lovely, whatever is admirable—if anything is excellent or praiseworthy—think about such things. —PHILIPPIANS 4:8

I have often said, "Think about what you're thinking about." This simply means to pay attention to your thoughts. The enemy and the world around you will bombard your mind with things for you to think about, and it's up to you to decide whether or not you will follow them. Thinking about the wrong things will drain your strength and vigor, while thinking about the right things actually energizes you.

Let me ask you today: Where do you put most of your mental energy? Do your thoughts cause you to relive painful circumstances or focus on situations that did not turn out as you had hoped? Do you recall past sins or mistakes? Or, in contrast, do you use your mental energy to focus on all that is good in your life, on making the most of the present and preparing for a great future?

Pay attention today to what you're thinking about. Don't let your mind wander anywhere it wants to go. Instead, discipline your thoughts in such a way that they will help you and strengthen you instead of holding you back or taking you into negative territory.

"Father, I don't want to pour any more effort into negative thinking. Help me to direct my mental energy in positive ways that will strengthen me. In Jesus' name. Amen."

DOUBT

Behold, I am with you and will keep [careful watch over you and guard] you wherever you may go, and I will bring you back to this [promised] land; for I will not leave you until I have done what I have promised you. —GENESIS 28:15 AMP

God wants us to be assured that He is with us and working on our behalf at all times. Satan wants us to doubt God's love, His presence, and His help. Our enemy wants us to think that God has abandoned us and that we are alone and helpless.

I want to encourage you today to believe God's Word more than you believe the way you feel. God doesn't always work according to our timetable, but as long as we continue believing, He keeps working. I urge you to believe today's scripture and let it encourage you and strengthen your faith.

Don't grow weary in doing what is right, because at exactly the right time, you will reap the rewards of your faithful obedience (Galatians 6:9).

"Father, help me to never doubt Your love and to always be confident that You are working in my life for my good. Thank You. In Jesus' name. Amen."

FOCUS

Therefore, strengthen your feeble arms and weak knees.

—HEBREWS 12:12

Life is filled with unexpected challenges. Every storm is not in the forecast. Sometimes we plan for a pleasant, sunny day, and suddenly, without warning, the rain begins to pour and the wind blows hard. Each time a storm arises in our lives, we have to choose what we will focus on.

If we focus on our disappointment and think too much about the problem, it seems to get bigger and bigger. But if we focus on God's goodness in our lives and trust that all things will work out for our good, it allows us to enjoy the day, even though it didn't work out as originally planned.

When we have physical pain, if we focus on the pain, it gets worse as every minute goes by. But paying attention to or focusing on something else almost always diminishes the pain to some degree. Think about things that benefit you and not about things that add to your misery.

"Father, help me focus on the good things in my life rather than the disappointments and challenges. Thank You. In Jesus' name. Amen."

KEEP YOUR PEACE

A furious squall came up, and the waves broke over the boat, so that it was nearly swamped. Jesus was in the stern, sleeping on a cushion. The disciples woke him and said to him, "Teacher, don't you care if we drown?" –MARK 4:37-38

Staying peaceful when your surroundings are calm and happy is easy. The challenge comes when your circumstances feel threatening or cause you to be angry or afraid. The disciples lost their peace in the middle of a storm that arose one night as they were in a boat on the Sea of Galilee (Mark 4:35–41). Most people would understand why they were afraid and upset in the midst of such a squall, but Jesus was on the boat with them, and He was sleeping through the storm.

When the disciples asked Jesus whether He cared about them, He got up, quieted the wind and the waves, and then asked them an important question: "Why are you so afraid? Do you still have no faith?" (Mark 4:40).

Because Jesus was with them in the storm, they had no reason to fear. One of the names of Jesus in Scripture is the Prince of Peace (Isaiah 9:6). And the apostle Paul writes that Jesus Christ "is our peace" (Ephesians 2:14). These verses tell us that Jesus always gives us peace. No matter what kind of storm you are facing today, remember that Jesus is with you, and keep your peace.

"Father, help me to keep my peace in every storm and to stay focused on Jesus, the Prince of Peace, who is my peace. In His name I pray. Amen."

WHEN YOU DON'T KNOW WHAT TO DO

If any of you lacks wisdom [to guide him through a decision or circumstance], he is to ask of [our benevolent] God, who gives to everyone generously and without rebuke or blame, and it will be given to him. —JAMES 1:5 AMP

At times, we all find ourselves needing to make a decision and not knowing what to do. Behaving emotionally is not the right answer, because that usually makes any situation worse.

When you are unsure about which direction to take, the first thing to do is to ask God for wisdom and acknowledge Him in all your ways (Proverbs 3:6). Trusting that God will guide you often leads you to a place of needing to step out and find out what will work. Understandably, you would like to be sure you are right before taking action, but in my experience, that rarely happens. I normally have to work with God to find the right course of action to take. I take a step in a direction and see if it works. If so, then I take another step, and then another, until I know if I am on the right path.

If I take a step in one direction and it doesn't work, then I simply step back, pray and think some more, and then try another direction when I feel the time is right.

Don't be discouraged if you try something and it doesn't work. That's often the only way you will ever know the right thing to do. When you carefully try different options, you quickly find out which choices to eliminate—and that ultimately leaves you with the right one.

"Father, I believe that You guide me in making decisions, but I also know that faith requires me to step out and find out. I ask for the confidence to step out and not be afraid of making mistakes. In Jesus' name. Amen."

TEMPTATION AND SIN

No temptation has overtaken you except what is common to mankind. And God is faithful; he will not let you be tempted beyond what you can bear. But when you are tempted, he will also provide a way out so that you can endure it. –1 CORINTHIANS 10:13

Satan likes to make us think that being tempted to sin is equal to committing a sin, but it isn't. We are all tempted. Even Jesus was tempted, but He never sinned (Hebrews 4:15). Satan may put in our mind a thought or an imagination so evil that we think we are not even saved. Be careful, because that is exactly what he wants you to think. Instead, you can cast down the evil thought and replace it with something good (2 Corinthians 10:5).

The Holy Spirit led Jesus into the wilderness, where the devil tempted Him repeatedly. He resisted each temptation, and when the testing was done, the devil left Him until a more opportune time (Luke 4:1–13). We will always be tempted to do wrong, but we don't have to yield to the temptation.

The moment you feel tempted to do wrong, pray immediately. I also suggest that you pray regularly about any area of your life in which you know you are weak or susceptible to the enemy. Being tempted to do wrong and choosing to do right in spite of the temptation is actually a victory. Each time you do it, you become stronger and stronger.

Remember, being tempted to sin is not sin; it is merely a test of faith.

"Father, strengthen me at all times to recognize and resist the temptation to sin. I rely on You for the strength to do what is right. In Jesus' name. Amen."

A STRONG FOUNDATION

When the foundations are being destroyed, what can the righteous do? —PSALM 11:3

The most important part of a building is its foundation. Everything about a building is built on the foundation, so if it is not strong, the whole structure is at risk for all kinds of problems. If it is not level or if it cracks, the building is not safe. Under certain circumstances, it could crumble or collapse.

Just as a building has a physical foundation, you have a moral and spiritual foundation, and you build your life on it. The world offers many options for your foundation. You may choose to build your life on your education, your gifts or talents, your professional success, your family, your achievements, your reputation with people, or any number of other things. But all of them will prove faulty. At some point, they will all weaken or crack.

The only firm foundation in life is God's Word. You can build every aspect of your life on His Word, and it will never crack or weaken. Nothing can destroy it, and nothing can take it away from you. As long as you have that foundation, you can walk in truth and power all the days of your life.

"Father, help me to build my life upon the firm foundation of Your Word. In Jesus' name. Amen."

GOD USES ORDINARY PEOPLE

Now when they saw the boldness of Peter and John, and perceived that they were uneducated, common men, they were astonished.

—ACTS 4:13 ESV

Sometimes people feel that they don't have enough ability to serve God, but He looks for availability rather than ability. If God wants us to do something, He can give us any ability we need to do the job. Our Lord frequently uses people who seem less than qualified for a particular job, but Paul teaches us that He chooses the weak and foolish things of the world to confound the wise (1 Corinthians 1:27–28). He wants people to be astonished at what He can do through those who are simply available.

Don't let the devil convince you that you don't have enough qualifications for God to use you. Tell God you are available for anything He wants you to do, and be assured that God's grace and His anointing (His power and presence) will help you do things that will amaze and astonish you.

Peter was so frightened that three times he denied even knowing Jesus. But a short while later, after the Holy Spirit came upon him, he boldly preached in the streets of Jerusalem, and people were astonished because they knew him as an ordinary man.

"Father, I want You to use me for Your glory. I know I am not qualified, but I ask You to give me the ability I need. I lean on and rely on You alone. Thank You. In Jesus' name. Amen."

WHAT ABOUT THE WICKED?

Be sure of this: The wicked will not go unpunished, but those who are righteous will go free. –PROVERBS 11:21

It is hard to understand why wicked people often prosper while they treat the godly in unjust ways. But be assured that they will not go unpunished. Our goal should be to keep doing right, no matter what others do, and to trust God to take care of our situations. We overcome evil with good (Romans 12:21), so I urge you to never return evil for evil, but instead, do all you can to bless others (1 Peter 3:9).

God has promised to vindicate us and give us a double recompense for former trouble and mistreatment (Isaiah 61:7). While we wait on God to fulfill His promise, it is important for us to forgive, pray for, and bless those who mistreat us when opportunity arises. Although this seems unreasonable, it reflects how God deals with us, and He expects us to deal with others the same way.

Perhaps you are being treated unfairly right now. If so, be assured that God knows and cares, and that He will deal with your enemies.

"Father, I am thankful that You are watching over me, and I trust You to deal with those who abuse and misuse me. I pray that they will know the truth and be set free. Thank You. In Jesus' name. Amen."

CHOOSE FREEDOM

The Spirit of the Lord is on me, because he has anointed me to proclaim good news to the poor. He has sent me to proclaim freedom for the prisoners and recovery of sight for the blind, to set the oppressed free, to proclaim the year of the Lord's favor.

—LUKE 4:18–19

Clearly, Jesus came to set us free. That's what today's scripture teaches us. But anytime freedom begins to replace bondage, a battle begins in our minds. Freedom is from God, and bondage is from the enemy. The enemy doesn't give up his territory easily. When he sees freedom coming, he will begin to whisper lies, such as "You'll never break free from that old habit," or "You will never heal from the pain of your past; what happened to you was so awful that even God can't help you," or "It's impossible to get unaddicted; you're going to crave that substance (or that behavior) for the rest of your life."

No matter how the devil tries to keep you in bondage, influencing your thoughts to work against you, you can choose to stand against him. According to James 4:7, when you submit to God and resist him, he will flee. You don't have to agree with what he wants you to think. You can choose to walk in the freedom Jesus offers you. Fill your mind with the truth of God's Word, and when the devil tries to keep you in bondage, speak those words of freedom to him. Keep choosing freedom, and you will experience it.

"Father, thank You for sending Your Son, Jesus, to set me free. Help me embrace the freedom You have provided for me. Amen."

DO YOU WANT TO CHANGE?

And I am sure of this, that he who began a good work in you will bring it to completion at the day of Jesus Christ. –PHILIPPIANS 1:6 ESV

Everyone who loves God wants to grow spiritually and be the best they can for Him. We can desire to change, study God's Word, and pray about our faults, but only God can change us. As a matter of fact, He is continually transforming us into the image of Jesus Christ and will continue doing so right up to the time of His return.

I pray that you will learn to celebrate your progress in the Lord instead of being upset about how far you still have to go. Not one of us has reached perfection, and we never will until we are out of our fleshly bodies and at home with the Lord. Satan wants us to focus on our faults, but God wants us to focus on Him and His unconditional love for us.

The more we focus on Jesus and spend time with Him, the more we will change. God is always with us, and as long as we continue believing, He continues working in and for us. Believe today that God is changing you and that you are becoming more and more like Him.

"Father, thank You for working in me and changing me. I trust that You will help me be the best I can be for Your glory. In Jesus' name. Amen."

TAKE CARE OF YOURSELF

Be not wise in your own eyes; fear the Lord, and turn away from evil. It will be healing to your flesh and refreshment to your bones.

—PROVERBS 3:7–8 ESV

God wants us to be healthy and energetic, but we forfeit good health if we don't take care of ourselves. We live in times of stress and pressure, and that is not likely to change, so we must make good decisions about how we should live and manage the time God has given us. If we pressure ourselves to do what everyone wants us to do, sooner or later our bodies will break down under the strain, and we may find that we have made ourselves sick while keeping others happy.

We all need to use wisdom and live balanced lives in which we work, rest, play, and worship. If we follow God's wisdom, it will promote healing and good health for us, but if we are foolish, we will pay the price for it eventually.

Taking time to take care of yourself—to rest and enjoy the fruits of your labor and do things that refresh you—is not selfish, but wise. Taking care of yourself will bring you great benefits in the future.

"Father, help me use wisdom in managing my time and energy. I want to be healthy all the days of my life and to serve You with my whole heart. In Jesus' name, I thank You for helping me. Amen."

THE DANGER OF ANGER

Whoever is slow to anger has great understanding, but he who has a hasty temper exalts folly. –PROVERBS 14:29 ESV

Most of us could find a reason each day to be angry with someone or about something. Life is filled with imperfections and injustices, but anger doesn't solve them. It only makes us miserable. The Word of God instructs us not to let the sun go down on our anger, because if we do, we give the devil a foothold in our lives (Ephesians 4:26–27).

Anger is an emotion that can and should be controlled. Love is not touchy or easily offended, but it is long-suffering and generous in mercy. One of the best ways to stay happy is to avoid anger. According to the writer of today's scripture, the person who is hasty to become angry is foolish, but the one who is slow to anger is wise and has great understanding.

If you are angry with anyone, I urge you to completely forgive that person. By doing so, you will set yourself free to enjoy the day. Remember that anger doesn't make any situation better; it only makes you miserable.

"Father, help me to be slow to get angry and always quick to forgive. Thank You. In Jesus' name. Amen."

KEEP THE JUDGMENT DOOR CLOSED

Do not judge, or you too will be judged. For in the same way you judge others, you will be judged, and with the measure you use, it will be measured to you. —MATTHEW 7:1–2

Most of us know that thinking critically about others and being judgmental is not kind or loving. But do we understand that it actually harms us and makes us vulnerable to the enemy? I believe that's what Matthew 7:1–6 teaches.

This passage simply instructs us not to judge or criticize others. This certainly applies to our words, and to our thoughts as well. When we judge others, Matthew 7:1 says, we will be judged too.

In Matthew 7:2, we see that we will be judged the same way we judge others. The Amplified Bible says that "in accordance with your standard of measure…judgment will be measured to you." For example, if you are very harsh and strict in judging others and cannot overlook even the slightest imperfection, others will judge you just as harshly.

I believe that judging other people opens the door for the devil, our enemy, to judge and accuse us. When we criticize or judge them, we are saying that we see nothing wrong with criticism and judgment. The enemy takes advantage of that attitude and turns it back on us.

We all need to do our best to keep the doors of our lives closed to the enemy. One way to do it is to walk in love, mercy, and grace toward others, refusing to criticize and judge them.

"Father, help me keep the judgment door to the enemy closed in my life by not criticizing or judging others. In Jesus' name. Amen."

GOD SEES

The eyes of the Lord are in every place, keeping watch upon the evil and the good. —PROVERBS 15:3 AMPC

Sometimes we feel that no one sees or understands what we are going through, and that can be a very lonely feeling. I want to encourage you today by reminding you that God is everywhere, watching over everything. He does have a good plan for your life, and as you continue to seek Him, that plan will become clear. Even the difficulties you experience will work out for your good and fit into God's plan.

None of us enjoy or understand injustice, but we all experience it as we journey through life. The good news is that God is a God of justice, which means that He eventually makes everything that's wrong right if we trust Him. You are not invisible to God. He sees right where you are, and He will strengthen you to keep moving forward as you rely on Him. You are not alone.

"Father, help me recognize Your presence in my life. Comfort me in difficult times. I put my trust in You. In Jesus' name. Amen."

SOWING AND REAPING

Do not be deceived: God is not mocked, for whatever one sows, that will he also reap. –GALATIANS 6:7 ESV

Beginning in the Book of Genesis and throughout Scripture, we read about the law of sowing and reaping. The kind of seed we sow determines the type of harvest we receive. Some people think they can sow bad seed (make bad choices) and then pray for a good crop (good results with no negative consequences), but it doesn't work that way.

Thankfully, God is merciful and patient, and He forgives our sins if we repent of them. But those who continually sow seeds of anger, selfishness, laziness, or other unrighteous deeds will eventually reap a harvest they will not enjoy. I love the law of sowing and reaping because it excites me to think that I can draw blessings into my life by blessing others. As we sow seeds of obedience to God, we can be assured that He will send a harvest of many good things our way.

Our thoughts, words, and deeds are equivalent to seeds sown. I encourage you to examine what you are sowing and to sow according to what you desire to reap in your life. The Bible says that if we sow to please our own flesh, we will reap corruption, but if we sow to please the Spirit, we will reap eternal life (Galatians 6:8). If you sow mercy, you will reap mercy; if you sow judgment, you will reap judgment; if you sow generously, you will reap generously. Get started today sowing more good seed than ever before.

"Father, I repent for all the bad seed I have sown, and I ask You to help me start today to sow good seed so I can reap a good harvest in my life. Thank You. In Jesus' name. Amen."

BE SLOW TO ANGER

Good sense makes one slow to anger, and it is his glory to overlook an offense. —PROVERBS 19:11 ESV

If we want to be angry, we can find plenty of things to be angry about or people to be angry with. But God teaches us to be slow to anger and quick to forgive. He is not asking us to do something that He doesn't do. God is long-suffering with us and forgives us over and over, often for the same offense.

Being angry makes us miserable, and when we are miserable, we usually make others around us miserable also. Anger doesn't solve a problem; it merely wastes our time; wears us out physically, emotionally, and mentally; and prevents us from entering into the peace and joy that Jesus died for us to enjoy. Can you honestly think of a time when being angry was a blessing and a benefit to you?

If you are angry about an injustice, ask God what you can do to help change it. If you are angry with someone, pray for that person and then let go of the offense. We should be assured that there are plenty of times when other people have to do that for us. Be slow to anger, and always remember that being angry hurts you and doesn't help or change anything.

"Father, I need Your grace to be quick to forgive and slow to become angry. I trust You to help me. In Jesus' name. Amen."

FULLY SATISFIED

As for me, I shall see Your face in righteousness; I will be [fully] satisfied when I awake [to find myself] seeing Your likeness.

—PSALM 17:15 AMP

Have you ever fallen into the trap of thinking, *If I could just buy that thing, I would be satisfied.* Or, *If my children would just behave, I would be satisfied.* Or, *If I could just get that job, I would be satisfied.* Or, *If my spouse would only do that, I would be satisfied.* Or, *If we could just get a bigger house, I would be satisfied.*

Most of us can come up with a long list of things we think would satisfy us. It's easy to do, but it doesn't work. The problem is that the satisfaction that comes from anything or anyone other than God is temporary. It might make you happy for a few days, but it would never give you deep, long-lasting joy.

As we read today's scripture, we see that David found the key to satisfaction, and it was in his relationship with God. That's the only place any of us will ever be satisfied. No matter what you long for, your heart's true craving is for God alone. I encourage you today to seek Him with all your heart and to spend time in His presence, talking to Him throughout your day and growing closer to Him.

"Father, only You can satisfy me completely. Thank You for being all that I want and all that I need. In Jesus' name. Amen."

WHY DO WE DO WHAT WE DO?

If I give away all I have, and if I deliver up my body to be burned, but have not love, I gain nothing. —1 CORINTHIANS 13:3 ESV

God is more concerned about why we do what we do than about what we do. He wants our motive (the reason we do what we do) in all things to be pure. When we give, we should do it out of love for God and appreciation for what He has done for us, not to gain something or out of fear that if we don't give, we will be cursed.

Everything we do should be led by the Holy Spirit and for His glory, not to boast or feel good about all we accomplish. Anyone who has an overly busy schedule could easily cut out many unimportant activities and make time for more important things if they would examine why they do what they do.

We should do what we do to please God, not to please other people or out of a sense of obligation. We should do all that we do in faith, because without faith it is impossible to please God (Hebrews 11:6). We should always be sure that our service to God is done because we love Him, not to get Him to love us. God already loves us, and nothing we do or don't do can add to or take away from that. Take some time and examine the reasons you do what you do. I believe this will help you find more joy in what you do.

"Father, I want all of my motives to be right. Reveal any wrong motives that I have and help me make any adjustments I need to make. Thank You. In Jesus' name. Amen."

GOD IS GOOD

Taste and see that the Lord is good; blessed is the one who takes refuge in him. –PSALM 34:8

It is important to believe at all times that God is good. When we have problems, or we are sick, or we experience loss of some kind, He is still good, and He will help us in our time of need.

How do we "taste and see" that the Lord is good? I believe we need to think and talk a lot more about the good things that God does for us all the time. We often give "coincidence" credit for circumstances that God has orchestrated and carefully planned for our good. Yesterday, I happened to be in the right place at the right time with the right people to see a need and be able to meet it. Did I just happen to be there? Did they just happen to be there? Or did God arrange the situation? I prefer to believe that God delights in being involved in even the tiniest details of our lives, and I hope to learn more and more how to "taste and see" His goodness.

I encourage you to be watchful, and before you say, "Wasn't that a good coincidence?" consider that it may have been the hand of God moving in your life.

"Father, help me give You credit for all You are doing in my life, and teach me to 'taste and see' that You are good. In Jesus' name. Amen."

BE WISE WITH YOUR WORDS

It is not what goes into the mouth that defiles a person, but what comes out of the mouth; this defiles a person. —MATTHEW 15:11 ESV

Since God gave us one mouth and two ears, I guess that means we should listen more than we talk. It is easy to blurt out whatever pops into your head, but that often causes problems, especially in relationships.

Old Testament Jewish law included many requirements about foods the Jews could not eat because they were considered to be unclean. But when Jesus came to earth, He said that what comes out of the mouth (words) defiles, not what goes into the mouth (food).

Many people don't realize the power of their words. Because of that they do not use caution regarding what they say about themselves, their future, their finances, their children, other people, and probably hundreds of other topics.

"Death and life are in the power of the tongue," according to Proverbs 18:21 (AMPC). Since that is true, we should certainly train ourselves to not speak without thinking. Our words may be one of our biggest problems. Start paying more attention to what you say, and ask God to help you speak only what is pleasing to Him. I think you will find that doing this will benefit you greatly.

"Father, I am sorry for all the words I have spoken that were not according to Your will. Please help me be more cautious moving forward, beginning right now. In Jesus' name. Amen."

BLESSING GOD AT ALL TIMES

I will bless the Lord at all times; his praise shall continually be in my mouth. —PSALM 34:1 ESV

When we experience a trial of some kind and it lasts a long time, blessing the Lord in the midst of it may become more and more difficult because of our physical or emotional pain. But blessing or praising Him actually helps relieve the pressure we feel and soothes our pain. God is the "God of all comfort, who comforts us in all our affliction" (2 Corinthians 1:3–4 ESV).

God is not in our life to make sure we never face difficulty, but to help us with and in our difficulties. The more we complain, the longer we remain in a situation we don't like. But the more we bless and praise the Lord, the better everything is—including our attitude.

No matter how bad things are, we can always find something for which to be thankful. I spoke this morning with a coworker who recently endured a painful bout with kidney stones. He has dealt with the same thing on and off for more than thirty years. He said, "I would prefer not to have them, but I thank God for doctors and medicine that help get me through it." This is the kind of attitude that glorifies God.

"Father, help me bless You at all times, because You are always good. There is always something good in my life to be thankful for. In Jesus' name. Amen."

OUR GREATEST PRIVILEGE

Pray at all times (on every occasion, in every season) in the Spirit, with all [manner of] prayer and entreaty. To that end keep alert and watch with strong purpose and perseverance, interceding in behalf of all the saints (God's consecrated people).

—EPHESIANS 6:18 AMPC

For the past three mornings, I have felt an urgency to meditate on the power of prayer and what a great privilege it is. We should never feel obligated to pray, but we should instead rejoice in being invited by God to do so. He hears our prayers, He delights in them, and He answers them.

We can pray anywhere, at any time. Through prayer, we can make petitions (make requests), intercede for others, give thanks, and put all of our concerns into God's hands. In addition, in Jesus' name, we can resist the power of the devil when we pray. Let us be diligent and take advantage of the great privilege of prayer.

Prayer doesn't have to be complicated. It is simply having a conversation with God. You can talk with Him about anything that concerns you and be assured that He is always interested. It can be simple, frequent, and powerful. Prayer gives us supernatural strength for each day.

"Father, thank You for the great privilege of prayer. I believe that You hear and answer my prayers. Teach me to watch and pray at all times. In Jesus' name, I pray. Amen."

GOD'S FAITHFULNESS

But I have trusted and relied on and been confident in Your lovingkindness and faithfulness; my heart shall rejoice and delight in Your salvation. –PSALM 13:5 AMP

David wrote the words of today's scripture when his enemies were all around him, threatening him. This had to have been frightening and discouraging for him. Maybe you know how he felt. You may feel surrounded right now by forces that are working against you. Perhaps you have a wayward child who resists every bit of sound advice you offer. You may be in the midst of financial problems or health struggles. You may be facing a future that looks bleak.

When you feel your enemies are surrounding you, no matter what they are—perhaps other people or maybe circumstances and situations that seem to be aligned against you—you may be tempted to worry. But that's not what David did. David reminded himself of God's faithfulness and determined that he would rejoice in God's salvation. The only way we can remind ourselves of something is to first experience it. I encourage you to trust God in the circumstances you face right now, and you will see His faithfulness. Every time He proves Himself faithful, you will find it easier and easier to trust Him in the future.

"Father, I choose to trust You, even though I feel my enemies are surrounding me. Help me to always remember how faithful You are. In Jesus' name. Amen."

ONE THING AFTER ANOTHER

Consider it pure joy, my brothers and sisters, whenever you face trials of many kinds. –JAMES 1:2

Facing an occasional trial wouldn't be so bad, but we often have times when we feel that difficulties come one on top of the other. We have heard people say, "If it isn't one thing, it's another," meaning that they have experienced a steady flow of disappointing and difficult circumstances.

Naturally, a series of troubles is more difficult than one problem here and another one there, but the more spiritually mature we are, the more we can remain peaceful and thankful even during those times.

I had been dealing with a physical problem that lasted several months. A few days after I started feeling well again, I hurt my back and was in pain because of that. My temptation was to get upset and start complaining, but experience and God's Word have taught me that neither of those glorify God or help me.

The Bible says we are to give thanks at all times in all things (1 Thessalonians 5:18; Ephesians 5:20). Let's set a goal of giving thanks for something every time we are tempted to complain. This will defeat the devil, glorify God, and ease our burden.

"Father, I am sorry for complaining. I ask Your forgiveness. I purpose to give thanks instead of complaining, but I need Your grace. Thank You for helping me. In Jesus' name. Amen."

KEEP SHOWING UP

And let us not grow weary of doing good, for in due season we will reap, if we do not give up. —GALATIANS 6:9 ESV

Our obedience to God must not be based on our circumstances, because the circumstances of our lives are not always enjoyable. I have determined that when I go through a difficult time, I will simply keep showing up. This means I continue doing what I would do if I had no trouble. I keep my commitments, spend time with God as usual, and make a practice of continuing to be good and kind to the people around me.

Is it easy? No, it isn't easy. Doing what is right is always easier if we feel like doing it, but we are to give thanks and "bless the Lord at all times" (Psalm 34:1 ESV). In addition, we are to continue to obey Him at all times.

Doing what is right when it is hard always helps us grow in Christian character. Jesus did this regularly, and we are called to be transformed into His image and let Him be our example in all things. If you are going through something difficult right now, just keep showing up and doing the right thing. In time, your trouble will pass, and you will have gained a victory over the enemy.

"Father, help me to be strong in You and keep showing up and doing what is right, no matter how I feel or what my circumstances are like. Thank You. In Jesus' name. Amen."

GOD'S VICTORIOUS POWER

Now this I know: The Lord gives victory to his anointed. He answers him from his heavenly sanctuary with the victorious power of his right hand. –PSALM 20:6

You have the opportunity to focus on many things today. You can focus on what you don't have or on what you do have. You can focus on what causes you to fear or on what makes you bold. You can focus on what you don't know or on what you do know. You can live this day as a victim of your circumstances or as a victor over them, depending on where you choose to focus.

In today's scripture, David declares: "Now this I *know*" (emphasis mine). He is thoroughly, unshakably confident in the fact that God gives victory to His people. This is a promise that you can depend on.

You can choose today to focus on areas of your life in which you seem to be losing, or you can focus on the fact that God will give you victory, no matter what battle you are fighting. I know that life's battles can be intense at times. They can drain your strength and cause you to want to give up. But I encourage you to be like David and have total confidence in the fact that God's victorious power is at work on your behalf.

"Father, help me focus on You and to have unshakable confidence in Your victorious power. In Jesus' name. Amen."

ARE YOU DISCOURAGED WITH YOURSELF?

But the path of the righteous is like the light of dawn, which shines brighter and brighter until full day. –PROVERBS 4:18 ESV

We all have faults, and because of our love for our Lord, we want to overcome them. But each time we gain a victory over one weakness or fault, it seems something else shows up—something we didn't even realize was a problem previously. This happens because the Holy Spirit doesn't deal with us about all of our weaknesses and faults at one time. If He did, it would be too much for any of us to bear without wanting to give up. He delivers us from our enemies and problems little by little (Deuteronomy 7:22).

As the Holy Spirit deals with us, we can easily become discouraged with ourselves, especially if we continue to struggle with certain faults long after we think we should have overcome them. The good news is that God does keep working with us as long as we continue believing His promises, and we always have the option to look at how far we have come instead of how far we still have to go.

The more we focus on Jesus instead of on what is wrong with us, the sooner we will be changed into His image. He will be working with us and in us, right up until the time of His return, so be thankful that He will never give up on you, and be determined not to give up on yourself.

"Father, thank You for the changes You have already made in me and for all the changes yet to come. Help me stay focused on You rather than on my faults. In Jesus' name. Amen."

YOU ARE UNIQUE

For as in one body we have many members, and the members do not all have the same function. —ROMANS 12:4 ESV

We are all unique, just as each part of our physical body is unique and has a unique function. We all look different, and we have different temperaments, abilities, and talents. Our enemy, Satan, often tries to make us feel that something is wrong with us if we are not like people around us, but that is absolutely not true.

God has uniquely created each of us with His own hand for a special purpose, and we need to embrace who we are and not try to be like someone else. Although other people may set good examples that we want to follow, it's a big mistake to reject ourselves and try to be someone other than who we are.

God's Word clearly says that He gives each of us different abilities and that we are to use them (Romans 12:6). We cannot be someone else, and trying to do so only frustrates us. I encourage you not to compare yourself with other people, but to be fully your own special, unique self.

"Father, thank You for making me unique. Help me use my abilities to glorify You and be a blessing to others. In Jesus' name. Amen."

REASONING

Trust in the Lord with all your heart, and do not lean on your own understanding. —PROVERBS 3:5 ESV

As human beings, we are naturally curious, and we want to know what will happen next in our lives. We can easily waste our time trying to reason or figure out the answers to questions that only God knows. But there would be no need for faith if we had no unanswered questions. We have something better than answers, because we have an invitation to trust God, who is always faithful and who never leaves us to bear our burdens without His help.

Some answers will be revealed in time, but others may never come. Ours is not to understand everything, but to trust God in everything. Naturally, we will ponder things we don't understand and search for answers, but when we grow confused and frustrated, we have gone too far and we need to stop the questions, trust God, and keep our peace.

If we had all the answers we would like, it would take the mystery out of life, and I think God has created us to love and even need a little mystery. I encourage you to trust God more and reason less. Whatever you don't understand will work out for your good if you keep your faith in God (Romans 8:28).

"Father, there is a great deal I don't understand, but thankfully You do understand it. I ask that You help me keep my trust in You until You know the time is right for You to give me understanding. In Jesus' name. Amen."

WORSHIP FIRST

A man with leprosy came and knelt before him and said, "Lord, if you are willing, you can make me clean." –MATTHEW 8:2

Sometimes, people read today's scripture and skip over its most important part. They first focus on the fact that the man had leprosy, a terrible disease that would have taken a miracle to cure. Then they turn their attention to his question and wonder if Jesus will be willing to heal him. We also need to pay attention to the fact that the man "knelt before him."

The fact that he knelt before Jesus reveals the condition of his heart. He was humble in the presence of the Lord, and he worshipped and honored Him before he asked Him for a miracle.

When we need something from God, we can easily become so focused on our situation that we completely overlook the importance of worshipping and honoring God. We jump straight into talking about what we need from Him and forget to thank Him for who He is.

No matter what you need today—whether it's something minor or something major—God can help you. But before you ask Him to do anything for you, take time to praise, worship, and honor Him for who He is.

"Father, help me to worship You before I ever ask You to do anything for me. In Jesus' name. Amen."

WHEN WILL MY BREAKTHROUGH COME?

My times are in Your hands. —PSALM 31:15 AMPC

God gives us dreams and visions (hope) for our lives, but He hides the exact timing of their manifestation. This He reserves for His wisdom. Why does God withhold the timing of our breakthrough from us? Waiting is definitely a test of our faith, and it helps develop patience in us. Moses waited forty years (Acts 7:30), Joseph waited thirteen years (Genesis 37:2; 41:46), and Abraham waited twenty-five years (Genesis 12:1–4; 21:5).

I waited many long years to see my dreams come to pass. During that time, I asked thousands of times, "When, God, when?" and never got any answer except that my times were in His hands (Psalm 31:15). I eventually learned to trust that God's timing would be perfect, but until I did, I was frustrated and anxious.

God must do many things to prepare us for the good things He has already prepared for us, and we should trust His process. If you are waiting for something right now and the waiting is frustrating you, I strongly encourage you to enjoy your journey, because God will not be rushed. Every day that passes brings you one day closer to seeing your dreams come true, so enjoy the wait and remember that we inherit God's promises through faith and patience (Hebrews 6:12).

"Father, help me be patient as I wait on You. Thank You. In Jesus' name. Amen."

RECEIVING FORGIVENESS

"I will remember their sins and their lawless deeds no more." Where there is forgiveness of these, there is no longer any offering for sin. —HEBREWS 10:17–18 ESV

Are you good at receiving forgiveness for your sins from God? Or do you repent of sin and then continue to feel guilty about it? If so, then you are asking but not receiving. The Bible says that we are to ask and receive that our "joy may be full" (John 16:24 ESV).

Jesus paid for our sins once and for all, and no more sacrifice is needed. When you repent of your sins, God wants you to receive His forgiveness, rather than sacrifice your joy or enjoyment of life because you are punishing yourself for your mistakes. I did that for years until God revealed to me that I was using guilt and refusing to enjoy life as a means of trying to pay for my sins. He also showed me that all my sins had already been paid in full and that nothing can be added to what Christ has done for us.

According to Scripture, God not only forgives our sins, but He also forgets them (Isaiah 43:25; Hebrews 10:17). This is difficult for us to take in and fully believe, but it is true. As humans, we often have difficulty forgetting hurtful things people have done to us. Thankfully, God is not like we are. I encourage you to make sure you not only ask for, but also fully receive, God's forgiveness when you admit your sin and repent.

"*Father, thank You for Your mercy, seen through Your forgiveness of sins. Please help me receive it fully and realize that I don't need to keep punishing myself for my mistakes, because Jesus took the punishment I deserved. In Jesus' name. Amen.*"

BREAKING UP WITH FEAR

Have I not commanded you? Be strong and courageous. Do not be frightened, and do not be dismayed, for the Lord your God is with you wherever you go. —JOSHUA 1:9 ESV

Deep down inside, I think we all want a life that includes adventure. But too often, fear is the ruling force in our lives, and it keeps us trapped in boring sameness. Perhaps fear has been with you through everything you have done in life. If so, then it has stolen the joy of what you were doing. Now is the time to break up with fear. It is time to take your life back and start living it by following the Holy Spirit.

God is extremely creative, as you may have noticed while observing His creation. Following Him will never lead you to boredom. It will, however, require that you take steps of faith and say goodbye to fear. Faith is taking step one before you know what step two will be. I encourage you to follow your heart and live courageously, which often means "doing it afraid"!

"Father, help me be courageous and guide me into the next step You want me to take in my life. In Jesus' name. Amen."

PURPOSEFUL QUIET

Come with me by yourselves to a quiet place and get some rest.

—MARK 6:31

The world we live in today is very noisy. In light of that, I think we must purposefully take time for periods of quiet. I love quiet, and it helps restore me when I am tired. Getting good quality rest is impossible without some quiet to go along with it. We can sit down in a chair or lie in bed to rest our bodies, but if our souls are busy worrying and we have no peace, we will not be rested when we get up.

This verse tells us that we need time alone—time that is quiet and restful. I have found that when we don't have quietness, stress builds up in us to a place where it can make us sick or unhappy. Quiet surroundings help us calm our souls.

Maintaining balance in our lives is vital. The King James Version of the Bible says, "Let your moderation be known unto all men" (Philippians 4:5). Excess is an open door for the devil to wreak havoc in our lives, and it always leads to problems of some kind. We need to think and plan, but excessive thinking and planning becomes a problem. We need activity, but we also need rest.

God has given us the fruit of self-control (Galatians 5:22–23), and we should use it to maintain balanced lives. In the midst of everything you do and while living your busy life, I urge you to plan quiet times to be alone and let your soul rest. Resting internally is just as important as resting externally. Our bodies do need to rest, but so do our minds and emotions. Plan a daily vacation for your soul. It will help you more than you can imagine.

"Father, please help me rest internally as well as externally. Teach me to love and enjoy quiet times in Your presence. In Jesus' name. Amen."

LOOK AHEAD

Let your eyes look straight ahead; fix your gaze directly before you.
—PROVERBS 4:25

Many people feel bothered by things in their past. Sometimes, this is simply an undercurrent of feeling uneasy and unable to completely relax. Sometimes, it's a nagging regret or an ongoing disappointment that infects people's hearts and minds each day. Whether you think your past has a little influence or a great impact on your present, let me say that the past does not have to negatively affect your current life. God forgives. God redeems. God heals. God restores.

Today's scripture offers clear direction about how to deal with the past. It basically says, "Don't look back." If your past weighs you down and keeps you from enjoying your present or looking forward to your future, spend some time with God, allowing Him to help you move beyond it, or you may want to get some professional counseling. Whatever you have to do to put your past behind you, I urge you to do it. Don't waste another day looking back, but look straight ahead, as today's scripture says, to the great future God has planned for you.

"Father, help me turn my focus away from my past and let my eyes look straight ahead to what You have planned for me. In Jesus' name. Amen."

GOD IS ON OUR SIDE

What, then, shall we say in response to these things? If God is for us, who can be against us? –ROMANS 8:31

It is very comforting for us to remember that God, who can do all things, is for us. He is on our side. We all have enemies—those who disapprove, those who judge, criticize, betray, and hurt us. In addition, the devil is against us, and it is he who works through the people who hurt us. But God is for us! This means that in order for something or someone to defeat us, they would have to defeat God first.

Find strength in the fact that God is with you and that He loves you unconditionally. Take courage in knowing that He is on your side, always fighting for you. The psalmist says, "The Lord is on my side; I will not fear. What can man do to me?" (Psalm 118:6 ESV).

Today, if you are hurting or dealing with a disappointment, I understand how you feel. If you have been waiting a long time for your breakthrough and it has not come yet, I also know how you feel. But even better, God knows how you feel, and He wants you to remember that His timing is perfect in your life. There are good things in your future.

"Father, thank You for reminding me that You are on my side. I put my trust in You and ask that You help me rest in You. In Jesus' name. Amen."

A PERFECT HEART

For when Solomon was old, his wives turned away his heart after other gods, and his heart was not perfect (complete and whole) with the Lord his God, as was the heart of David his father.

—1 KINGS 11:4 AMPC

How could David have a perfect heart toward God since he had committed adultery and murder? Acts 13:22 says that David was a man after God's own heart. It is obvious from this example that having a perfect heart does not mean perfect behavior. Throughout God's Word, we see examples of weak and sinful men and women whom God used mightily. Peter is an example of this. He denied three times that he even knew Jesus, yet went on to be a great apostle and leader in the early church.

We can see that weakness is quite different from wickedness. David, Peter, and others had weaknesses, but their hearts were perfect toward God. What does this mean? I think, first and foremost, it means that they loved God with all their hearts. Jesus said the most important command is to love God with all our heart, soul, and mind (Matthew 22:37–38). He also said that if we love God, we will love other people as we love ourselves, which is the second command, after loving God wholeheartedly (Matthew 22:39–40). If we love Jesus, we will obey Him (John 14:15).

Perhaps if we focused more on loving Jesus and less on behavior modification, we would make more rapid progress in spiritual maturity.

God doesn't look for people who demonstrate perfect

performance when He wants to use someone, but for those who have perfect hearts toward Him (2 Chronicles 16:9). If you are not perfect (just like everyone else on earth), yet you love God with all your heart, you want to please Him, and you repent of your sins, then you are in a position for Him to use you in a powerful way.

"Father, I am sorry for my sins, and I repent of them, yet I do love You with my whole heart. I have weaknesses, but my heart toward You is not wicked. Help me focus on and love You more and more. In Jesus' name. Amen."

ENJOY WHAT YOU HAVE

I know that there is nothing better for people than to be happy and to do good while they live. —ECCLESIASTES 3:12

Solomon, the writer of Ecclesiastes, reminds us several times to enjoy life and says there is nothing better than to enjoy life and do good. Are you enjoying your life, or are you merely going through the motions of each day, doing your duty but never stopping to enjoy any of the blessings God has given you? Every day that goes by is one you will never get back, and the only way to live without regrets is to make the most of each day you have.

Work is an important part of our lives, and Solomon tells us to enjoy our work and the fruit of our labors. As a parent, I delight in seeing my children enjoy their lives. It makes me sad when they are sad, and I am sure our heavenly Father feels the same way about us.

Be purposeful about enjoying the blessings you have instead of always pursuing something you don't have. Enjoy life today! Enjoy God, yourself, and the people in your life. Each day you have is a gift from God, and I encourage you not to waste this one.

"Father, thank You for today! Help me see how blessed I am and to enjoy all that You have given me. In Jesus' name. Amen."

A NECESSARY STEP IN SPIRITUAL MATURITY

Then he called the crowd to him along with his disciples and said: "Whoever wants to be my disciple must deny themselves and take up their cross and follow me." –MARK 8:34

The process of spiritual maturity is exciting in many ways. We feel happy when we feel close to God. We feel strong when our confidence in Him is high. We enjoy being able to choose peace instead of worry as we become more established in our faith, and we experience joy in His presence. But becoming spiritually mature also has its challenges and today's scripture addresses one of them.

One of the steps of spiritual growth is to deny ourselves. I've never met anyone who enjoyed self-denial, but in order to follow Jesus, we must discipline ourselves to do it. Denying ourselves involves—but is not limited to—doing God's will when we do not understand it and when we would rather not obey Him. It also includes overcoming ungodly attitudes, inconveniencing ourselves in order to help someone in need, putting aside our personal desires or plans to do something God is calling us to do, and aligning our thoughts and words with the way God would have us think and speak. It involves forgiving those who have hurt us and praying for and being kind to our enemies.

Following Jesus is not always easy, but it always has great rewards.

"Father, make me willing to die to myself and to give up anything You ask me to sacrifice in order to follow You. In Jesus' name. Amen."

THE RESTED SOUL

Anxiety in a man's heart weighs it down, but an encouraging word makes it glad. —PROVERBS 12:25 AMPC

When we think of Jesus, we see a picture of perfect rest and peace. Although He often encountered situations that could have upset Him, He always remained at peace. This was because He trusted His Father with everything in His life. It seems today that most of us hurry, scurry, and worry about a multitude of things. But interestingly enough, all the hustle and anxiety are a waste of time and never accomplish anything good.

I invite you today to cast your care on God and let Him take care of you (1 Peter 5:7). Stop incessantly thinking and talking about your problems, and go about the business of living and enjoying your life while God takes care of your problems. If worry were effective, I would urge you to do it, but every result of worry and anxiety is negative. It can cause health problems, relationship problems, and emotional problems.

Instead of worrying, God's Word invites us to "be anxious for nothing," and in all things to pray and be thankful (Philippians 4:6 NKJV). The result of this is peace. Instead of thinking about your problems, start thinking about your blessings, and you will soon see that your life is not so bad after all. God has helped you in the past, and He will do it again.

"Father, I'm sorry for all the time I have wasted worrying. Forgive me and grant me grace for a new beginning today. I want my life to be filled with gratitude, not complaining. In Jesus' name. Amen."

CHOICE OVERLOAD

Let your moderation be known unto all men. –PHILIPPIANS 4:5 KJV

A standard supermarket now carries an average of 48,750 items. The cereal aisle alone is enough to confuse anybody. A missionary I know came home to visit in America after serving several years in Africa. When she went shopping for cereal, she went home empty-handed because the number of choices was so confusing to her. Where she lived in Africa, only one cereal was available in the grocery store.

I often stand in my closet way too long trying to decide what to wear. The choice is difficult because I have so many clothes. When I was a teenager, I had eight outfits and two pairs of shoes. There was no confusion about what to wear. I wore the blue on Monday, the brown on Tuesday, the red on Wednesday, and so on. Life was much simpler then.

Today, technology offers us many benefits, but it also complicates our lives in various ways. Each of us must choose how much complication we want in our life and not allow more than we can manage peacefully.

How often do you stand in front of an open refrigerator door, unable to find anything you really want to eat? In most of the world, especially poverty-stricken countries, people would think your refrigerator was a gold mine, and they would happily eat anything in it.

I encourage you to simplify on purpose. Minimize for the sake of your sanity. Have what you need and some of what you want, but don't keep collecting more and more merchandise just for the sake of having more.

"Father, help me do all things in moderation. I don't want to be frustrated because of choice overload in my life. Help me be a decisive person who is led by Your wisdom. Thank You. In Jesus' name. Amen."

THE STRESS OF COMPARISON

I praise you because I am fearfully and wonderfully made; your works are wonderful, I know that full well. —PSALM 139:14

God created each of us uniquely and wonderfully. We should never compare ourselves with other people, because trying to be anyone other than ourselves only causes stress.

Satan works diligently to draw us into the comparison trap, and he has a purpose in doing so. As long as we are trying to be someone we will never be, we cannot enjoy being who we are.

You may not have the same gift as someone else, but you have something that they don't have, and God wants you to use it. We all benefit from one another's gifts, but only when we are focused on being our unique and amazing self. Yes, I said you are amazing! No one else in the universe is exactly like you. You are special.

Anytime we try to do something that God has not given us the ability to do, we invite stress into our lives, because God will never help us be anyone other than ourselves. Nothing good comes from trying to imitate, compete with, or outdo someone else. The more you compare your life to the lives of those around you, the less you'll enjoy the life God has given you.

"Father, thank You for creating me uniquely. Help me be fully and completely myself and to never compare myself with others, thinking I need to be like they are in any way. In Jesus' name. Amen."

DON'T STOP BELIEVING

Yet he did not waver through unbelief regarding the promise of God, but was strengthened in his faith and gave glory to God.

—ROMANS 4:20

Today's scripture refers to Abram (later called Abraham) and the miraculous promise he received from God. God had told him that He would give him a vast expanse of land—as far as he could see in every direction—and that He would make his descendants as numerous as the dust of the earth (Genesis 13:14–18). This kind of promise would be a lot for anyone to grasp, but it was especially difficult for Abram because he and his wife, Sarai, were very old—way too old to have a child. In addition to that, about twenty-five years passed between the time of God's promise and its fulfillment.

But Abraham did not let his natural circumstances or the passing of time negatively affect his faith in God. Even Paul, who wrote the Book of Romans about two thousand years after Abraham lived, knew the strength of Abraham's faith.

I encourage you today not to waver in your faith. Don't let the devil pull you into unbelief. Be strengthened in your faith by studying God's Word, confessing it aloud, and remembering that God still works miracles today, just as He did in Abraham's time. Even if you have to wait longer than expected, as Abraham did, keep in mind that God's timing is perfect.

"Father, I believe You are still a miracle-working God. Strengthen me in my faith so I will not waver or give in to unbelief. Amen."

THE FIRST DAY OF THE REST OF YOUR LIFE

The steadfast love of the Lord never ceases; his mercies never come to an end; they are new every morning; great is your faithfulness.

—LAMENTATIONS 3:22–23 ESV

Do you ever stop to think that today is the first day of the rest of your life, and that what you do with this day that you have been given is very important? You have the ability to choose what kind of day this will be for you. Don't let the regrets of yesterday ruin today, but receive God's mercy. God loves new beginnings, and His mercy is new every day. Let go of everything behind you, and focus on this amazing day.

Choose to live with hope today. Hope is the aggressive expectation that something good is going to happen in your life. The other choice is to be hopeless, sour, and negative, but why would anyone choose to live that way? We choose it sometimes because Satan deceives us into thinking that we are the only ones who can solve our own problems, and we work to try to do what only God can do.

God gave you this day to enjoy, not to be miserable, frustrated, and negative. If you have fallen for those temptations in the past, today can be the turning point for you. God wants to work in your life, but He cannot work through a negative attitude. God works through your faith. Put your faith in Him and look for the good things in life. Make it a habit, starting today.

"Father, I'm sorry for the days I have wasted being negative and discouraged. Today is a new day, and I choose, with Your help, to be hopeful, to be positive, and to be a blessing everywhere I go. In Jesus' name. Amen."

I CAN'T DO IT WITHOUT YOU

Apart from me you can do nothing. —JOHN 15:5

We wear ourselves out trying to do things that only God can do, or that only He can help us do. We need His strength at all times, and those who wait on Him (who spend time with Him) have their strength renewed (Isaiah 40:31). I urge you to take time each morning to tell God that you are helpless without Him and that you want Him involved in everything you do.

Little children are happy to let their parents and other people do everything for them, but eventually they grow and want to do things by themselves, even things they can't possibly do. This is all part of growing up and should not be discouraged, but we can draw a parallel from this example and ask ourselves, "What am I trying to do by myself that I can't do without Jesus?"

Our frustration comes from struggling with things that we want to happen, yet no matter what we do, they stay the same. Frustration and struggle should be a sign that we are out of God's will. We may want something that isn't His will, or we may be trying to get it in our timing or in our own way. This is a recipe for misery. Perhaps today is your day to fully surrender to God and realize that if He doesn't help you, you will fail at everything you try to do. But if you surrender and allow Him to be your Helper, you will be amazed at what He will do and how much peace He brings to your life.

"Father, I don't want to be frustrated anymore because I try to live without inviting You into everything I do. I repent for the times I have ignored You, and today I surrender fully to Your Lordship. I wait on You for strength and help. Thank You. In Jesus' name. Amen."

IT'S ALL UP TO ME

God is our refuge and strength, an ever-present help in trouble.

—PSALM 46:1

Have you ever tried to suggest to someone who is seriously stressed out that they learn how to delegate some of their responsibilities to other people? If so, have you ever heard them answer, "If I don't do it, it won't get done"? I have heard those words, and I have also felt that way personally.

It is fairly easy to keep picking up responsibilities as we go through life, but sometimes we have a false sense of responsibility, and the end result is stress that can cause many problems. A lack of joy is only one of a long list of stress-related struggles. If you are feeling controlled and overwhelmed by your schedule, remember that you are the one who makes it, and only you can change it.

Some people keep the "it's all up to me" attitude because it makes them feel important and needed. But our sense of worth and value should never come from what we do; it comes from who we are in Christ.

Ask yourself if you need to let some things go so you can enjoy your life. It is true that depending on other people is often disappointing, because they don't always do what you depend on them to do, but there are many wonderful, faithful people who can be trusted and won't let you down. If your first attempts at delegation do not work, keep trying until you find something that works for you.

"I'm sorry, Father, for thinking that everything in my life is up to me. I see now that this mindset has caused stress and stolen my joy. Grant me the grace to let go and trust others to do some of the things I have been doing. In Jesus' name. Amen."

A VITAL KEY TO RELIEVING STRESS

Whoever wants to be my disciple must deny themselves and take up their cross and follow me. —MARK 8:34

We spend a great deal of energy trying to take care of ourselves and obtain what we want and need. Believe it or not, this is very stressful. Why? Because God has not designed us to be selfish and focused on ourselves. He wants to take care of us while we focus on being a blessing to other people.

John Bunyan said, "You have not lived today until you have done something for someone who can never repay you." How much time do you put into thinking about what you can do for someone else? We might say, "The more the merrier." In other words, the less you focus on yourself and the more you focus on others, the happier you will be.

Obsession with self is a breeding ground for stress, pressure, and anxiety. But blessing someone else and worrying about yourself at the same time is nearly impossible. God's Word is full of instructions about how we should treat others. It is time we start taking these directives seriously, realizing that if Jesus mentions our treatment of others so often, He must want us to pay attention to it. The reason He emphasizes the way we relate to other people is that He wants us to enjoy the life He has provided for us, and He knows we cannot ever do so if we are self-focused.

Tell God what you need and want, and then leave it in His hands as you spend your time blessing others.

"Father, help me be less self-focused and more focused on being a blessing to others. Thank You for helping me. In Jesus' name. Amen."

UNWAVERING TRUST

O my God, in You I [have unwavering] trust [and I rely on You with steadfast confidence], do not let me be ashamed or my hope in You be disappointed. –PSALM 25:2 AMP

We read in today's scripture about having "unwavering trust" and "steadfast confidence" in the Lord. Most of us would think, *Oh, yes, I want to have unwavering trust and steadfast confidence in God!* We instantly know that such firm, unshakable trust in Him would increase our peace and stability. But this kind of trust and confidence does not form overnight. It takes time.

As we journey through life, most of us develop habits of worry, anxiety, and fear. We may also become self-reliant to some degree, trusting our own abilities instead of trusting God. We may learn to seek confidence in the things of the world, even though they continually prove faulty. Overcoming ingrained habits in our thoughts or emotions is a process, and unweaving them usually happens step by step over a period of weeks, months, or years.

This is why perseverance is so important. When your trust in God does waver, don't feel condemned. Simply repent and choose to trust Him again. Every time you trust Him, and every time He comes through for you, your trust and confidence will grow stronger.

"Father, help me to grow continually in unwavering trust and steadfast confidence in You. In Jesus' name. Amen."

BE RESPONSIBLE FOR YOUR OWN JOY

Rejoice in the Lord always. I will say it again: Rejoice!

—PHILIPPIANS 4:4

When we are unhappy, we usually blame it on someone or something else. It rarely occurs to us that we must be responsible for our own joy, but that is indeed what we must do. If my joy is based on having all the people in my life do as I please and on always having pleasant circumstances, I have little hope of enjoying very many days. However, if I take responsibility for my joy and realize I can choose to be joyful regardless of my circumstances, then I can enjoy every day of my life.

The longer I live, the more I realize that everything in life is a choice. My enjoyment of life does not depend on what happens to me, but on how I respond to it. We can't control what other people do, nor what our circumstances will be from day to day, but we can control ourselves, with God's help. He has given us the gift of self-control as one of the fruit of the Holy Spirit (Galatians 5:23). This fruit resides inside of us and is like a muscle: The more we use it, the stronger it becomes.

For many years, if I wasn't happy, I usually blamed my emotional state on something Dave was or wasn't doing. But God has taught me that my joy is my responsibility, not anyone else's. Blaming others for our problems only puts off the inevitable. Sooner or later, we must take responsibility for our lives if we want to enjoy them. The sooner we do, the more days we can enjoy in the future. Let's stop making excuses for our ungodly behavior, take ownership of it instead, and ask God to help us change for the better.

"Father, help me take responsibility for my own joy by no longer blaming others if I am unhappy. I recognize that I have self-control as a gift from You, and I ask that You help me start using it on a regular basis. Thank You. In Jesus' name. Amen."

IT ISN'T FAIR

For I, the Lord, love justice; I hate robbery and wrongdoing. In my faithfulness I will reward my people. —ISAIAH 61:8

When we feel we have been mistreated, the next step is usually anger and then bitterness. This is especially true if the situation is not resolved to our satisfaction. Maybe the offending party won't admit they were wrong, or perhaps they blame you for their behavior. If you are a Christian, you will know that according to God's Word, He expects you to forgive the person or people who abused or mistreated you. That's when our soul screams, "It isn't fair!"

I won't argue about what is or isn't fair. I can only say that a great deal that happens in life isn't fair, but the good news is that we love and serve a God who loves justice. This means that if we are obedient to Him, He will make wrong things right in due time. Being expected to forgive someone who has hurt us and perhaps won't apologize or take responsibility for what they've done does feel unfair, but that is exactly what God commands us to do. Why? Because when we forgive, we are not doing our enemies a favor; we are doing ourselves a favor.

As long as we hang on to resentment, anger, and bitterness, we are tormented. In reality, we are allowing the one who hurt us to continue hurting us until we finally let go of the situation and trust God to make it right. For your own sake, if you have anything against anyone, please release it, let it go, and forgive as God has forgiven you.

"Father, help me forgive those who have hurt me, and help me to pray for and bless them as You command me to do. I choose to trust You to bring justice in my life. In Jesus' name. Amen."

JEALOUSY

Anger is cruel and fury overwhelming, but who can stand before jealousy? –PROVERBS 27:4

Jealousy is often referred to as the "green-eyed monster." It is a monster because it devours the life of those who permit it in their hearts. God has a special, individualized plan for each of us. Being jealous of another person is pointless, because no matter how much we wish it, we cannot ever have anyone else's life. Neither can we have the specific aspect of their life that makes us jealous of them.

A jealous and envious person is never content, and God wants us to be content always, trusting that He is doing—and will continue to do—great things in our lives. Being jealous of what others have or can do prevents us from seeing the blessings in our own lives. Jealousy is not new; it has been around since people began to inhabit the earth. Early in the story of Genesis, Cain was jealous of Abel, and he murdered him because of it. In 1 Samuel, King Saul was so jealous of David that he continually tried to kill him, and at times the jealousy drove him mad. In addition, some of Jesus' twelve disciples were jealous of one another, asking Him which of them was the greatest.

The Bible tells us that jealousy can even make us sick: "A heart at peace gives life to the body, but envy rots the bones" (Proverbs 14:30). Being jealous or envious is foolish and a total waste of time. Wisdom recommends that we live at peace, be content with what we have, and be thankful in all things.

"Father, I'm sorry for being jealous and envious of other people. You have blessed me, and I want to be very thankful for what You have done and are doing in my life. Help me in the future to resist jealousy in the power of the Holy Spirit. In Jesus' name. Amen."

GOD'S REWARD

But without faith it is impossible to please Him, for he who comes to God must believe that He is, and that He is a rewarder of those who diligently seek Him. —HEBREWS 11:6 NKJV

God is a rewarder. I love the thought of that, don't you? Instead of seeing God as someone who is waiting to punish us for each mistake we make, we should see Him as He really is. He is one who rewards our faithfulness and the right choices we make. God can get angry, but He is not an angry God. He is full of mercy and loving-kindness, always ready to forgive. God is love, and His love is unconditional.

Some things God asks us to do are difficult, such as forgiving our enemies and waiting on Him to bring justice in our lives instead of seeking revenge ourselves. But we have the promise of reward. I have experienced the rewards of God, as have many other people, and God's rewards are wonderful. It is amazing when you see God do something for you that you know you could not have done for yourself. His justice is sweet.

If you are going through difficulties at this time in your life, remember that God is your rewarder. This powerful truth can lift you out of the pit of discouragement and despair. Of course, you must wait for God's rewards and you don't know their exact timing, but they will come because God promises them, and it is impossible for God to lie.

"Father, I am encouraged to realize that You bring rewards in our lives, and I am waiting for mine. Keep me strong, trusting in Your perfect timing. While I wait, let me serve You with all of my heart. In Jesus' name. Amen."

I AM MAD AT ME

Grace and peace to you from God our Father and the Lord Jesus Christ. —PHILIPPIANS 1:2

Are you angry with yourself? Many people are. They have made mistakes, and even though they have asked for God's forgiveness, they refuse to forgive themselves. This actually means they refuse to receive the gift of forgiveness that God is offering them. Our heavenly Father has already punished Jesus for our sins and mistakes, and He doesn't want us to punish ourselves for a debt we do not owe. Surely, if God, who is perfect, can forgive us, we can receive His gift and forgive ourselves.

Let me encourage you today: Don't be so hard on yourself, and don't live with unrealistic expectations of yourself. You will make mistakes, and that is exactly why you need Jesus who freely offers you His grace and peace.

Any anger in your heart will come out of you one way or another. I know a woman who has an explosive temper, and it made everyone around her uncomfortable. When she finally got to the root of her anger, she discovered she was not angry with someone else, she was mad at herself. Each day she set unrealistic goals for herself, so every day she felt like a failure, and this made her more and more angry. She had to face her perfectionism and learn that her worth wasn't in finishing her to-do list, but in Christ. She has since dealt with the problem and now enjoys a peaceful life. If you are mad at yourself, the same freedom is available to you, and it is available today.

"Father, I pray that I would always receive Your forgiveness and not be angry with myself because of weaknesses, sins, and failures. Help me know that Your love is unconditional, and grant me grace to love myself in a godly and balanced way. Thank You. In Jesus' name. Amen."

DREAD DRAINS YOUR STRENGTH

For sighing has become my daily food; my groans pour out like water. What I feared has come upon me; what I dreaded has happened to me. I have no peace, no quietness; I have no rest, but only turmoil. —JOB 3:24-26

How many times have you said something like this: "Oh, I just dread having to work in the yard this weekend," or "I'm really dreading the Friday afternoon meeting with my boss"? Most of us have made remarks such as these when we know we must do something we do not enjoy. What we really mean is that we do not look forward to the task ahead of us and would rather not do it. But when we dread things, we drain ourselves of strength, perhaps without realizing that's what we're doing.

Dread is a symptom of a negative attitude, not the fruit of a positive attitude, and it affects our joy in a negative way. Dread is also a close relative of fear.

We can't feel dread and joy at the same time. We all enjoy doing some things more than others, but we can choose to remain joyful and upbeat even while we do things we don't particularly like. When we stay happy and positive, we usually do things faster and better, and we can then move on to other activities.

Whatever you need to do today, even if you are not looking forward to it, decide right now that you will not dread it. Instead, ask God to help you do it with a positive attitude. Don't let an item on your to-do list decrease your joy, because "the joy of the Lord is your strength" (Nehemiah 8:10).

"Father, help me not to dread anything, but to have a positive attitude toward everything I need to do. In Jesus' name. Amen."

THE SOLUTION FOR SIN

In him we have redemption through his blood, the forgiveness of sins, in accordance with the riches of God's grace that he lavished on us. —EPHESIANS 1:7–8

Do you live each day knowing that you are righteous before God because of your faith in Jesus, meaning that you are in right standing or right relationship with Him? One of the Holy Spirit's roles in a believer's life is to convict (meaning, to convince) of sin and righteousness. He reminds us and enforces the truth that we are righteous because Jesus shed His blood to forgive our sins and to make us right with God, who loves us unconditionally.

We need to understand that we do not lose our relationship with God when we sin, but we do need to repent and receive His forgiveness when we sense the conviction of the Holy Spirit. The solution for sin is that Christ died for our sins and paid in full the penalty they should have incurred. This is the reality in which we need to live.

God's grace meets us where we are, but never leaves us where it found us. When you feel convicted of sin, repent, receive God's forgiveness, and move forward in the righteousness Jesus died to give you.

"Father, thank You for sending Your Son to provide the solution for my sin and to put me in right relationship with You. In Jesus' name. Amen."

ARE YOU LETTING AN UNHAPPY PERSON MAKE YOU UNHAPPY?

Do not make friends with a hot-tempered person, do not associate with one easily angered, or you may learn their ways and get yourself ensnared. —PROVERBS 22:24-25

I advise not getting into deep personal relationships with hot-tempered, angry people, but if you already are in one and can't get out of it, you can learn not to let the unhappy person make you unhappy. The angry person could be your boss, your spouse, one of your children, a parent, or someone else. In our world today, there is no shortage of angry people.

You cannot control what others do, but you can learn, with God's help, not to let them control you. As a matter of fact, the worst thing you can do for an angry person is to allow them to control you because that will keep them stuck in the same place.

When Dave and I married, I was an angry woman due to the abuse I suffered during my childhood. Of course, Dave never saw my anger while we were dating because I hid it, but eventually it did reveal itself. He tried for a while to make me happy and finally decided that, no matter what he did, I was not going to be happy, so he told me he was finished trying. He said that he was going to be happy and enjoy his life and hoped that I would decide to join him. But if I didn't, he continued, he was not going to let it affect him.

Of course, what he said to me made me even angrier than I already was for a while, but eventually it gave me the desire to get to the root of my problem and let God help me change. Dave always loved me, but he didn't let me control him. If you are dealing with an angry person, I recommend that you do likewise.

"Father, give me the strength to remain peaceful and joyful, no matter how the people around me behave. Help me show them Your love without letting them affect my joy with their bad attitudes. Thank You. In Jesus' name. Amen."

LOVE IS KIND

Therefore, as God's chosen people, holy and dearly loved, clothe yourselves with compassion, kindness, humility, gentleness and patience. —COLOSSIANS 3:12

Kindness is wonderful! When we are kind, we are generous, friendly, and considerate. People who are kind are kind to everyone, not just those they love and admire. In fact, random acts of kindness are some of the most beneficial. Being kind to a friend or family member might be expected, but being kind to a stranger is even better. An act of kindness may be the very gesture that touches and even changes and softens that person's heart.

I recall showing kindness to a stranger in a coffee shop. She later saw me somewhere else and said, "Why are you the kindest person I have ever met?" It gave me an opportunity to witness to her about Jesus, and she was receptive to the idea. As children of God, we are His representatives on the earth, and He has given us the assignment of showing the world what He is like.

It is easy to be hard-hearted and harsh, especially when people make mistakes or anger us, but kindness is a godly trait that goes beyond our natural tendencies and feelings. I urge you to be kind to everyone. Be generous, friendly, and considerate. Treat other people as you want to be treated.

"Father, I want to be kind as You are kind. Help me develop this fruit of the Spirit by giving me opportunities to show kindness instead of harshness. In Jesus' name. Amen."

THE EMOTION OF ANGER

Do not let the sun go down while you are still angry, and do not give the devil a foothold. –EPHESIANS 4:26-27

Anger is an emotion, and although it is a strong one, we do not have to let it control us and dictate how we will behave and treat people. God said not to let the sun set while you are still angry, so obviously we do have a choice about what to do when we are upset. We can remain angry, or we can let go of the anger and trust God to take care of whatever is bothering us.

Emotions can flare up quickly. We are not expected not to have them, but we are expected not to let them rule us. We can manage our emotions and learn to live beyond how we feel. Sometimes, when we are angry, we feel justified in it, but that is a big mistake. Anytime we justify or make excuses for something, we will probably keep doing it.

Uncontrolled anger has caused many people to do things that they deeply regretted later, but had no opportunity to undo. Murder is the result of anger, as are many other crimes and abusive treatment toward people. In a moment of anger, we have all spoken words that we deeply wish we could take back, but once they have been uttered, they may be forgiven, but they can never be unsaid.

If you are easily angered, realize that you are a new creature in Christ—not an angry person, but a righteous one in Him (2 Corinthians 5:17, 21). As you see yourself as the new creation you've become in Christ, your behavior will begin to change.

"Father, when I am angry, help me let it go quickly before it damages my health, my relationship with You, and my relationships with the people I love. In Jesus' name. Amen."

SEIZE THE DAY

And God blessed them and said to them, Be fruitful, multiply, and fill the earth, and subdue it. –GENESIS 1:28 AMPC

When we seize something, we take hold of it forcibly and suddenly; we take control of it or subdue it; we bring it under our control.

Each day that God gives us is a gift, and if we waste it, we can never get it back and make it useful. We all have the same number of hours in a day, but some people seem to do much more with their time than others, because some don't seize the day and others do. Wise people do something fruitful with each day.

What do you want to do with your life? Mother Teresa said, "Yesterday is gone. Tomorrow has not yet come. We have only today. Let us begin." I encourage you not to procrastinate but to take advantage of the time you have now and begin working toward your goals.

Set long-term and short-term goals for yourself. When you have accomplished one goal, take time to celebrate the accomplishment, even if it means simply relaxing for thirty minutes with your favorite beverage. You are capable of great things, but you must begin!

I am not encouraging you to work all the time. A goal for today may be to work on a project you need to finish, but it might also be a full day of rest that you desperately need. Let God guide you, and be purposeful about how you spend your time.

"Father, I don't want to waste my time. Guide me daily to do what I should be doing. Once I make a decision, help me stick to it without becoming distracted. Thank You. In Jesus' name. Amen."

WHERE DID THE TIME GO?

Lord, remind me how brief my time on earth will be. Remind me that my days are numbered—how fleeting my life is. –PSALM 39:4 NLT

How often do we say at the end of a year, "I can't believe this year is over!" Or, "Time flies!" How often do we comment at a graduation or a wedding, "My children are grown, and I can barely remember their growing-up years!" We make statements such as these because time does go by quickly, especially for those of us who are busy. Let's remember that God never commanded us to be busy, but to be fruitful (productive). We can be busy doing nothing, or busy doing something that will add value to our life or to someone else's.

Consider these words, which Paul wrote to the Ephesians about how to live: "Look carefully then how you walk! Live purposefully and worthily and accurately, not as the unwise and witless, but as wise (sensible, intelligent people), making the very most of the time [buying up each opportunity], because the days are evil. Therefore do not be vague and thoughtless and foolish, but understanding and firmly grasping what the will of the Lord is" (Ephesians 5:15–17 AMPC).

I want to be an "on purpose" person—one who thinks about what I want to do and what God wants me to do, and then disciplines myself to do it. It is very frustrating to me to have a good plan of action for the day and then find, at the end of the day, that I have done nothing I intended to do and instead have wasted my time on things I can't even clearly remember doing.

Let us be more purposeful and ask God to help us stay on target and focused each day.

"Father, help me to be an 'on purpose' person. Guide me to use my time wisely and bear good fruit. In Jesus' name. Amen."

RESIST THE DEVIL

Submit yourselves, then, to God. Resist the devil, and he will flee from you. —JAMES 4:7

In order to resist the devil, we must recognize when he is attacking us. His character is that of a liar. He only knows how to lie, and what he says to us by putting thoughts into our minds is never in agreement with God's Word unless he is taking it out of context.

The more we know God's Word, the quicker we will recognize the lies of Satan. If we submit to God by honoring His Word above all else, we can then resist the devil, and he will flee from us.

Romans 12:21, which says that we overcome evil with good, is one of my favorite scriptures. The devil only steals, kills, and destroys (John 10:10), but no matter what he tries to do, if we continue obeying God and being good to people, we will always defeat him.

"Father, help me to recognize and resist the work of the enemy against me and to live each day according to the truth of Your Word. In Jesus' name. Amen."

STARTING YOUR DAY RIGHT

I love those who love me, and those who seek me early and diligently shall find me. —PROVERBS 8:17 AMPC

Seeking God "early" in this scripture probably means seeking Him in the early part of each day, but I also believe it is advisable to seek God early, or at the beginning of any project. Hudson Taylor wrote, "Do not have your concert first, and then tune your instrument afterwards. Begin the day with the Word of God and prayer, and get first of all into harmony with Him."

God is our source (1 Corinthians 8:6), and because He is, seeking Him and spending time with Him daily is not a devout obligation, but a divine privilege. Every day is a journey with God, and we find strength for our journey by spending time with Him. Nothing is more vital to living an effective, intentional, "on purpose" life than daily time with God.

When you start your day right by spending time with God, it is more likely to go well and end well. Just imagine how different our lives would be if everyone spent time with God before they left their homes and began to interact with other people. It would put an end to the miseries that stem from selfishness, crime, violence, injustice, and oppression—just to name a few.

Don't wait to find time for God. Make time for God, and your life will improve greatly.

"Father, I am sorry for all the times I have ignored You. Forgive me, and help me be diligent to start each day right by spending time with You. Thank You. In Jesus' name. Amen."

PERSPECTIVE

So we fix our eyes not on what is seen, but on what is unseen, since what is seen is temporary, but what is unseen is eternal.

—2 CORINTHIANS 4:18

Yesterday I had what I would call a very challenging day. Four very disappointing things happened one right after another. I kept turning them over to the Lord, but they kept coming back to my thoughts and stirring up my emotions. I'm sure you have things like that too. When these days come, what should we do?

One thing that really seems to help me is to put my problems in perspective. I may have a problem (or three or four), but thankfully, I also have the privilege of praying to the Creator of all things and the assurance that He hears me and will answer. It also helps me to remind myself that these challenges will not last forever. While I am waiting for these situations to improve, I count my blessings, which far outnumber my problems.

We can trust God to do the best for us when we ask for His help. He may not always give us what we want, but He will always give us what we need. I encourage you today to remember that your problems are temporary, and God is working on them right now.

"Father, help me not to worry when trouble comes, but to keep my problems in their proper perspective compared to the rest of my life. In Jesus' name. Amen."

THE UNHURRIED LIFE

I said, "Oh, that I had the wings of a dove! I would fly away and be at rest." —PSALM 55:6

In Psalm 55, David is apparently weary of dealing with enemies and life's challenges. He wants to be at rest. One of the primary hindrances to rest is, of course, worry, and another one is hurry. When I think of Jesus, I never think of Him as hurrying from one place to another. I think of Him as rested. Jesus was always at rest, no matter what He was doing.

We know that trusting God helps us enter into rest. I also find that not rushing inwardly, not allowing my mind to flit from one thing to a thousand others in a day, helps me enter rest. In addition, I've discovered that not hurrying outwardly is vital to enjoying rest. I have had a bad habit of rushing, and I notice that lots of other people do too. The question is, what are we rushing to do? Could we not walk a little slower and still arrive at our destination?

I find that slowing my pace physically helps me to slow down my mind. This helps me to be more rested than rushing inwardly and outwardly most of the time. I encourage you to also try slowing down—externally and internally—to see if it helps you feel calmer.

"Father, I want to live an unhurried life, and I need Your help to do it. When I am rushing, remind me to slow down. I ask this in Jesus' name. Amen."

JUST PRAY

One day Peter and John were going up to the temple at the time of prayer—at three in the afternoon. –ACTS 3:1

We see in today's scripture that in the days of the early church, three o'clock in the afternoon was a designated time of prayer. I wonder, does your schedule include a time of prayer? Do you have a certain portion of each day reserved to stop what you are doing and pray? It doesn't have to be at three o'clock in the afternoon. It doesn't even have to be at the same time each day, so don't feel guilty if your schedule won't allow that. God delights in the fact that you want to pray and seek Him, and while having regular prayer times is very important, the schedule does not need to become a rule that you struggle to follow.

Prayer is simply talking to God, and praying every day will benefit you greatly. Ephesians 6:18 says we are to "pray in the Spirit on all occasions with all kinds of prayers and requests." I say, "Pray your way through the day," which means that I like to live a lifestyle of prayer—offering prayers in all kinds of situations and praising God in my heart wherever I am, in addition to having dedicated set-apart times of prayer and fellowship with God each day.

The most important thing about prayer is that we do it often and that we grow in it, becoming more and more confident that God hears and answers us.

"Father, strengthen me in my prayer life as I seek You each day. In Jesus' name. Amen."

ACCEPTED

Whoever believes in him is not condemned, but whoever does not believe stands condemned already because they have not believed in the name of God's one and only Son. –JOHN 3:18

If you are like most people, you want to be accepted. When people hear that they have been accepted to a certain school or organization, they often become very excited. Something about being accepted makes us feel confident and good about ourselves.

Today's scripture reminds us that when we believe in Jesus Christ and trust Him as our Savior, we are not condemned. In other words, we are accepted. We don't have to work to be accepted. In fact, we can't earn God's favor or acceptance through good works or through any human effort.

People who believe that God's acceptance is based on good works or on doing everything perfectly struggle and feel condemned because they try to behave perfectly and cannot do it. Everyone makes mistakes. But no matter how many mistakes we make, if our hearts are pure toward God and we sincerely repent, He forgives us.

When we believe in God's Son and acknowledge Him as our Savior, we can be sure of God's unconditional love and acceptance. Love and acceptance are not based on anything we do or don't do. They are based on what Jesus has already done by dying for our sins.

"Father, thank You for sending Your Son, Jesus, to die for my sins. Because I believe in Him as my Savior, I know that You love and accept me completely. In Jesus' name. Amen."

AVOIDING DECEPTION

Be alert and of sober mind. Your enemy the devil prowls around like a roaring lion looking for someone to devour. –1 PETER 5:8

It is important for us to remember that the devil is a real enemy and that he works constantly trying to deceive us and take us captive through his lies. The more knowledgeable we are of God's Word, the less likely he is to succeed at deceiving us. To be deceived means to believe a lie. What we believe becomes our reality, even if it is not true.

For example, you may believe someone doesn't like you, but the truth is that the person doesn't have an opinion of you one way or the other. Satan wants us to think people are against us, hoping we get so caught up in trying to gain their favor that we take our eyes off Jesus and the purpose He has for us.

Ask God to show you what, if any, lies you may believe. Guard your heart with all diligence and pay attention to what goes on in your mind. If your thoughts do not agree with God's Word, then cast down (or reject) those wrong imaginations or thoughts and replace them with God's Word (2 Corinthians 10:4–5). Jesus died so that we could enjoy our lives and live a full, abundant life (John 10:10). Whenever we think thoughts that oppose or prevent what Jesus wants for us, we should examine them closely to determine their source.

"Father, help me to keep my mind free from lies that deceive and filled with the truth of Your Word. Thank You. In Jesus' name. Amen."

BUILD OTHERS UP

You, therefore, have no excuse, you who pass judgment on someone else, for at whatever point you judge another, you are condemning yourself, because you who pass judgment do the same things.

—ROMANS 2:1

Our enemy, the devil, wants us to be faultfinders, focusing on the shortcomings of others while being blind to our own faults. If we see nothing wrong with ourselves and a great deal wrong with others, then the devil has won because we are opening doors for him to work in our lives through our lack of love. Jesus said, "Take the plank out of your own eye, and then you will see clearly to remove the speck from your brother's eye" (Matthew 7:5).

We can and should pray for others, but we cannot change them. Only God can change people. We can, however, work with the Holy Spirit to make positive changes in our lives if we are not overly focused on what we think is wrong with everyone else.

Faultfinding is the fruit of pride. The devil wants us to be proud and haughty, thinking more highly of ourselves than we do of others. We may often feel superior to other people, and that always causes us to look down on them and treat them in a belittling manner.

We should build others up and help them feel good about themselves. If we choose to do so, we can find a compliment for each person with whom we come in contact. Then we will be joyful, and we will reap a harvest of good things in our own lives.

"Father, I want to please You in all my ways. Help me to think good thoughts about others and never judge them critically. Teach me how to pray for them and love them as You do. In Jesus' name. Amen."

GOD'S ANOINTING

Now I know that the Lord saves His anointed; He will answer him from His holy heaven with the saving strength of His right hand.

—PSALM 20:6 AMPC

God's anointing is His presence and power. His anointing enables us to do great things. The prophet Samuel told Saul that when God's anointing came on him, he would be turned into another man (1 Samuel 10:6), meaning that he would have new abilities and power. God's anointing is very valuable and should be protected. Psalm 133 says that where there is unity, there will also be anointing and blessing.

I believe Acts 10:38 makes it clear that God's anointing and generosity work together. I desire a greater anointing on my life, and I have learned that in order to have it, I need to work for unity constantly, and I need to be aggressively generous. I encourage you to learn all you can about God's anointing and do all you can to protect and enhance it in your life.

"Father, I need Your presence and power in my life. I pray that You will teach me to be aware of Your presence and sensitive to You at all times. Thank You. In Jesus' name. Amen."

FIRST FORGIVE, THEN PRAY

If I had cherished sin in my heart, the Lord would not have listened.

—PSALM 66:18

The devil does not want us to pray, because prayer is more powerful than we know. It invites God and His power into the situations in our lives. Through prayer, we can also invite Him to work in other people's lives. We can accomplish more in five minutes of sincere prayer than we can in five years of effort spent trying to make things happen in our own strength.

God answers prayer, but there are hindrances to having our prayers answered. Today's scripture mentions one of them. We cannot have hidden or unconfessed sin in our heart and expect God to answer our prayers at the same time. Let's ask ourselves: Are we harboring any of God's enemies in our hearts—perhaps sin, unbelief, anger toward another person, an unwillingness to forgive, jealousy, or envy?

As we approach God in prayer, I believe we should first repent of any known, and even unknown, sin. King David prayed that God would forgive him for unconscious sins (Psalm 19:12). When we pray, we should be sure that we have no unforgiveness in our heart toward anyone. Let us be honest with ourselves in the presence of God and approach Him with our requests only after a time of soul-searching to root out anything that may hinder our prayer.

"Father, help me begin each day with a time of soul-searching, laying my heart open before You and giving You the opportunity to speak to me about anything You want to. Thank You for the privilege of prayer. In Jesus' name. Amen."

GOD WILL ANSWER

Lord, I wait for you; you will answer, Lord my God. —PSALM 38:15

When you call a friend or family member on the phone, you expect that person to answer if at all possible. If they don't answer, you can leave a message, and they will usually return your call. If you need a quick response to a question, you can always text them. Even if they can't talk on the phone, they may be able to answer you, and you can go on with your day. Technology has made getting answers almost instant in many cases.

But God doesn't work the way technology does. He may not always answer us instantly. In His wisdom, He answers us according to His perfect timing, not according to our schedules. He knows and sees everything, even things we cannot imagine, so He knows best how and when to answer us. I encourage you to wait patiently on the Lord today, trusting that He will answer you when the time is right.

"Father, thank You for hearing my prayers. I will wait on You to answer in Your perfect timing. In Jesus' name. Amen."

EXTREMES

Be well balanced (temperate, sober of mind), be vigilant and cautious at all times; for that enemy of yours, the devil, roams around like a lion roaring [in fierce hunger], seeking someone to seize upon and devour. —1 PETER 5:8 AMPC

Satan seeks to push us to extremes at all times. He wants us to be either unaware of him or excessively focused on him. He wants us to be unaware of our faults or obsessed with them. Once you become aware of a sin or fault in your life, confess it to the Lord, repent, and ask for His help to overcome it. Don't focus on what is wrong with you, because in Christ, there is more right with you than there is wrong. If you focus only on your faults, you may begin to think you do nothing right and fall into condemnation, and that is not God's will.

We see extremes in all kinds of practical situations of everyday life. One person may work too hard and not get enough rest, which leads to all kinds of problems, while another may not work enough and sink into passivity and laziness. Some people spend too much money and go into debt, while others become miserly and are unwilling to spend when they need to.

Maintaining balance can be quite difficult, because our fleshly tendency is to think that if a little of something is good, a lot of it should be better. But this is not always the case. Eating a little dessert occasionally is tasty and enjoyable, but eating it excessively adds unwanted pounds and can make us lethargic.

The only way to maintain balance is to regularly examine your life in the light of God's Word. If anything is out of balance, seek God's help in restoring it to its proper place.

"Father, forgive me for being extreme at times. Help me to always maintain a perfect balance in my life, doing enough of everything but never too much of anything. Thank You. In Jesus' name. Amen."

EMOTIONS

For we live by faith, not by sight. −2 CORINTHIANS 5:7

People who live according to their feelings will never truly enjoy their lives. Feelings can sometimes be good, and they also can be bad. I often say that they show up when you don't want them and disappear when you need them. People share their feelings with me more than anything else, and I probably do the same to others.

Our natural tendency is to follow our feelings, but God wants us to be led by the Holy Spirit. Feelings will never go away; we have to deal with their ebb and flow throughout our lives. Emotions seem to have a mind of their own and change without notice. We can have feelings, but we must not let them have us. We cannot let them take the lead or make decisions for us. We can learn to manage our emotions and live beyond our feelings.

We can do what we know is right, instead of doing what we feel like doing. I fulfill many responsibilities that I would fail to carry out if I always did what I felt like doing. I am sure you are the same way. Emotions are the number one enemy of the child of God. They lie to us, and if we follow them without examining whether or not they are healthy, we will experience great difficulty in life. We can manage our emotions with God's help and learn to recognize when the devil is using them to lead us down the wrong path.

"*Father, help me not to let my feelings boss me around. I want to follow Your Holy Spirit, not my feelings, but I need Your help to do it. I trust You to teach me how to walk by faith in You, not my feelings. In Jesus' name. Amen.*"

LORD, MY STRENGTH

I love you, Lord, my strength. The Lord is my rock, my fortress and my deliverer; my God is my rock, in whom I take refuge, my shield and the horn of my salvation, my stronghold. –PSALM 18:1-2

Let me encourage you to reread today's scripture. David says simply, "I love you, Lord, my strength." Then he goes on to declare who God is to him. When we think carefully about these truths, we get just a glimpse of God's greatness and power, and we can easily see why David would say, "I love you, Lord, my strength."

What was true for David is true for you and me today. When you face a difficult situation and you aren't sure how to pray, I encourage you to turn to this passage and say it to the Lord from your heart. Tell Him that you love Him. Declare that He is the rock in whom you take refuge, your fortress, your deliverer, your shield, the horn of your salvation, and your stronghold. This kind of praise and declaration of truth is very powerful in the spiritual realm, and it brings change in the natural realm.

"I love You, Lord, my strength. In Jesus' name. Amen."

WHAT IS LOVE?

Whoever does not love does not know God, because God is love.

—1 JOHN 4:8

God is love, and His love is poured out in our hearts by the Holy Spirit (Romans 5:5). We have God's love inside of us, and God wants it to flow through us to others.

Someone recently asked me, "What is love?" It is a word that we use frequently but inappropriately. We say we love ice cream, our new car, sunshine, God, and countless other things. But the kind of love the Bible talks about cannot be applied to ice cream or a car. The love of God is patient and kind; it is not envious; it is not proud or boastful; it does not dishonor others and is not self-seeking nor easily angered. Love keeps no record of wrongs; it rejoices in truth, it always protects, it believes the best of everyone, it always hopes, and it never gives up. Love never fails (1 Corinthians 13:4–8).

God demonstrates His love for us through the way He treats us, and we show our love for others through the way we treat them. I have heard and repeated this often: People don't always remember what you said to them, but they always remember how you made them feel. We have the God-given ability to make everyone we meet feel valued and special, and we should endeavor to do so. It is easy to love those who love you or do what you want them to do, but it's much more difficult to love an enemy or someone who has disappointed you.

Jesus gave us one new command—to love others as He has loved us (John 13:34). In all your dealings with people, ask yourself what Jesus would do and how He would treat them, and follow in His steps.

"Father, I know that loving You and loving others is Your highest command. I am sorry for all the times I have failed to do so. Forgive me, help me grow in the kind of love You give to me, and give me a greater desire and ability to give it to others. In Jesus' name. Amen."

BE KIND

And now these three remain: faith, hope and love. But the greatest of these is love. —1 CORINTHIANS 13:13

The world needs kindness, and being kind is one of the best ways you can show love to others. I saw on the Internet an eight-year-old's definition of love. It said that love is when your grandmother loves her toenails painted but has arthritis and can't bend over anymore, so your grandfather paints them for her all the time, even after he got arthritis in his hands.

Kindness is not merely a word or an empathetic feeling; it is action. Kindness does things for others, often for no reason at all. In other words, the person being shown kindness has not done anything to deserve it.

Let me encourage you to try some random acts of kindness this week. Be kind to someone you don't even know. Help an elderly person or a pregnant woman get groceries from the store into their car. When you notice someone in a restaurant who looks like they could use a blessing or someone in a coffee shop who seems frustrated or sad, anonymously pay for their food or drink.

The Bible teaches us to "aim to show kindness and seek to do good to one another and to everybody" (1 Thessalonians 5:15 AMPC). I love the words *aim* and *seek*. They tell me I will need to be kind and good on purpose—that I should look for opportunities to show kindness. Those opportunities are everywhere if we will simply look for them. The more we make others happy and stop trying so hard to please ourselves, the happier we will be.

"Father, don't let me pass up any opportunity to be kind to another person. You are kind to me, and I want to be kind to others. Thank You. In Jesus' name. Amen."

WISDOM SPEAKS

Out in the open wisdom calls aloud, she raises her voice in the public square; on top of the wall she cries out, at the city gate she makes her speech. —PROVERBS 1:20-21

Wisdom is the proper application of knowledge. What good is it to know something if we do not apply that knowledge when and where we need it? I look at wisdom in two ways. First, it is sanctified common sense, and second, wisdom means doing now what we will be satisfied with later on. Foolishness is the opposite of wisdom. It seeks immediate gratification and lives as though there is no tomorrow. A fool is said to be morally deficient, and foolish people are gullible and without moral direction and inclined to evil.

The Book of Proverbs urges us repeatedly to be wise and avoid folly if we want to have a good and enjoyable life. As I have studied Proverbs and taken a deeper look at wisdom, I have become convinced that wisdom must be waited on. We cannot hurry and rush through life and expect to hear from wisdom. We may momentarily and impulsively think we want to do a certain thing, but later find out that it was the wrong thing to do.

Take time to let wisdom—either from God's Word or from the experience you have gained on your journey through life—speak to you. Consider the decisions you make, and ask yourself if you are listening to wisdom. Although following wisdom may not always initially be easy, it will always be the best thing to do.

"Father, I'm sorry for all the times I have acted foolishly, and I ask You to grant me the grace to always follow wisdom in the future. Thank You. In Jesus' name. Amen."

BUILD YOUR ARSENAL

For the word of God is alive and active. Sharper than any double-edged sword, it penetrates even to dividing soul and spirit, joints and marrow; it judges the thoughts and attitudes of the heart.

—HEBREWS 4:12

I speak and write often about the power of God's Word. I know it to be one of the most powerful tools on earth, and if we use it properly and often, we cannot be defeated. Our enemy, the devil, uses many strategies to steal our joy, our strength, and our confidence. Today I simply want to remind you of three biblical truths you can use to counter the enemy's lies, along with corresponding scriptures you can speak aloud to remind you of God's truth.

First, know that God loves you (Ephesians 3:17–19).

Second, remember that your battles belong to the Lord (2 Chronicles 20:15, 17).

Third, be confident that God will give you victory in every situation. The apostle Paul writes in 1 Corinthians 15:57: "But thanks be to God! He gives us the victory through our Lord Jesus Christ."

I encourage you to mark this page with a bookmark or take a photo of it to keep on your phone so you can refer to it quickly when you need it. In this way, you can build an arsenal of weapons from God's Word and use them to gain victory over the enemy.

"Father, thank You for the power of Your Word. Help me to use it often, knowing that it never fails. In Jesus' name. Amen."

NOTHING GOOD HAPPENS ACCIDENTALLY

Therefore, as we have opportunity, let us do good to all people, especially to those who belong to the family of believers.

—GALATIANS 6:10

Tragedy that has caused pain and suffering is often attributed to an accident, such as an automobile accident, a fall, a broken limb, or some other random situation. But I have never heard anyone say of a good deed, "It was an accident." Good things happen on purpose. Someone decides to be good to someone else, and then they take corresponding action.

Most people in the world are starved for love. They need affirmation, kindness, compliments—anything that helps them feel valued. Because of what Jesus has done for us, we have the ability to do that for other people, and I think it should be one of our great purposes in life. It should be something we live to do, rather than something we do on rare occasions.

We can live on purpose for a purpose. Loving God and loving people is our highest purpose in life. When you spend time with people, ask yourself how you could compliment them and then do it. When you are shopping or eating out, tell the people serving you that they did a good job. And always remember that you can never say thank you too often.

"Father, I want to help everyone I come in contact with feel valued and loved. I ask You to help me take action aggressively in this area of my life. Thank You for Your help. In Jesus' name. Amen."

FRIENDS

Greater love has no one than this: to lay down one's life for one's friends. You are my friends if you do what I command. I no longer call you servants, because a servant does not know his master's business. Instead, I have called you friends. —JOHN 15:13–15

What a great honor it is to be called a friend of the sovereign all-powerful God. Scripture teaches us to have reverential fear of God and to be in awe of Him (Proverbs 1:7). It also teaches us, in today's scripture, for example, that we are also called His friends; therefore, God can be our friend.

Some people never experience an intimate relationship with God because of the way they see Him. He is not sitting in heaven waiting to punish us every time we make a mistake. Although He can and does become angry with sin, He is not an angry God. He is love, and He loves you! He is quick to forgive and generous in mercy.

You can talk to God about absolutely anything. Be assured that He will understand you and never reject you. I urge you to begin to be more aware of the fact that God is present with you at all times and to develop the habit of talking with Him throughout the day about everything you do.

"Father, I am grateful to know that You see me as Your friend, and I want to see You the same way, as my friend. Please draw me closer to You and teach me to grow in friendship with You. In Jesus' name. Amen."

THE POWER OF WORSHIP

Jehoshaphat bowed down with his face to the ground, and all the people of Judah and Jerusalem fell down in worship before the Lord. –2 CHRONICLES 20:18

One of my favorite Old Testament stories is the story of Jehoshaphat, a king who led God's people to a mighty victory because he understood two key principles. First, he understood that the battle was not his, but God's. Therefore, he knew that God would fight for him (2 Chronicles 20:15). Second, he understood the power of worship.

As Jehoshaphat and his people prepared for battle, the Spirit of God spoke to them, saying, "You will not have to fight this battle. Take up your positions; stand firm and see the deliverance the Lord will give you, Judah and Jerusalem. Do not be afraid; do not be discouraged. Go out to face them tomorrow, and the Lord will be with you" (2 Chronicles 20:17). We might think, in response to these words, that the people grabbed their weapons and ran to their positions on the battlefield. But they didn't. Jehoshaphat and all the people fell before the Lord and worshipped Him. In addition, the Levites began to praise "with a very loud voice" (2 Chronicles 20:19). And of course, they won the battle, just as the Spirit of God had told them they would.

Whatever battle you are facing today, take your position in praise and worship. Praising and worshipping God will strengthen you and defeat the enemy. There is real power—spiritual power—in worship.

"Father, I choose today to face my battles with praise and worship. Thank You for fighting for me, for being with me, and for giving me victory. In Jesus' name. Amen."

BELIEVING GOD

And the scripture was fulfilled that says, "Abraham believed God, and it was credited to him as righteousness," and he was called God's friend. –JAMES 2:23

Believing God is very important. I am not talking about simply believing that God exists, but believing everything He says and being obedient to what He asks you to do. Abraham was even obedient when God asked him to sacrifice his son (Genesis 22:2). Later, the Bible refers to him as God's friend. In addition, the writer of Hebrews understood that believing is the key to entering the type of rest God offers us (Hebrews 4:2–3, 9).

Jesus went to visit Mary and Martha because their brother, Lazarus, had died (John 11:1–44). He had already been dead and in his tomb for four days, but Jesus commanded them to roll away the stone anyway. Martha expressed her unbelief by saying it was too late to do anything, and Jesus told her if she would only believe she would see the glory of God (John 11:40).

God asks us to believe, and as we do, we will see His glory, enter His rest, and be called His friend. Abraham's belief was credited to him as righteousness, and our belief in Jesus makes us "the righteousness of God in Him" (2 Corinthians 5:21 NKJV).

I encourage you today to enter God's rest, relax in His presence, and enjoy your relationship with Him.

"Father, help me enter Your rest and believe everything You say in Your Word, regardless of my circumstances. In Jesus' name. Amen."

CHRIST IN YOU

To them God has chosen to make known among the Gentiles the glorious riches of this mystery, which is Christ in you, the hope of glory. –COLOSSIANS 1:27

Many people who sincerely love God sometimes feel that He is far away, in a place they cannot reach. But He is actually in us and with us at all times. He desires an intimate, close relationship with you. James writes that if we draw near to God, He will draw near to us (James 4:8). Jesus did not die so we could be religious, but so that we might have a personal, comfortable relationship with God.

Do you desire to be closer to God? Does your soul long and thirst for God, as the psalmist writes in Psalm 42:1–2? If so, then begin telling Him how much you desperately require His presence in your life. Realize that He is with you all the time and is interested in everything about you and all that you do. Invite Him to share your life, or, as I like to say, "Do life with God."

Closeness with God requires spending time with Him, not merely once a day for a set period of time, but throughout each day, in addition to setting time apart for Bible study and special prayers. God is never more than one thought away from you, so think of Him often and talk with Him verbally or silently throughout your day.

God loves you very much, and He desires to be the center of your life. When you put Him first, everything else will work much better.

"Father, I long to be closer to You and experience a loving friendship with You. Grant me Your presence at all times. In Jesus' name. Amen."

ABIDE IN CHRIST

I am the vine; you are the branches. Whoever abides in me and I in him, he it is that bears much fruit, for apart from me you can do nothing. —JOHN 15:5 ESV

To abide in Christ means to live, dwell, and remain in Him. Abiding with someone is not an occasional get-together, or even a short daily visit, but a continuous dwelling with that person. Dave and I abide (live, dwell, and remain) together and have for fifty-four years. We know everything about each other, and our lives are intricately intertwined to the point where it would be hard to separate them. This is the kind of relationship that Jesus wants to have with you.

Today's scripture says that if you abide in Christ, you will bear much fruit. Also, if you abide in Christ, you can ask what you wish, and it will be done for you (John 15:7). As we abide in Christ, we come to know Him more deeply and intimately, and His continual influence changes us into His image.

True change does not come from struggling to modify your behavior, but from abiding so deeply in Christ that you become like Him and begin to bear the same good fruit He bears. Do everything you do with and for Him, and you will be amazed at the positive changes in your life.

"Father, teach me to abide in You at all times. I desire You more than any other, and apart from You, I can do nothing. I ask for the gift of Your manifest presence. In Jesus' name, thank You. Amen."

LET NOTHING BE WASTED

When they had all had enough to eat, he said to his disciples, "Gather the pieces that are left over. Let nothing be wasted."

—JOHN 6:12

Just as the disciples had broken pieces left over after feeding the five thousand, I believe we all have broken pieces of our lives left over from pain (emotional or physical) we have experienced. I also believe that if we give those pieces of pain to God, He will find a good use for them in our lives. I was sexually abused by my father for many years, but God has used the story of my recovery to help countless others find freedom.

The Lord wants to use you and all your experiences in life. You may look at your past and think, *I've wasted so many years,* but they don't have to be wasted if you will gather them up and release them to God for His use. He promises to give you beauty for ashes (Isaiah 61:3), but you cannot keep the ashes and also get the beauty. Release your pain and the injustices in your life; release rejection, abandonment, and anything else that has hurt you; and start watching what God will do.

God works all things together for good to those who love Him and want His will in their lives (Romans 8:28). Broken hearts can be mended, and broken relationships can be restored and work out for your good in the future. Stop running from the pain in your past. Take God's hand and let Him walk you into freedom.

"Father, I offer You all the broken pieces of my life. I pray that You will not let them be wasted. In Jesus' name. Amen."

STRENGTHEN YOUR STRENGTHS

But in fact God has placed the parts in the body, every one of them, just as he wanted them to be. If they were all one part, where would the body be? As it is, there are many parts, but one body.

—1 CORINTHIANS 12:18–20

Aren't you glad that everyone on earth is not exactly the same? We all have different abilities, different preferences, different opinions, and different strengths and weaknesses. Some people are not confident in their uniqueness, though, and they try to do what others do well, even if they are not gifted to do so. This is sad to see, because those people have strengths of their own. When they ignore their strengths and try to develop other strengths, they only become frustrated. If they resisted the temptation to be like someone else, they would enjoy their lives more.

I encourage you today to know your strengths and your weaknesses. Focus on developing your strengths and using them to serve God and others to the best of your ability. God has given you your particular strengths for a reason, and He wants you to make the most of them. Some people may suggest that you improve in an area of weakness, but I say don't waste your time doing something you are not gifted to do that will require a great struggle for you to succeed. If you need help in an area in which you are not strong, God will send people to help you.

"Father, help me to accurately assess my strengths and my weaknesses and to grow in my strengths. In Jesus' name. Amen."

ADOPTED BY GOD

Although my father and my mother have abandoned me, yet the Lord will take me up [adopt me as His child]. –PSALM 27:10 AMP

My parents abandoned me. They didn't physically leave me, but they certainly didn't treat me as a child should be treated. My mother knew that my father was abusing me sexually, and she did nothing to stop it because she was afraid of him. So in essence, she abandoned me in my time of need. However, I remember even as a very young child talking to God and being aware of Him, but I was an adult before I realized that He was comforting me in my situation and giving me the grace to get through it.

Regardless of what you have been through, be assured that the Lord is with you and that He accepts you and cares for you, no matter what anyone else does. We are never alone, because the Lord has promised to never leave us or forsake us (Hebrews 13:5). I know how hard it is when you feel that the people who should help and comfort you abandon you. But instead of getting angry with them, turn the situation over to the Lord and let Him take care of you.

God can do more for us in a few moments than a human being can do for us in a lifetime. All things are possible with God, but people are limited in their ability to help us. Even if they want to help, they are not always able to do so. I urge you to give yourself to the Lord and ask Him to be in charge of your care.

"Father, I give myself to You—all my pain and joy, everything I am, and everything I am not. People have disappointed me, but I now trust You to take care of me. Thank You. In Jesus' name. Amen."

GUARD YOUR INTIMACY WITH GOD

For if you forgive other people when they sin against you, your heavenly Father will also forgive you. But if you do not forgive others their sins, your Father will not forgive your sins.

—MATTHEW 6:14–15

Forgiving people when they have hurt or offended us is not easy. In fact, it can be so difficult and painful that people often decide not to do it. This is a serious mistake. The reason choosing not to forgive is such a mistake is that harboring unforgiveness does not affect the person who hurt us at all. But it does hinder our relationship with God. In fact, unforgiveness is one of the quickest and most effective ways I know of for a person to decrease their intimacy with Him.

God's Word says that when we refuse to forgive others, God does not forgive us (Matthew 6:14–15). When He does not forgive us, our sin stands between Him and us, causing us to struggle to hear His voice and sense His presence. We feel far away from Him, and that is a terrible way to feel.

Clinging to unforgiveness keeps people from hearing God's voice, and it serves as a barrier to answered prayer. It steals our peace and joy, and it has a negative impact on our general health and well-being. When Jesus tells us that we must forgive others, He offers this instruction for our benefit—no one else's. Staying in close fellowship with God is always in our best interest, so guard your heart against unforgiveness, and when you feel it creeping in, deal with it quickly.

"Father, even when forgiving someone is not easy for me, give me the grace to do it in obedience to Your Word. I don't want anything to stand between You and me. In Jesus' name. Amen."

WAITING ON GOD

Wait for the Lord; be strong and take heart and wait for the Lord.

—PSALM 27:14

To wait on the Lord doesn't necessarily mean to sit somewhere and do nothing. It means to wait expectantly on God. I encourage you today to have an expectation that God will do something amazing in your life at any moment.

Waiting on God can include just spending time with Him, telling Him that you expect Him to show Himself strong in your life and to do what no one else can do for you. Spending time with God is very important to developing a personal relationship with Him. You may study or read the Bible during that time. You may read spiritually fulfilling books that teach or explain lessons from the Bible. You may also simply sit and look out the window and thank God for His creation. The good thing about spending time with God is that there are no rules concerning how to do it.

The time you give God is much more important than what you do during that time. Just set your heart on the Lord and enjoy Him. Sometimes I like to sit and think of all the things I can remember that God has done for me in my life and thank Him. Sometimes I like to just sit in the quiet and enjoy His presence.

Waiting on God gives you strength and courage to carry you through any situation while you are waiting for your breakthrough.

"*Father, thank You for inviting me to wait on You. Help me develop the habit of doing so regularly. I am excited to see what You will do in my life as I wait for and expect You. In Jesus' name. Amen.*"

CLOSER THAN YOU THINK

On that day you will realize that I am in my Father, and you are in me, and I am in you. –JOHN 14:20

Jesus is closer to you than you may think. He is not only with you, but He is living inside of you. You are the temple of the Holy Spirit (1 Corinthians 6:19). Every time I think about this powerful spiritual truth, it amazes me more and more, and knowing He is close to me makes me feel closer to Him.

Too often, we think of God as being far away, in His holy place, and of ourselves as trying to reach Him. Although our Father is in heaven and Jesus is seated at His right hand, He also lives in us through His Spirit. We should never doubt that God is always near to us and ready to help us.

I encourage you to dwell on God's promise to never leave you (Hebrews 13:5). Meditate specifically on today's scripture, which reminds you that Jesus is in the Father, that you are in Jesus, and that Jesus is in you. Practice thinking about how close He is to you, and talk with Him throughout the day, as you would speak to anyone else who is with you all the time. Develop a holy friendship with Him, always being respectful and reverent yet also relaxed and comfortable in His presence.

"Father, thank You for never leaving me and for being close to me at all times. I'm amazed that You choose to live in me and grateful for my relationship with You. In Jesus' name. Amen."

THE WORK OF GOD'S HANDS

The heavens declare the glory of God; the skies proclaim the work of his hands. —PSALM 19:1

I encourage you today to simply notice and appreciate the beauty of God's creation around you. If you don't have a very good view from your home or office, take a moment to search the Internet for photos of mountains, oceans, deserts, sunrises, sunsets, pastures, or whatever represents natural beauty to you. Watching documentaries about nature is another good way to remember and appreciate all God has created and how amazing it is.

Today's scripture reminds us that the glory of God—His excellence—is on display all around us. Even the sky above us proclaims the awesome work of His hands. Genesis 1 teaches us about the process of creation and shows us how carefully God made the heavens and the earth. He made them for you and me to enjoy, and He invites us to remember Him whenever we see something beautiful in nature.

"Father, thank You for the beauty of Your creation. Help me to see You everywhere I look. In Jesus' name. Amen."

DON'T LET YOUR HEART BE TROUBLED

Do not let your hearts be troubled. You believe in God; believe also in me. —JOHN 14:1

The situations about which we can worry—if we choose to—are endless. The world is a complicated place, and people are often difficult to deal with, so we may be anxious about our lives. Our families and loved ones may be making bad choices, and we worry about them. Financial pressures weigh us down, causing us concern. But thankfully, worry is not our only option. We can cast our care on God, knowing that He is eager to take care of us (1 Peter 5:7).

Why not try replacing worry and anxiety with prayer? If you do, you will see that it is a much better choice. When we worry, we don't help anything or anyone, but when we pray, God can help everyone and do anything. What is impossible with human beings is possible with God (Luke 18:27). I urge you to give God an opportunity to work in your life and in the lives of those you love through prayer. Anytime you have a problem or see a need, the first thing to do is to pray.

Prayer makes tremendous power available to us (James 5:16 AMPC) and opens the door for God to work. Pray in faith, believing and expecting to see God move and do what only He can do. When we pray, we may not see instant change, but Jesus says that when we "ask and keep on asking," we will receive (Matthew 7:7 AMP). While you are waiting for God to work on your behalf, talk with Him about how you are feeling and remember that He always understands (Hebrews 4:15).

"Father, thank You for the great privilege of prayer. Being able to talk with You about anything and knowing that You care is a great blessing. I love You. In Jesus' name. Amen."

SEEK GOD'S KINGDOM FIRST

But seek first his kingdom and his righteousness, and all these things will be given to you as well. –MATTHEW 6:33

When you have a question, a need, or a dilemma—or when you are hurting because someone has treated you unjustly—what's the first thing you do? Do you run to God? Or do you pick up the phone, write in your journal, or take a long walk, rehearsing the situation in your mind with every step? When you get paid, what do you do first? Do you go shopping, or do you give a portion of your resources to God? People handle their circumstances in many different ways, but we should always put God first. God's Word is very clear about that.

Today's scripture teaches us to seek first God's kingdom. To seek God's kingdom simply means to endeavor to know God and His ways. Whatever happens in your life, go to God with it first, and seek to know His will and His way to deal with it. When you have a question, look for your answer first from Him and from His Word. When choosing how to spend your money, your time, and your other resources, give to God first. When we seek God's kingdom first, He will take care of everything else we need.

"Father, in every situation, help me to seek You and Your kingdom first, before I do anything else. In Jesus' name. Amen."

BE GENEROUS IN GRATITUDE

Give thanks in all circumstances; for this is God's will for you in Christ Jesus. —1 THESSALONIANS 5:18

When we express gratitude and thanksgiving, we can be sure we are obeying God's will for us. The more we focus on the good things God has given to us and done for us, the happier we will be, and God will be glorified. As soon as you wake in the morning, start expressing gratitude by thanking God for another day. When you get up, pay attention to all the things God has provided for you, such as running water, heat and air-conditioning, clothes to wear, food to eat, and thousands of other things. When we have never had to do without certain things, taking them for granted is easy, but we can purpose to notice them and be thankful for them.

We should be generous in every way, just as God is generous. Being generous in gratitude is a beautiful thing. Gratitude keeps us positive and opens our hearts to receive even more from God. Think of your own children. Would you give the grumbling, complaining child more, or would you be inclined to give more to the most thankful child? A lack of gratitude shows spiritual immaturity and feeds self-centeredness, but gratitude shows the opposite.

The Bible tells us to be thankful and say so (Psalm 107:1–2). Being thankful is good, but voicing our gratitude to people and to the Lord is even better. We "enter his gates with thanksgiving" (Psalm 100:4), so we know that thanking God takes us into His presence and allows us to experience intimacy and closeness with Him.

Begin now to form the habit of being generous in gratitude. This will put a smile on your face and on the Lord's.

"Father, You have been very good to me, and I repent for any complaining I have done. Please help me form the habit of being generous in gratitude. Thank You. In Jesus' name. Amen."

AVOIDING STRIFE

Make it your ambition to lead a quiet life: You should mind your own business and work with your hands. —1 THESSALONIANS 4:11

Today's scripture tells us to mind our own business, and I am sure we would all experience much less strife and fewer relationship problems if we were obedient to God in this area. People often say, "I have a right to my opinion," and this is true, but we don't have a right to give our opinion unless it is asked for. Proverbs 18:2 says that only a fool delights in revealing all of his opinions.

Pride is what causes us to want to give our advice and opinions, but humility is what God requires. We may offer an opinion if we are trying to prevent someone from harming themselves, but even then, if that person rejects our point of view, we should not continue trying to press it. This is often a difficult transition for parents to make when their children are grown and wanting to make their own decisions. Unless parents can make the change gracefully, it often causes their adult children to feel resentment.

I will admit that I am opinionated, but I have made a lot of progress in keeping my opinions to myself unless someone asks for them. This has made my life much more peaceful. I want to continue growing in this area, and I hope that you do also.

"Father, help me mind my own business and be humble enough not to offer my opinion where it is not wanted. Help me live a quiet life that is filled with peace. In Jesus' name. Amen."

TRUE JOY

You make known to me the path of life; you will fill me with joy in your presence, with eternal pleasures at your right hand.

—PSALM 16:11

We often think we will be happy when certain things happen—when we get married, when we land our dream job, when we buy our dream house, when we achieve our ideal weight, when we go on vacation, when we have children, when the children leave the house...the list goes on and on.

Depending on circumstances to make us happy is understandable. Lots of people do it, but focusing too much on future developments and events can cause us to miss the joy of each day. As we grow spiritually, we learn to appreciate each day more and more, looking forward to the future with a positive attitude, but not letting our goals for the future steal our happiness in the present.

In the early days of my ministry, I had certain milestones in mind, and I believed I would be happy when I reached them. But God showed me that I would never find true joy in achieving goals or reaching milestones. Having them is not wrong, but putting them ahead of God is. True joy is found only in God's presence, and in serving Him according to His will. Have you found that worldly pursuits have not delivered the happiness you long for? Then spend time with God today and let Him show you what true joy is.

"Father, I do not seek happiness in my circumstances. In Your presence is where I find true joy. In Jesus' name. Amen."

LOOK FORWARD TO THE FUTURE

However, as it is written: "What no eye has seen, what no ear has heard, and what no human mind has conceived"—the things God has prepared for those who love him. –1 CORINTHIANS 2:9

Today's verse is a very exciting scripture. God's plans for us are so wonderful that we cannot even imagine them! Believing this allows us to live with hope—the aggressive expectation that something good is going to happen.

For too many years, I lived with evil foreboding, which is the expectation that something bad will surely happen. This type of thinking can easily take hold of someone who has had a lot of pain or misfortune in life. That was me. Because I had been abused during my childhood and married the wrong man at the age of eighteen, the first twenty-three years of my life were one long series of disappointments. I grew to expect trouble, but thankfully, God has taught me that He is good and is ready to do good things in my life, as He is in yours.

What is the most wonderful thing you can imagine God doing for you? Now remember that He can do even more than that. God has good things prepared for His children, and I encourage you to wait for them with expectancy.

"Father, You are good beyond anything I can describe, and I am grateful for Your blessings. I am excited to see what You will do in my future. In Jesus' name. Amen."

AUGUST 6

DEALING WITH DISAPPOINTMENT

They cried out to You and were delivered; they trusted in You and were not disappointed or ashamed. —PSALM 22:5 AMP

Are you dealing with a disappointment right now? Did you expect a situation to turn out one way, and now it's ended up another way? Were you hoping to hear a yes in a certain situation and you have heard a no instead? Have you been praying that God would do one thing, and it is clear He has chosen to do something else? If so, it is understandable that you may feel disappointed.

We all face disappointment at times. Some disappointments are minor, while others are quite significant. Feelings of disappointment are not unusual or wrong in any way, but the way we handle those feelings makes a big difference in our lives.

Today's scripture holds a key for dealing with disappointment. The people who cried out to God "trusted in [God] and were not disappointed or ashamed." The remedy for disappointment is to trust in God. Trust that He knows every detail of your situation. Trust that He cares for you more than you can imagine. And trust that He is always working in your very best interest, even when you cannot see it.

"Father, help me to deal with disappointment by trusting in You and believing that You are always working for my good. In Jesus' name. Amen."

GOD'S CHOICES SURPRISE US

But God chose the foolish things of the world to shame the wise; God chose the weak things of the world to shame the strong. God chose the lowly things of this world and the despised things—and the things that are not—to nullify the things that are, so that no one may boast before him. –1 CORINTHIANS 1:27-29

Are you sometimes surprised by the people God chooses to use and through whom He works? I have been surprised that He chose me, and you may feel the same way. God chooses people who love Him and whose hearts are with Him, and they are not always the most educated or most talented.

God's anointing (His presence and power in our lives) qualifies us for His use—not who we know, what we own, how much education we have, or how naturally gifted we are. This is good news, because it means that God can and will use everyone who makes themselves available. We don't have to have ability, just availability. When we realize that God chooses those who are least likely to be chosen, it causes us to give God all of the glory for what He does through them. It also prevents us from boasting about ourselves.

Never count yourself out. Just give yourself to God and ask Him to use you as He desires—and then get ready for anything. All things are possible with God!

"Father, naturally speaking, I don't have much to offer, but I give You all that I am and all that I am not. I ask You to use me as You desire. In Jesus' name. Amen."

HOW TO HANDLE CRITICISM

If anyone will not welcome you or listen to your words, leave that home or town and shake the dust off your feet. —MATTHEW 10:14

Jesus spoke the words of today's scripture to His disciples when He sent them out to minister two by two. He was aware that not everyone would receive them or be kind to them. He knew that some would mock or criticize them and reject their message.

You may also encounter criticism or rejection, and the instruction Jesus gave His disciples is good advice for you too. He basically said, "Shake it off!"

Jesus knew about criticism and rejection. Isaiah prophesied long before Jesus was born that He would be "despised and rejected by mankind, a man of suffering, and familiar with pain" (Isaiah 53:3). When He was criticized and mocked during His life on earth, He typically ignored it (Matthew 27:11–12).

Many times the best way to handle criticism is to keep quiet and keep moving forward. I encourage you to stay calm and not become angry, knowing that peace is a powerful spiritual weapon. Resist the temptation to be defensive, knowing that God is your vindicator, and walk in forgiveness toward those who try to hurt you or damage your reputation, knowing that forgiveness is God's will for you (Matthew 6:14–15).

"Father, help me shake off criticism and rejection. When I must deal with it, help me to do so wisely and in accordance with Your will. In Jesus' name. Amen."

THE ENEMY'S CRAFTY ATTACK

Now the serpent was more crafty than any of the wild animals the Lord God had made. He said to the woman, "Did God really say, 'You must not eat from any tree in the garden'?" –GENESIS 3:1

One way your enemy, the devil, will try to keep you weak and ineffective is to cause you to question God's Word. In his very first attack on the human mind, he asked Eve, "Did God *really* say?" (emphasis mine). Eve's first mistake was to take the enemy's bait and engage in conversation with him.

As today's scripture says, the devil is crafty. He doesn't always come against our minds in ways that are so blatantly ungodly that we immediately recognize that he is at work. He is slyer than that. Instead of directly mocking or challenging what God had said to Eve, he simply questioned it. When Eve responded, he countered with lies and an appeal to her ego (Genesis 3:4–5).

I encourage you today to be so strong in the Word of God that a question from the enemy will not sway you. The minute the thought comes to your mind, "Has God really said…?" respond by speaking the Word. Don't engage the enemy in conversation, but reinforce your thoughts and words with the truth of Scripture.

"Father, help me not to take the enemy's bait when he questions Your Word, but to stand firm on what You have said. In Jesus' name. Amen."

TAKE CARE OF YOURSELF

Do you not know that your bodies are temples of the Holy Spirit, who is in you, whom you have received from God?

—1 CORINTHIANS 6:19

It is amazing to think that God makes His home in His children. When we receive Christ as our Savior, He comes to live in us, and our bodies become His temple. It is therefore prudent and wise for each of us to take good care of our bodies.

I am sorry to say that I spent many years pushing myself too hard and not taking care of my body, a temple of God, before I realized how important it is.

I hope to spare you the same mistakes I made. I urge you to respect your body and give it proper rest, sleep, hydration, and nutrition. God wants to not only live *in* you, but also to work *through* you. However, if you feel bad all the time because you don't take care of yourself, He won't be able to do that.

I encourage you to meditate on how amazing it is that God lives in you. You are the home of God. Prayerfully, this will urge you to keep the house of God—your body—in good condition. We are representatives of God, and He makes His appeal to the world through us (2 Corinthians 5:20). Let's commit to representing Him well.

"Father, forgive me for not taking better care of myself. I want to represent You well, and I ask You to help me work with You to repair any damage done to my body. Thank You. In Jesus' name. Amen."

WHY DO YOU DO WHAT YOU DO?

Be careful not to practice your righteousness in front of others to be seen by them. If you do, you will have no reward from your Father in heaven. —MATTHEW 6:1

God is more concerned with why we do what we do than with what we do. God sees our hearts, and only good works done from a pure heart will bring a reward. We often fall into the trap of trying to impress people who ultimately don't matter because they don't truly care for us and will likely abandon us if we don't live to please them. We need to pay attention to what is really important, and the most important thing is that we please God, not other people.

Beware of doing good works to be noticed, gain applause, or be admired and well thought of. Do your good works in obedience to God and to help others because you love them. Good works cannot get us into heaven, but they can bring us rewards from God when they are done with pure motives.

Take time to examine everything you are doing, and be bold enough to ask yourself why you are doing it. As your motives become clear, you may decide to cross a lot of things off of your to-do list and become more energized to do the things that you are doing with a pure motive.

"Father, thank You for revealing any impure motives I may have, and help me do what I do with a pure heart. Thank You. In Jesus' name. Amen."

ALWAYS BE HONEST

The Lord detests dishonest scales, but accurate weights find favor with him. —PROVERBS 11:1

Today's scripture speaks of the use of dishonest scales. In our society, this would mean to never overcharge anyone for a service or product. Jesus is the Truth (John 14:6), and He expects us to be like Him in our financial dealings and in all areas of our lives.

Always being honest is a godly character trait, and we should make sure it characterizes us. Many people in the world today are quick to compromise, but we should always remember that although we are in the world, Jesus tells us not to be like the world (John 17:11, 14–16).

We should always speak the truth, even if it could cause trouble for ourselves or perhaps anger someone else. A friend or coworker might ask us to lie for them in order to keep them from getting into trouble, but our answer to such a request must always be a firm no, even if we lose a friendship because of it. Our first allegiance is always to God and His Word.

Thinking again about today's scripture, let me encourage you to be honest in all your financial dealings. If you are shopping and a clerk gives you back too much change or fails to charge you for an item, be sure to return to the store and make it right. Doing so will be a good witness of the love and integrity of God to the clerk.

"Father, if I am being dishonest in any area and don't realize it, I pray that You will reveal it to me. Help me be honest in every area of my life. In Jesus' name. Amen."

FIND A QUIET PLACE

Then, because so many people were coming and going that they did not even have a chance to eat, he said to them, "Come with me by yourselves to a quiet place and get some rest." –MARK 6:31

Can you relate to the scene in today's scripture? Do you know what it's like to be so busy that you do not even have a chance to eat? Some days are that way. Sometimes, we have entire weeks or months that feel too busy, and we simply want to get away from the people and the pressure. In the midst of such a busy season, Jesus offers us the same invitation He gave to His disciples: "Come with me by yourselves to a quiet place and get some rest."

The world is a busy place right now, and you may have a very busy life. You may wish things would change, but if things don't change, you can change. You can begin today to handle the busyness of life differently. You can start by carving out time to be alone with God. That time alone with Him can offset the stress of an overscheduled day, filled with interruptions.

You may crave a few hours or a whole weekend alone with Him, but whatever it is, He will meet you there, and you will find it beneficial. Spend time alone with Him as often as you can, and you will feel His peace in you and around you, no matter how busy the day may be. Even a five-minute visit with God will refresh you and give you strength for the next task you need to do.

"Father, help me to find time to be alone with You today. In Jesus' name. Amen."

DON'T LET YOUR HEART BE TROUBLED

Peace I leave with you; my peace I give you. I do not give to you as the world gives. Do not let your hearts be troubled and do not be afraid. −JOHN 14:27

We often pray for peace. But according to today's scripture, we already have Jesus' peace. He gave us that peace before He departed this world. However, we must hold on to it by staying in peace and not being anxious, worried, troubled, or afraid.

You might think that you cannot control how you feel, but I've found that if Jesus tells us not to do something, there is a way not to do it. For me, identifying the things that cause me to lose my peace and avoiding them has greatly increased my peace. For instance, if I'm too rushed, I end up frustrated. Or, if I get involved in something that is none of my business, it usually causes strife and problems I could have avoided.

Fear is one of the biggest problems people have today, because the world has become a dangerous place. However, believers in Christ do not need to fear because we have the privilege of trusting Him to take care of us. This does not mean that we can always avoid trouble, but even if something unpleasant does happen, God has promised to bring good out of it (Romans 8:28). Hold on to your peace today and every day, and don't let your heart be troubled.

"Father, I am thankful that You have given me Your peace, and I ask You to help me hold on to it and not be anxious, fearful, or troubled. Thank You. In Jesus' name. Amen."

I WILL NOT FEAR

Even though I walk through the darkest valley, I will fear no evil, for you are with me; your rod and your staff, they comfort me.

—PSALM 23:4

Today's scripture reminds me of 2 Timothy 1:7: "God has not given us a spirit of fear, but of power and of love and of a sound mind" (NKJV). When we become fearful, we can be sure that the enemy is at work, not God. Sometimes we think of fear as a human emotion, but it is actually a spirit. The spirit of fear often operates as a thought or a whisper telling you that you have every reason to be afraid and that God has forgotten you or will not help you.

David, who wrote the words of Psalm 23:4, says to God that the reason he can walk through the darkest valley is that "you are with me." If the enemy can use fear to make us think that God is not with us—that He does not care about what we are going through or that He does not love us—he can begin to win the battle for our hearts and minds. No matter how fear comes against you, remember that it comes from the enemy, and remember that God is always with you and has not given you a spirit of fear.

"Father, help me to resist the attacks of fear that the enemy launches against me and to remember in every situation that You are with me. In Jesus' name. Amen."

BE CAREFUL WHAT YOU THINK ABOUT

The worries of this life and the deceitfulness of wealth choke the word, making it unfruitful. –MATTHEW 13:22

God's Word teaches us to study it and meditate on it. The more thought we give to the truth we read or hear, the more we will get out of it. Meditating on God's Word can turn the information we read into the revelation we need.

When the seed of God's Word is sown in our hearts, Satan comes immediately to try to steal it (Mark 4:15). He doesn't want us to hear or study the Word, but if we do, he doesn't want us to think about it. He knows that if we do ponder the Word, it will become part of us, and we will obey it.

He will try to distract us by giving us something to worry about, but we can choose to hold on to our peace and trust God with every problem that arises. Satan also lies to us about the importance of wealth and deceives us into chasing it instead of keeping God and His Word first place in our lives. Let us remember that Jesus says if we seek first the Kingdom of God and His righteousness, everything else will be added to us (Matthew 6:33).

"Father, help me keep my mind full of thoughts about Your wonderful Word and all the magnificent things You have done and are doing every day. In Jesus' name. Amen."

CHOOSE FRIENDS WHO MAKE YOU BETTER

As iron sharpens iron, so one person sharpens another.

—PROVERBS 27:17

The people with whom we spend our time are very important, because we often pick up some of their habits and character traits. If we spend a lot of time with people who compromise morally, we may begin to think compromise is acceptable for us too.

We cannot avoid all immoral people—otherwise, we would have to get out of the world entirely, and we do want our lives to be a witness for Christ to them. I often say that spending time with people who don't know Christ is good, as long as we affect them without allowing them to infect us. We spend different amounts of time with different people, but the ones we spend much time with should lift us up and make us better.

If your friends are stingy and greedy, they will not help you become generous. If your friends gossip about others, you may find yourself gossiping or spreading rumors too. However, if your friends are kind, patient, loving, and always ready to help others, you will find yourself wanting to grow in these godly qualities. Choose your friends wisely, and if you are spending too much time with the wrong kind of people, make a change for the better.

"Father, I want friends who make me a better person. I pray for divine connections. I ask You to guide me to people who are godly rather than worldly and to give me favor with them. In Jesus' name. Amen."

STAY BALANCED

I am sending you out like sheep among wolves. Therefore be as shrewd as snakes and as innocent as doves. —MATTHEW 10:16

We would struggle to think of two animals more different than snakes and doves, yet Jesus tells us in today's scripture to be like both. I believe He uses this example to teach us the importance of maintaining balance in our dealings with other people. The snake represents shrewdness and wisdom, while the dove represents innocence and gentleness. The Amplified Bible says that to be "innocent as doves" means to "have no self-serving agenda."

People who are innocent without also being wise usually open their hearts to people without knowing whether those people are trustworthy. They don't use reasonable caution in relationships and often end up being hurt or betrayed. In contrast, people who are shrewd or wise without also being innocent and gentle may be overly suspicious of others, always expecting people to take advantage of them. They may end up with few deep, meaningful relationships or even with no true friends at all. Being out of balance in either direction—too innocent or too shrewd—can keep people from cultivating and enjoying relationships God may want to give them.

The Holy Spirit will help us be appropriately wise and appropriately innocent at the same time so that we can develop healthy, balanced relationships with others.

"Father, help me to be wise like a serpent and gentle like a dove toward everyone I meet. In Jesus' name. Amen."

CREATED IN GOD'S IMAGE

Then God said, "Let us make mankind in our image." –GENESIS 1:26

Science often tells us that human beings have evolved from primates, but God says that we are created in His image. Knowing that God created you to be like Him, that He created you because He wanted you, and that you are not merely an accident makes a big difference in the way you feel about yourself. Having God-given confidence in who He has created you to be is important to your own enjoyment of life and to God's plan for His kingdom.

One of the biggest problems troubled and unhappy people have is that they don't like themselves. They feel they have no purpose or value, but that is completely untrue. God carefully created each of us with His own hand in our mother's womb (Psalm 139:13). You are a special, one-of-a-kind, amazing person, and God loves you unconditionally. He has you on His mind all the time, and every plan He has for you is good.

Learn to see yourself as God sees you. Talk about yourself the way God talks about you in His Word. Love who you are! We don't always do the right thing, but we are always loved by God, and we can enjoy ourselves where we are on the way to becoming more and more like Jesus.

"Father, I love You. I am thankful that You created me in Your image and that You love me. Help me see myself the way You see me and to be confident in You. In Jesus' name. Amen."

UNDERSTANDING THE CONVICTION OF THE HOLY SPIRIT

And He, when He comes, will convict the world about [the guilt of] sin [and the need for a Savior], and about righteousness, and about judgment. —JOHN 16:8 AMP

The word *convict* in its various forms, such as *convicted* and *conviction*, can be used in a negative sense, such as in a trial, when someone is convicted of a crime. They can also be positive, such as when they describe a person of "strong moral convictions," meaning strong moral principles or beliefs.

In biblical terms, the word *conviction* is used in connection with the ministry of the Holy Spirit. He convicts us of sin—not so we will feel terrible about what we've done when we fall short of God's standard, but so we will repent, experience God's grace, and find freedom.

Feeling convicted is not the same as feeling condemned. When you feel the conviction of the Holy Spirit, you know you have done something that is not pleasing to God, but you also know He loves you, and you are certain you will be forgiven. When people feel condemned, they feel a burden of guilt that they cannot seem to escape, and they feel hopeless. Condemnation is from the enemy, but conviction is a gift of the Holy Spirit, and it leads to forgiveness and freedom.

"Father, thank You for sending the Holy Spirit. Help me yield to His conviction so I may enjoy Your forgiveness and freedom. In Jesus' name. Amen."

USE YOUR WORDS WISELY

Set a guard over my mouth, Lord; keep watch over the door of my lips. —PSALM 141:3

The power of life and death is in the tongue (the words we speak), and we eat the fruit of what we say (Proverbs 18:21). This is an amazing truth, and if we truly believe it, we will use more wisdom concerning the words we speak. No one can tame the tongue without God's help (James 3:7–8); therefore, we are wise to pray regularly for God to help us in this area.

Almost daily, I pray as David did in Psalm 141:3 and ask God to set a guard over my mouth. I need His help in my speech, and so do you. Words can lift up or tear down, they can give hope or steal hope, and they can minister life or death to those who hear and speak them.

When we talk, we hear what we say, just as others do, and those words do have an impact on us. I think that if we spend most of the day gossiping, complaining, and being negative, we will feel depressed and perhaps even angry.

I firmly believe that some people suffer with depression simply because they think and speak negatively most of the time. I urge you to start today to speak words filled with life. Be positive and hopeful at all times, and ask God regularly to help you say what He would say in every situation.

"Father, I need Your help with my words. Put a guard over my mouth and help me think before I speak. In Jesus' name. Amen."

NEVER FORSAKEN

The chief priests accused him of many things. –MARK 15:3

Before Jesus went to the cross, people made many false accusations against Him. He stood strong in the face of the unfair charges, refusing to answer His accusers (Mark 14:55–61; 15:3–5). But by the time He hung on the cross, the bitterly harsh and accusing language and injustice He endured, along with the physical agony He suffered, made Him ask aloud if God had forsaken Him.

Perhaps you have experienced being falsely accused. Maybe you are wondering right now if God has forsaken you or left you alone in a certain situation. The answer is no! God did not forsake Jesus, and He has not forsaken or abandoned you today. In fact, He is always close to you, and He always will be. Jesus knows exactly how it feels to suffer, and He can relate to your pain.

Just as God had a plan for Jesus to be gloriously resurrected after His experience on the cross, He has a great plan for you too. On the other side of your struggle, you will be stronger than ever before. He is with you, and He loves you more than you realize.

"Father, help me to remember that You never leave me. You are always with me. I never have to go through a difficult time alone. In Jesus' name. Amen."

THE MOST EXCELLENT WAY

And now these three remain: faith, hope and love. But the greatest of these is love. —1 CORINTHIANS 13:13

The Bible teaches us that walking in love is the most excellent way to live (1 Corinthians 12:31). God is love, and when we walk in love, we are walking and living in Him (1 John 4:16). Love is more than a word we use when speaking to other people. It is seen in our actions, especially in how we treat other people.

Jesus gave us one new command, which is for us to love one another just as He loves us. As we show that love, others will know that we are His disciples (John 13:34–35). God's love for us required Him to sacrifice His only Son, and if we truly want to love people, there will be times when we will also need to sacrifice for them.

According to 1 Corinthians 13:4–8, love is not self-seeking; it is patient, kind, humble, and not envious. It does not dishonor others, is not easily angered, keeps no record of wrongs, and doesn't delight in evil. It rejoices with the truth. It always believes the best of everyone, and it never fails. If we focus on loving God and loving other people, we will live the life that He desires for us to live.

No matter what so-called good works we may do, if we don't have love, we simply make a lot of noise and amount to nothing (1 Corinthians 13:1–3).

"Father, I want to walk in the kind of love You show to me, but I need Your help. Teach me what love is and how to show it to other people. In Jesus' name. Amen."

GOD HAS CALLED US TO LIVE IN PEACE

I have told you these things, so that in me you may have peace. In this world you will have trouble. But take heart! I have overcome the world. —JOHN 16:33

I think we would all agree that the world today is not a very peaceful place. This should not surprise us, because Jesus says in today's scripture that in the world, we will have trouble. He also gives us some good news, which is that in Him we can have peace.

God has called us to live in peace and to be peacemakers. The older I get, the more I value peace. I had twenty-four hours this week that were not peaceful, and when the turmoil was settled and peace returned, I was so thankful. I love peace!

We all say we want peace, but wanting peace and doing what we need to do in order to have it may be two different things. If you are lacking peace, ask God to show you what you can do or change to bring peace into your life, and then be willing to do it.

I've learned that having fewer opinions helps me maintain peace and that humility always brings peace. Not hurrying helps me stay at peace, as does getting proper rest. There are things you can do to increase your peace, and I encourage you to identify them and start doing them today.

"Father, I want to enjoy Your peace. I ask You to show me anything in my life that I need to change in order to have it. Thank You. In Jesus' name. Amen."

A PROPER PERSPECTIVE ON CORRECTION

For those whom the Lord loves He corrects, even as a father corrects the son in whom he delights. —PROVERBS 3:12 AMP

Part of the process of spiritual maturity is receiving the correction of the Lord when we need it. Many times, our experience with earthly parents or people in authority leaves us feeling ashamed, guilty, or inept as a result of correction. People do not always administer correction lovingly or with our best interests at heart—but God does. Often, correction from other human beings is designed to punish us and cause us to fear them so they can control us, but God's correction is designed to ultimately bless us. According to today's scripture, His correction is a sign of His love, not an indication of His displeasure.

The more we mature spiritually, the more we realize that God's correction is motivated solely by His love and His desire for us to live the best life we can possibly live. As we grow in Him, we understand that He corrects us in order to help us, not to hurt us. When we understand this, we will welcome His correction and be eager to make the changes He leads us to make.

"Father, help me to understand that Your correction is intended to help me become the best I can possibly be and to live the best life I can possibly live. In Jesus' name. Amen."

LOVE ONE ANOTHER

This is my command: Love each other. —JOHN 15:17

The command to love each other is repeated throughout Scripture. Loving one another is one of the best ways we can show the world that we are Christ's disciples. One way we can show love is through forgiveness, and another is through showing mercy.

Is there anyone in your life right now who you need to forgive? Perhaps that person has treated you unjustly. Forgiving them may be difficult, but you can do it by God's grace.

Be merciful and good to those who don't deserve it, for that is what God has done for us in Christ. Our goal should be to become like Christ in all our ways, and He is quick to forgive and plenteous in mercy.

Love is much more than a feeling; it is action. Love is seen in how we choose to treat people—including people who have wronged us. God's Word teaches us that if our enemy is hungry, we should feed him, and if he is thirsty, we should give him something to drink (Romans 12:20). This means we should be willing to meet his needs even if we don't feel he deserves to have them met. Doing good in order to have good come back to us means nothing, but doing good to those who don't deserve it is doing what God does.

"Father, I want to love as You love, and I ask You to teach me how to do it. Help me to be merciful, kind, and forgiving, just as You are. In Jesus' name. Amen."

WHO RULES YOUR MIND?

The mind governed by the flesh is death, but the mind governed by the Spirit is life and peace. —ROMANS 8:6

What kind of thoughts do you think most of the time? Are they thoughts that God would approve of? Do you realize that you can exchange wrong thoughts for right ones? For many years, I didn't pay any attention to what I was thinking. But when I started thinking about what I was thinking about, I found the source of many of my problems.

Our thoughts are very important, because they become the words we speak and the actions we take. In 2 Corinthians 10:4–5, Paul instructs the Corinthians to cast down, or reject, wrong thoughts and imaginations and to bring every thought captive to the obedience of Jesus Christ.

I believe that where the mind goes, the man follows. Proverbs 23:7 indicates that as our thoughts are, so we become. You can change your life by changing your thoughts. If you want to be happy, then think good, happy thoughts. Thinking positive thoughts based on God's Word will release joy in your life. Think good things about other people, and always believe the best of them. Let your mind be governed by the Spirit, not the flesh.

"Father, I want my mind to be governed by Your Spirit, and I ask You to help me recognize when my thoughts are not as You want them to be. In Jesus' name. Amen."

ARE YOU COMFORTABLE BEING INTIMATE WITH GOD?

There is a friend who sticks closer than a brother. —PROVERBS 18:24

The title of today's devotion may seem like a strange question. I ask it because I think many people are not comfortable in an intimate relationship with God. They may approach Him as one who is far away in heaven, and they may not feel they are worthy of intimacy with Him.

God referred to Abraham as His friend (Isaiah 41:8), and He spoke to Moses "face to face, as one speaks to a friend" (Exodus 33:11). These people were not perfect. They made mistakes just as you and I do, but they had an intimate relationship with God.

I encourage you to be comfortable talking with God about anything. After all, He already knows everything about you, and He loves and accepts you unconditionally.

The more open you are with God concerning everything in your life, the closer to Him you will feel. I believe God is calling you closer, and I pray that you will enter into His presence knowing that you are welcome there.

"Father, I want to be as close to You as I can be. Help me not to be ashamed or to feel uncomfortable in any way in Your presence. In Jesus' name. Amen."

HAVE A GREAT DAY

Very early in the morning, while it was still dark, Jesus got up, left the house and went off to a solitary place, where he prayed.

—MARK 1:35

Have you ever gotten up in the morning and everything seemed to go wrong? Perhaps you didn't sleep well, or you know you have to do something that you don't want to do, or you simply feel grumpy. When that happens, the entire day usually feels "off." Hardly anything seems to go right. But when you wake up feeling healthy, strong, and happy, the morning seems to flow smoothly, and the rest of the day tends to go well.

Many times, the way we feel in the morning sets the tone for the day. This is why it's important to be intentional in the mornings. When we choose to be positive and confident, we influence the day instead of allowing the enemy to interfere with it.

I encourage you to begin each day in God's Word and in prayer, asking Him to give you a positive mindset toward all that is on your schedule and grace for everything that will come your way. Put your faith in God and His goodness, and expect your day to go well. The day may or may not go as planned—and often something unexpected will arise—but even if your plans must change, you can keep a good attitude and trust God to do something even better than you originally hoped.

"Father, I expect to have a great day today, whether it goes as planned or not. In Jesus' name. Amen."

STRENGTH FOR THE WEARY

He gives strength to the weary and increases the power of the weak…those who hope in the Lord will renew their strength.

—ISAIAH 40:29, 31

We all grow weary and feel weak in our faith or weak in physical strength at times, but God understands and is ready to help us. According to today's scripture, those who put their hope and expectation in God will renew their strength. They will be able to do all they need to do and not grow weary because His grace (strength) is sufficient for every situation in life (2 Corinthians 12:9; Philippians 4:13).

Run to the Lord and ask for what you need, and then wait in His presence, believing that you receive it from Him. If we ask and believe we receive by faith, then we will have what we request (Mark 11:24).

As you wait on God, wait with expectation that He will meet your need. Be excited each day to see what He will do for you. We receive from God through faith and patience (Hebrews 6:12), so be patient, and know that God will not be late. His timing may not be what you would like it to be, but it will be perfect.

"Father, renew my strength as I wait on You. I pray that You would meet all of my needs in Your perfect timing. Thank You. In Jesus' name. Amen."

HOW THE TRUTH MAKES YOU FREE

Then Jesus said to those Jews who believed Him, "If you abide in My word, you are My disciples indeed. And you shall know the truth, and the truth shall make you free." –JOHN 8:31-32 NKJV

The world tells us there are many sources of truth. It also tells us truth is relative, or dependent on circumstances. The world tries to get us to follow its truth, and the devil tries to convince us that what he says is truth. He wants us to receive as truth the thoughts he plants in our minds, but we know that he does nothing but lie (John 8:44). There is only one source of eternal truth—the truth that will change our lives and set us free—and that is God's Word.

In today's scripture, Jesus did not tell the Jews that they would know the truth and that it would make them free if they casually read His Word or knew a few verses of Scripture. He said, "If you *abide* in My word" (emphasis mine). According to the Amplified Bible, abiding means "continually obeying" His teachings and "living in accordance with them."

I believe this is one of the great keys to spiritual strength and to victory in any form of spiritual warfare. Only by abiding in (obeying) God's Word will we know the truth to the point that it will make us free. God's Word is truth (John 17:17), and it is powerful in our lives if we receive it in our hearts and apply it to our lives each day through obedience.

"Father, thank You for the unshakable truth of Your Word. Help me to abide in it and know it as truth so it will make me free."

VINDICATION

The Lord will vindicate me; your love, Lord, endures forever.

—PSALM 138:8

Has someone mistreated you? Have you suffered an injustice for which you want revenge or vindication? God says that He is our Vindicator and that vengeance is His (Romans 12:19). Most of the time, when people hurt you, they cannot pay you back. They have taken something from you that only God can return.

My father abused me sexually, and because of that I felt for years that I had been cheated in life. I wanted someone to repay me, but then I discovered in Scripture that people could not pay me back, but God could. He is a God of justice, which means that if we trust Him, He will make wrong things right. Being patient and waiting on God rather than taking matters into your own hands may be difficult to do, but God's reward will be better than any revenge you or I could exact for ourselves.

I urge you today to forgive all those who have hurt you and turn the situation over to God. Then, patiently wait and watch Him work amazing things in your life. He will give you beauty for ashes, joy for mourning, happiness for sadness, and peace for turmoil. God will restore your soul and give you every good thing He has for you.

"Father, I trust that You are my Vindicator, and I forgive my enemies and turn my situations over to You. I wait on Your justice in my life. Thank You. In Jesus' name. Amen."

BE GOOD SOIL

Still other seed fell on good soil. It came up, grew and produced a crop, some multiplying thirty, some sixty, some a hundred times.

—MARK 4:8

According to Mark 4:1–8, there are four types of people who hear God's Word. God's Word is like seed, and people's hearts are like soil.

Mark 4:3–4 says that the first type of person hears God's Word, but birds (symbolizing the devil) immediately steal it. The second type of person, described in Mark 4:5–6, receives God's Word and is excited about it, but they do not develop the spiritual strength to hold on to it. The Amplified Bible says that they accept it, but "only superficially" (Mark 4:16). The third type of person allows cares, concerns, and the things of the world to distract them from the truth of God's Word (Mark 4:7, 18–19).

The fourth type of person is what I hope you and I will always be. Let us be mature Christians who hear the Word, receive it, obey it, guard it, and allow it to work in us so that our lives bear good fruit for God, meaning that we do something that honors Him and benefits others with the time, talents, and resources He has given us.

Make sure you are good soil for God's Word by guarding your heart against the enemy, persevering and holding tight to its truth when troubles come your way, and refusing to allow worry or worldly things to distract you from it.

"Father, help me to be good soil—to have a heart in which Your Word will take root, grow, and multiply. In Jesus' name. Amen."

TAKING TIME FOR ENJOYMENT

God saw all that he had made, and it was very good. −GENESIS 1:31

God not only worked and created things, but He also looked them over and said they were good. He took time to enjoy the work He had done. Do you do that? Do you just work and work, but never take the time to stop and enjoy what your labor has produced?

Jesus said that He came that we might have and enjoy life in abundance (John 10:10), but in order to enjoy life, we have to take time to do so. Most people today are busy, busy, busy—rushing here and there, but not really taking time to enjoy the wonderful life God has given them.

God worked for six days. On the seventh day, He rested from all of His labors (Genesis 2:2). We should also have a day of rest, not as a law we follow, but as a freedom God has given us. Rest is a gift from God, and it is necessary if we want to live long and healthy lives. Work is good, but we can turn a good thing into a bad thing if we do it excessively. I encourage you to schedule rest into your calendar just as you schedule other important responsibilities and activities, and take time to enjoy God, your family, and your life.

"Father, I want to live a well-balanced life, and I need Your wisdom to do it. Show me what changes I need to make in my life in order to enjoy regular periods of rest and quiet. In Jesus' name. Amen."

REINFORCE YOUR PRAYERS

And now you will be silent and not able to speak until the day this happens, because you did not believe my words, which will come true at their appointed time. –LUKE 1:20

God responded in a surprising way when Zechariah struggled to believe Him after He sent an angel to tell him that he and his wife, Elizabeth, would have a son. That's understandable in a way, because they were way too old to have children. But God had spoken. And Zechariah questioned. That was a problem. Because of his lack of faith, God made him unable to speak until the baby was born.

This story teaches us that the way we respond to God's promises is very important. When we pray in faith, believing He will answer, we are not to stop praying and then go about our business, wondering if He heard us and if He will move on our behalf. We are to keep our faith strong, expecting Him to answer, and we are to think and speak in agreement with our expectation. He is a God who keeps His promises and answers prayer, and He wants us to keep this truth in the forefront of our minds.

When you are praying about something, don't let doubt enter your heart and weaken your prayers—or cause you to forget about them. Instead, let your confidence in God reinforce your prayers as you trust Him to answer at the right time and in the right way.

"Father, when I pray, help me to reinforce my prayers with faith and expectation. In Jesus' name. Amen."

STAY FOCUSED

Let your eyes look straight ahead; fix your gaze directly before you.
—PROVERBS 4:25

Many things scream for our attention. If we want to accomplish anything important in life, we need to learn how to stay focused on what is truly important to us at the time.

Distraction is a scheme of the devil to keep us from succeeding at doing what God wants us to do. Even when we try to study God's Word or pray, the devil brings many distractions to prevent us from focusing.

When I am writing, for example, it is important for me to be able to focus on that one thing, so I go to a place that is quiet and where I am not likely to be interrupted. If someone breaks my focus by asking me questions, or if the phone rings and I answer it, then it takes time for me to regain my focus and get back into what I was doing.

We all have a purpose in life, and it is important not to let distractions derail us. Don't waste your time on trivial things while ignoring the things that are important.

"Father, I want to fulfill my purpose each and every day. I ask You to help me ignore the many distractions that try to steal my focus. Give me grace to do one thing at a time and give it my full attention. Thank You. In Jesus' name. Amen."

THE BELIEVER'S WORK

Then they asked him, "What must we do to do the works God requires?" Jesus answered, "The work of God is this: to believe in the one he has sent." –JOHN 6:28-29

Most of us want to know what we can do to please God. We should be ready to serve Him in any way He leads us, but we should not feel that we must offer Him our works in order to be acceptable to Him. We are made acceptable to Him through Christ, and our work is to believe in Him. Any service we offer God should be done in faith because we love Him, not to be accepted by Him. God is not for sale.

In today's scripture, Jesus' disciples asked Him what they could do "to do the works God requires." He gave a very simple answer, telling them all they needed to do was to believe in Him. By faith, we should always obey God and follow His lead. Take every opportunity you can to serve God, but always remember that the work you do isn't what makes you acceptable; it is your faith in Jesus Christ.

"Father, more than anything else I do to serve You, help me to believe. In Jesus' name. Amen."

GOD SEES ALL

For your ways are in full view of the Lord, and he examines all your paths. –PROVERBS 5:21

It is interesting to think about the fact that God sees everything we do. If we were more aware of that truth, perhaps we would be more careful about how we behave.

Nothing is hidden from God. He even knows what we will do, think, and say before we do it. We should do everything we do in Jesus' name, and if we can't, then we should not do it. God doesn't live in a building called a church that we visit once a week. We ourselves are the temple of the Holy Spirit (1 Corinthians 6:19). God lives in us. We are His home and His personal representatives, and He makes His appeal to the world through us (2 Corinthians 5:20).

The Lord never leaves us. He is with us all the time. The more we realize this, the more exciting life becomes. God wants to do life with you and be involved in every facet of it. He is not merely interested in only the spiritual aspect of your life, but He wants to be involved in all you do.

"Father, thank You that You love me and want to be with me all the time. Help me to recognize Your presence in all things and to realize that I am never alone. In Jesus' name. Amen."

GOD OPENS DOORS

These are the words of him who is holy and true, who holds the key of David. What he opens no one can shut, and what he shuts no one can open. —REVELATION 3:7

Trusting God to open the right doors and close the wrong ones for us brings much peace into our lives. I've tried pushing open a door I wanted to walk through, and the only result was frustration because it didn't work. However, I have learned to trust God not only to open the right doors for me, but also to close the wrong ones.

When God opens a door for you, He makes things easy. When He closes a door, it is very difficult to continue trying to do what you have been doing. I have enjoyed many open doors in my life and ministry, but I have also had to learn that when God closes one, I need to walk away from it and trust Him for what is next.

God always has bigger and better plans for us if we will follow His lead. We don't usually do the same thing all of our lives, because God promotes the faithful. Perhaps you are trying to hang on to something that God is finished with. If you will let it go, you will see that a new door will open and it will lead to something better than what you were trying to hold on to. God is faithful, and you can put all of your trust in Him.

"Father, I want to trust You to open right doors for me and close wrong ones. Help me recognize what You are doing in my life and to follow Your guidance. In Jesus' name. Amen."

GOD, WHAT ARE YOU DOING?

As you do not know the path of the wind, or how the body is formed in a mother's womb, so you cannot understand the work of God, the Maker of all things. –ECCLESIASTES 11:5

In life, many things happen that we do not understand. If we could understand everything, there would be no need for us to trust God. Bad things happen to good people, and this confuses us. Ours is not to reason, but to trust.

There are things that we do not know, but we do know that God is good and that He is faithful. He promises us, "All things work together for good to those who love God, to those who are the called according to His purpose" (Romans 8:28 NKJV).

I spent years in confusion because I was constantly trying to figure out what God was doing in my life or why this thing or that thing had happened. Thankfully, God has taught me that I am not to lean to my own understanding, but to acknowledge Him in all my ways, and He will direct my paths (Proverbs 3:5–6).

Give your questions to the Lord and patiently wait on Him to reveal anything you need to know. At the same time, be satisfied with what you don't know, because God is in control.

"Father, I repent for all the times I have questioned and not trusted You. Forgive me, and help me trust You in the future without having to know what You are doing. In Jesus' name. Amen."

AGAIN AND AGAIN

Evening and morning and at noon I will pray, and cry aloud, and He shall hear my voice. –PSALM 55:17 NKJV

When you want to become stronger in a certain way, you can approach it both spiritually and naturally. Spiritually, you can pray and ask God to help you, and you can read scriptures or books that encourage you. Naturally, meaning in a practical way, the way to gain strength in any area of your life is through repetition.

People who want to gain strength physically do so by working out several times a week. They may walk, swim, use weights, do yoga, or join an exercise class. But if they exercise only one time and never do it again, it will not benefit them at all. They have to do the same thing time after time after time. Eventually, that repetition will get them the results they desire.

To gain strength in any area of your life, ask God to show you what you need to do in order to become stronger—and then do it, and do it, and do it, and do it again.

"Father, I ask for Your supernatural help to grow stronger in the areas of my life in which I need strength. Help me also to do everything I need to do in the natural realm to become the person of strength You want me to be. In Jesus' name. Amen."

GOD'S FORGIVENESS

If we confess our sins, he is faithful and just and will forgive us our sins and purify us from all unrighteousness. —1 JOHN 1:9

Admitting our sins and being willing to turn away from them is all that is necessary to receive God's complete forgiveness for all of our wrongdoing. I spent years feeling guilty and condemned, and you may have done the same. But condemnation is not from God. He not only forgives our sins, but He forgets them (Hebrews 10:17), and He removes them "as far as the east is from the west" (Psalm 103:12).

When you or I sin, no more sacrifice is needed other than the sacrifice Jesus has already made. We don't need to sacrifice our peace or our joy and feel guilty as a way of trying to pay for our sins. God's forgiveness is complete. It washes away all sin and all guilt. So if we still feel guilty after repenting of sin, it is a false guilt with which Satan is trying to burden us.

I encourage you not only to ask for forgiveness, but also to take time to receive it. At times I even say out loud, "I receive Your forgiveness, Lord, and I thank You for it." If guilt tries to visit me after that, I simply keep saying, "I am forgiven," until the devil gives up.

"Father, thank You very much for Your mercy and forgiveness, and for freedom from guilt and condemnation. In Jesus' name. Amen."

LEAD A QUIET LIFE

Make it your ambition to lead a quiet life: You should mind your own business and work with your hands, just as we told you, so that your daily life may win the respect of outsiders and so that you will not be dependent on anybody. –1 THESSALONIANS 4:11-12

Today's scripture is full of good, practical advice. How much more peace could we enjoy if we all would mind our own business and pray instead of judging what we don't understand or agree with? The apostle Paul affirms the benefits of a quiet life, rather than one filled with strife and turmoil.

How often do we offer our opinion regarding something about which we have no knowledge? Too often, I think! Instead of giving unsolicited opinions and getting involved in situations that don't concern us, Paul tells us to stay busy with our own hands. We should tend to our own work, and that will keep us busy enough that we will have no time to get involved in unfruitful things that cause turmoil.

When offering our opinions, we often say, "I am just trying to help." But in order for anyone to receive our help, they must first want it. And most of the time, they don't want it if they haven't asked for it. I encourage you to follow the simple guidelines Paul provides in today's scripture. As you do, you'll find greater peace and enjoyment in your life.

"Father, I recognize that I often give my opinion when it is not asked for, and I want to change. Help me learn to be quiet, mind my own business, and do my own work. In Jesus' name. Amen."

IN THE MORNING

In the morning, Lord, you hear my voice; in the morning I lay my requests before you and wait expectantly. –PSALM 5:3

I believe the best way to start each day is by talking to God. Apparently, this is what the psalmist David did, and he was confident that God heard his voice. David set the tone for his day by letting God know what he needed and choosing to wait expectantly for God to answer.

How do you start each day? Do you begin by turning your heart toward God in prayer, confident that He hears you and believing He will answer? Or do you begin by thinking about getting children off to school, or the work piled up on your desk, or the weeds you need to pull in the garden? Do you think about a difficult conversation you will need to have that day or about an important decision you need to make?

You do not have to let life's stresses set the tone for your day. You, like David, can begin the day by laying your requests before God and waiting with confident expectation that He will answer in just the right way at just the right time. Decide today that from now on, based on today's scripture, you will get your days off to a good start.

"Father, I believe You hear me when I pray, and I wait expectantly for You to answer me. In Jesus' name. Amen."

DOING THE RIGHT THING

But be doers of the word, and not hearers only, deceiving yourselves.

—JAMES 1:22 NKJV

The Bible is filled with various instructions that will help us live better, more fruitful (productive), more enjoyable lives. But simply reading the instructions won't help us. We need to obey them and incorporate them into our daily lives.

James 1:2–3 teaches us to be joyful in trials, knowing that the testing of our faith brings out patience. James also urges us to persevere through our troubles and ask God for wisdom concerning how to handle them (1:4–5).

God promises to give us wisdom "liberally and ungrudgingly, without reproaching or faultfinding" (James 1:5 AMPC). In other words, even if we have created trouble through disobedience, God will still help us if we ask Him to do so. No matter what we have done wrong, God never stops loving us. If we are willing to repent of our sins, He totally forgives us and helps us get out of the messes we have created.

I urge you to begin to do what you know you should do. That's the right thing to do, and not doing what you know to do is sin (James 4:17). Be wise and do now what you will be satisfied with later.

"Father, I ask You to forgive my disobedience. Grant me wisdom concerning how to confront my problems and help me get my life back into Your will. In Jesus' name. Amen."

AN EXCELLENT LIFE

As for the saints (godly people) who are in the land, they are the majestic and the noble and the excellent ones in whom is all my delight. –PSALM 16:3 AMP

David writes about godly people in today's scripture, describing them as "the majestic and the noble and the excellent ones." If we want to live up to this description, we begin in the mind. A noble and excellent life starts with noble, excellent thoughts. Paul echoes this idea in Philippians 4:8: "Finally, believers, whatever is true, whatever is honorable and worthy of respect, whatever is right and confirmed by God's Word, whatever is pure and wholesome, whatever is lovely and brings peace, whatever is admirable and of good repute; *if there is any excellence*, if there is anything worthy of praise, *think continually* on these things [center your mind on them, and implant them in your heart]" (AMP, emphasis mine).

God has called all of us to be excellent in all we do. In this way, we represent Him well to the people around us. Examine your thoughts today, and embrace only the ones that are excellent.

"Father, help me to think excellent thoughts so I can live an excellent life. In Jesus' name. Amen."

PAYDAY IS COMING

I am he who searches hearts and minds, and I will repay each of you according to your deeds. –REVELATION 2:23

Salvation is a gift of God's grace, and we receive it through faith in Jesus Christ. It is not based on anything we have done, although we will be rewarded in heaven for our works. In Hebrews we read, "Without faith it is impossible to please Him," and that when we come to Him, we "must believe that He is, and that He is a rewarder of those who diligently seek Him" (Hebrews 11:6 NKJV).

I don't want to miss anything that God has for me, because I know it will be something wonderful. I am sure you feel the same way. Scripture teaches us that we reap what we sow (Galatians 6:7). This is a very sobering thought to me, but it is also an exciting one. When we do what is right because of our love for the Lord, He will reward us. If we do what is wrong, we will miss our reward.

At times, you may grow weary in life, but thinking of all the rewards God has stored for you in heaven and being excited to see what they are will keep you strong and refreshed.

"Father, help me sow good seed so I can reap a good harvest. I want to use wisdom in all that I do so that I will not miss the reward that You have for me. In Jesus' name. Amen."

THE REAL CHALLENGE OF BEING A CHRISTIAN

Why do you call me, "Lord, Lord," and do not do what I say?

—LUKE 6:46

For many people, doing what they know is right to do is the only thing that stands between them and a tremendous victory in their lives. Listening to a sermon or reading the Bible is good, but if we do not do what we learn to do, it does us no good in practical ways. This is the real challenge of being a Christian. It is easy to put a bumper sticker with a cross or fish on your car, but it is more challenging to behave as a Christian should behave. It is easy to carry your Bible to work, but the real test comes in treating your fellow employees as God instructs.

Knowledge alone can fill us with pride. Although knowledge is good, it is useless if we don't act on it. Paul told the Corinthians that knowledge puffs one up, but love edifies (1 Corinthians 8:1). This means that love builds up and encourages people to grow into being more like Christ. You may be the only representative of Christ some people know, so it is important that you represent Him well.

Doing what is right often brings pain before it brings pleasure. The flesh wants what is easy. But if we follow the Spirit, we will always do what is right, no matter how hard it is, knowing that God's blessings will come in due time.

"Father, help me always do the right thing. I want to represent You well, and I need Your help to do it. Forgive me for compromising in the past, and give me a new beginning. Thank You. Amen."

GOD REWARDS OUR WORK

Look, I am coming soon! My reward is with me, and I will give to each person according to what they have done. –REVELATION 22:12

Sometimes, we try our best in certain situations because of our love for the Lord, but things don't seem to work out in our favor. When this happens, we can easily become discouraged. We may need to do the right thing for a long period of time before we see the right results, but as I always say, "Payday is coming."

God never forgets our labor for Him. The Bible says, "He is a rewarder of those who diligently seek Him" (Hebrews 11:6 NKJV), and "there is great reward" for those who keep and obey His teachings (Psalm 19:11 NKJV).

Some of our rewards are realized here on earth, and some are set aside for us in heaven. We don't know exactly what these rewards are, but we know that God is good and that everything He prepares for us is also good. I encourage you to look forward to your reward from God. Be steadfast, be strong in the Lord, and continue to do what is right. You will never regret it.

"Father, thank You for Your goodness in my life. I look forward to my reward, not because I deserve anything, but because You are faithful. Help me remain strong and never give up. In Jesus' name. Amen."

A CONTENTED ATTITUDE

Let this same attitude and purpose and [humble] mind be in you which was in Christ Jesus: [Let Him be your example in humility].

—PHILIPPIANS 2:5 AMPC

People who have humble hearts are appreciative and content. They appreciate all that God has done for them, and they are satisfied because they know that He loves them and has provided everything they need at the current time in their life. They trust that when the time is right for them to have more, God will give it to them. They wait patiently.

Being content does not mean that we do not want to see change or make progress. It means we are not unhappy with what we have now because we trust God's timing in our lives. To be content means to be satisfied to the point where we are not upset or disturbed.

"Godliness accompanied with contentment…is great and abundant gain" (1 Timothy 6:6 AMPC). Contentment is one of the greatest blessings a person can have. It is much more valuable than possessing more things yet not being content. True contentment can only come from being in right relationship with God and seeking Him above all else. Discontented people dishonor God, but those who are content show Him honor, and their actions declare that they trust Him.

"Father, I love You and I want to be content at all times. Forgive me for the times I have murmured and complained due to discontentment, and help me always recognize how good You are to me. In Jesus' name. Amen."

THE DANGER OF PRIDE

Pride goes before destruction, and a haughty spirit before a fall.

—PROVERBS 16:18 AMPC

Pride causes people to boast, to be high-minded, to think more highly of themselves than they should, or to take more credit than they are due. It is characterized by an excessive degree of self-esteem and an unreasonable sense of superiority in talents, beauty, wealth, accomplishments, social position, or professional status. When people operate in pride and think proudly, they put on lofty airs. Proud people are often contemptuous of others, and insolent or rude in the way they treat others.

The pride of our hearts deceives us (Obadiah 3). It distorts our perceptions, and we don't see things as they truly are. We don't see other people's value, nor do we see our own flaws.

God wants us to have a humble heart, which is the opposite of a proud heart. People who are humble do not think too highly of themselves, but they lean on God and know they are nothing without Him. They are courteous, have a modest evaluation of their own worth, and are conscious of their defects. They think highly of other people and have good manners.

God tells us in His Word that if we humble ourselves under His mighty hand, He will exalt us in due time (1 Peter 5:6). If we refuse to humble ourselves, God will have to do it for us. He lifts us up as long as we remain humble, but He can also quickly bring us down if we become filled with pride.

"Father, I ask that You continue to work with me to keep me humble. I repent for pride and I recognize that I am nothing without You. Help me to always treat others well and never to think I am better than anyone else. In Jesus' name. Amen."

YOU ARE NEVER REJECTED

All that My Father gives Me will come to Me; and the one who comes to Me I will most certainly not cast out [I will never, never reject anyone who follows Me]. –JOHN 6:37 AMP

In today's scripture, Jesus promises not to reject anyone who comes to Him. Isn't that a wonderful assurance? When we come to Him—no matter what shape we are in or what we have been through or what we have done in the past—we are guaranteed a welcome, and we can be confident that we are loved and wanted in His presence.

I don't know anyone who has not been rejected by other people at some time. Perhaps a father or mother rejected you. Perhaps classmates at school or colleagues at work have not been kind or welcoming to you. Maybe other people have rejected you for so long and in such painful ways that you now reject yourself instead of loving yourself in a healthy way. Rejection can be extremely painful and affect our lives in very negative ways.

With God, we never have to fear or experience rejection. He welcomes us each time we come to Him; He delights in us and even sings over us (Isaiah 62:4; Zephaniah 3:17). Be at peace today and rejoice, because God never rejects you.

"Father, thank You for always making me welcome in Your presence and for never rejecting me. In Jesus' name. Amen."

FAULTFINDERS

Do not complain, brethren, against one another, so that you [yourselves] may not be judged. —JAMES 5:9 AMPC

All people can come to God as-is. We all have flaws, and we are tempted to complain about the flaws in others while disregarding the ones in ourselves. Lately, I seem to be noticing what is wrong with everyone. I don't like the way that makes me feel, so I asked God to show me how to deal with my bad attitude, and He did.

The best way to enjoy being in community with others is to focus on their strengths rather than their weaknesses and flaws. Don't focus on what people don't do for you, but instead focus on the good and helpful things they do. The kinds of thoughts and words that we sow, or express, toward others are the ones that will come back to us. So, if we want people to be patient with us and not complain about us, then we need to do the same for them.

Satan tempts us to judge people critically, but God gives us the ability to love them, with His help. Let's all put on our "God glasses" and learn to see people the way He does.

"Father, forgive me for finding fault with others and help me see people the way You do. Thank You. In Jesus' name. Amen."

GOD SEES YOU

For God is not unjust so as to overlook your work and the love that you have shown for his name in serving the saints, as you still do.
—HEBREWS 6:10 ESV

When we are working hard and serving God, we may often feel that no one really appreciates our labor and sacrifices, but God sees us and knows everything we do. He appreciates our labor for Him, and He rewards us in due time.

The apostle Paul encourages us not to "become weary in doing good," because in due time, "we will reap a harvest if we do not give up" (Galatians 6:9). I'm sure Paul experienced the same feelings of weariness that we feel at times, but he pressed on. His goal was to finish what God had given him to do, and that should be our aim also.

When you feel like giving up, just remember what Jesus went through so you could be forgiven for your sins and live with Him forever. Any difficulty you face is minor compared to what He endured. Any good thing you do for others is counted as something you have done for Jesus. Keep that in mind, and your work for Him will energize you and give you peace and joy.

"Father, thank You for allowing me to serve You by serving others. Help me to always appreciate each opportunity and to find joy in my labor. In Jesus' name. Amen."

KEEP YOUR COMMITMENT TO GOD

Joshua told the people, "Consecrate yourselves, for tomorrow the Lord will do amazing things among you." –JOSHUA 3:5

When we make a commitment to God, it is important that we don't turn back from it when difficulty comes. Hannah dedicated or consecrated her son, Samuel, to the Lord and did not draw back or change her mind when losing him caused pain in her heart (1 Samuel 1:24–2:11).

When we dedicate something to God, we set it aside for His use; we give it to Him to use as He pleases. We may dedicate ourselves, our finances, our time, and many other things to the Lord, and when we do, so we should always keep those commitments.

The Bible is filled with stories of men and women who dedicated themselves to God and did not shrink back when keeping their commitment to Him became difficult. Daniel, Joseph, Esther, and Ruth are just a few of them. Each of these people dedicated themselves to God, and although they faced difficulties, they did not back down. As a result, they were rewarded for their faithfulness.

Don't make commitments without thinking seriously about whether or not you are willing to finish what you begin. If you are in a place where you are about to give up on a commitment you have made, I encourage you to press on, because the end result will be worth the sacrifice.

"Father, I ask You to grant me the strength to go all the way through to the finish in everything I have committed to do. I want to always finish what I start and keep my word. In Jesus' name. Amen."

BECAUSE HE SAYS SO

When he had finished speaking, he said to Simon, "Put out into deep water, and let down the nets for a catch." Simon answered, "Master, we've worked hard all night and haven't caught anything. But because you say so, I will let down the nets." –LUKE 5:4-5

Have you ever done something you believed to be good and right, but not gotten the results you expected? Maybe you believed it was something God told you to do, but it didn't seem to work. If so, then you understand how Simon (also known as Peter) felt about his fishing expedition recorded in Luke 5. He and his friends had fished all night and caught nothing, so they had little hope that casting their nets again would be productive.

But notice Simon's response when Jesus told them to fish one more time. His first answer was to reason with Jesus, saying, "We've worked hard all night and haven't caught anything." But his next words reveal his obedience: "*But because you say so*, I will let down the nets" (emphasis mine).

What will you say to the Lord when you have worked for a long time with no results and He asks you to try again? Will you let reason take over your thoughts and tell Him that you have already been doing it for weeks, months, or years—and nothing has happened? Or will you respond as Simon did, saying, "But because you say so," I will try again.

When Simon let down his nets after Jesus told him to, he hauled in his biggest catch ever. When you obey God, there's no limit to the wonderful things He will do through you.

"Father, whatever You tell me to do, I will do—because You say so. In Jesus' name. Amen."

SLOW AND STEADY

The plans of the diligent lead to profit as surely as haste leads to poverty. —PROVERBS 21:5

My husband is very patient, while I have a tendency to want things done quickly. He has said for years, "Fast and fragile. Slow and solid." Being hasty can end up causing us a lot of trouble. We say things we wish we had not said, we make commitments that are difficult to keep, and we buy things we regret purchasing once we have to make payments on them. The hasty person always loses instead of gaining in the end.

Thankfully, God is very patient with us, and He never gives up on us. Patience is a fruit of the Spirit. We have it because the Holy Spirit lives in us, but we need to exercise it in order to develop and strengthen it. We inherit God's promises through faith and patience (Hebrews 6:12).

I have become more patient as the years have gone by because I have learned from experience that being impatient does not make God hurry. His timing is perfect, and we should learn to wait for it, enjoying our lives while we wait.

What are you waiting for right now? Whatever it is, God sees your heart, and if it is the best thing for you, He will give it to you at just the right time.

"Father, I appreciate Your patience with me, and I ask that You help me exercise patience instead of being hasty. In Jesus' name. Amen."

GROW IN LOVE

And this is my prayer: that your love may abound more and more in knowledge and depth of insight. −PHILIPPIANS 1:9

Loving God and loving people are the primary responsibilities of the believer. Love is much more than a theory or a word. It is action, and we demonstrate it in the way we treat people. Are we patient with those who are weak or those who are not like we are? Are we kind to everyone with whom we come into contact? Are we good to people whether they deserve it or not? Paul teaches us to never miss an opportunity to do good to people, especially those "of the household of faith" (Galatians 6:10 NKJV).

Focusing on loving God and loving others keeps us from being selfish and self-centered, and that is very important to our joy. We cannot be selfish and happy at the same time. God has created us to receive from Him and then share what He has given us with other people.

We cannot merely love those who love us, because God's Word requires us to love even our enemies and to pray for them and bless them (Matthew 5:44). At first, this seems difficult to do, but once we begin doing it, we realize that it is truly the best way to keep the poison of unforgiveness out of our souls.

Paul not only tells us to love others, but to "abound" in love. God wants us to keep growing in love and to love others more and more. If you are angry with anyone, I urge you to forgive quickly and remain at peace.

"Father, I want love to fill my heart and flow out to You first and then to everyone I know. Thank You for loving me first, so that I am able to love You and others. In Jesus' name. Amen."

CHANGE AS THE HOLY SPIRIT LEADS

How can you say to your brother, "Let me take the speck out of your eye," when all the time there is a plank in your own eye?

—MATTHEW 7:4

Everyone we meet has flaws and weaknesses, but everyone has good qualities too.

Today's scripture encourages us not to criticize other people's imperfections without first looking at our own weaknesses. If we concentrate on the areas in which we need to improve ourselves, we probably won't have time to judge other people for their flaws.

When we think about ways we need to grow and change, we need to do it in a healthy way. Some people are overly concerned about their weaknesses, to the point that they become obsessed with fixing them. For example, some people feel they are overweight and become obsessed with losing weight to the point that they develop eating disorders. Some people face criticism or even punishment for talking too much, so they reach a point that they become excessively quiet and withdrawn. When I mention strengthening ourselves in our areas of weakness, I am not talking about going to extremes, but about making changes as the Holy Spirit leads us, and He always leads us in ways that are healthy and balanced.

Is there an area of your life in which you need to be changed and strengthened? Ask God to help you today.

"Father, help me to appropriately assess my weaknesses, not so I can obsess over them, but so I can become stronger in those areas as You lead me. In Jesus' name. Amen."

SPIRITUAL POWER

But you will receive power when the Holy Spirit comes on you.

—ACTS 1:8

Part of our privilege as believers in Christ is to receive the power of the Holy Spirit. Without that power, nothing we do is effective. Spiritual power is the influence that leads people to accept Christ as their personal Savior and follow Him. We may teach and preach God's Word, and do so eloquently, but still be devoid of the power of the Holy Spirit. Our words may even move people emotionally, but they do not move them spiritually. Paul reminded the Thessalonians that the gospel did not come to them in word only, but in power (1 Thessalonians 1:5).

The Holy Spirit is the third person of the Trinity. He brings us the power of God and enables us to do great things. He speaks through those who speak the Word and ministers to those who hear it. We should depend on the Holy Spirit to strengthen us and to help us in everything we do. He is the one who walks alongside us, lives in us, and enables us to do all that we need to do in life.

Pray daily to be filled with the power of the Holy Spirit and to enjoy the benefits of all of the gifts of the Spirit. His power and gifts will enable you to help people who are lost and in need of Christ. Jesus promised us this power right before He ascended to heaven, and we should never be content to live without it.

"Father, I desperately need the power of the Holy Spirit filling me every moment of every day. I ask that You baptize me with the Holy Spirit and grant me the gifts He desires for me to have so I may effectively serve You and help increase Your kingdom. In Jesus' name. Amen."

VALUE EVERYONE

Do nothing out of selfish ambition or vain conceit. Rather, in humility value others above yourselves. –PHILIPPIANS 2:3

In God's eyes, we are all equal and valuable. We should always show respect for all people, for they are all important to God. First Peter 2:17 says that we should "show proper respect to everyone," and I realize there are some people that are very difficult to respect because of their ungodly actions. However, instead of judging them, we should pray for them in the hope that their hearts would be open to God (Matthew 5:44–45).

If we are selfish and filled with pride, we always feel we are more important than others, and we will look down on them rather than valuing them. Pride causes us to think more highly of ourselves than we should rather than seeing ourselves according to the grace of God.

Always remember that whatever you are good at or gifted to do is only a strength for you because God has made you that way. Don't take credit for yourself, but give glory to God always. Instead of allowing your abilities to make you feel that you are better than others, let them humble you in amazement that God has been so good to you. None of us deserve the goodness that God shows to us. I encourage you to be a vessel that God can use to help others feel valued and important.

"*Father, I believe it is very important to You that I treat all people the way You would treat them. Please help me do this, and help me always remember that any good I do is only because of Your grace. In Jesus' name. Amen.*"

RECEIVING COMFORT

Then the church throughout Judea, Galilee and Samaria enjoyed a time of peace and was strengthened. Living in the fear of the Lord and encouraged by the Holy Spirit, it increased in numbers.

—ACTS 9:31

To be encouraged by the Holy Spirit means to be comforted by Him. We all know how wonderful it is when we are hurting emotionally to have a loved one or a friend comfort us. If their comfort helps us, just imagine how wonderful the comfort of the Holy Spirit is. Many of us have experienced it, but some have not. I believe that we do not have or experience certain things because we do not ask for them (James 4:2).

I have learned not to run to my friends or family first when I need to be comforted or encouraged, but to go to God and ask Him to give me what I need. Often, He does so by working through another person, but there are also times when His comfort comes without human instrumentation. The Holy Spirit is "the Comforter" (John 14:26 AMPC). He comforts us so that we will be able to comfort others with the comfort that He has given us (2 Corinthians 1:3–4).

The world is filled with hurting people who need others to come alongside them and encourage them along the way. Look for these people and make it your mission to allow the comfort of the Holy Spirit to flow through you to them.

"Father, I am grateful for the comfort of the Holy Spirit. I pray that I will be able to comfort and encourage others, as You have comforted and encouraged me. Put people in my path who need to be comforted so You can use me to minister to them. In Jesus' name. Amen."

SURRENDERED

Going a little farther, he fell with his face to the ground and prayed, "My Father, if it is possible, may this cup be taken from me. Yet not as I will, but as you will." –MATTHEW 26:39

The first condition of receiving divine guidance is a surrendered life. Before we can know God's will, we must first surrender our own will. He promises to guide and to teach those who are meek (Matthew 11:29). We must also be ready to obey. There is no point in His giving us direction unless we intend to follow it. We may not always understand why God wants us to do or not to do a certain thing, but we must trust His guidance.

At times, the answers to our prayers may seem to lead us away from, instead of toward, the direction of our expectation, but God's ways are perfect. If His plan is different from ours, it will be better. Sometimes, we may feel that God is slow to provide what we desperately feel we need. In those seasons, we should remember that a surrendered life is one that surrenders not only to God's will, but also to His timing.

We are privileged to live by divine guidance, but learning to properly discern God's voice from our own and all others takes practice. Often, we learn by making mistakes, but God will redeem even the mistakes of a surrendered person. Ask God daily for His guidance, and be ready to follow it when He gives it.

"Father, I ask that You would guide me in every aspect of my life. Your will be done, not mine. I choose to surrender my entire being to You, and I ask for the grace to follow through with Your will and remain surrendered when it is difficult to do so. In Jesus' name. Amen."

EXPECT GOD TO MOVE

Seeing in the distance a fig tree in leaf, he went to find out if it had any fruit. When he reached it, he found nothing but leaves, because it was not the season for figs. Then he said to the tree, "May no one ever eat fruit from you again." And his disciples heard him say it. —MARK 11:13–14

One of the Bible stories that can be confusing to people is the story of the fig tree. They wonder why Jesus cursed it to the point that it withered and dried up. I think the reason is simple: It wasn't doing what God designed it to do. Because it had leaves, it should have had fruit too.

The day after Jesus cursed the tree, He and His disciples passed it again, and the disciples were shocked to see that it had died. Seeing their shock, Jesus told them, "Have faith in God" (Mark 11:22). He then went on in Mark 11:23–24 to talk about the sheer power of faith.

As believers, we can choose to respond to what God says the way the disciples responded when Jesus spoke to the fig tree, and we can be surprised when His Word actually comes to pass. Or, we can be filled with faith. When we read God's Word or hear His voice, we can immediately begin expecting it to happen.

Fill your mind today with thoughts of faith and confidence in God, not with thoughts of doubting Him, questioning Him, or wondering if He means what He says.

Believe God's Word, and keep believing it until you see Him fulfill His promises.

"Father, may I never be surprised when what You say actually happens. May I live looking for You to move and expecting You to do what You say You will do. In Jesus' name. Amen."

THE BLOOD OF JESUS CHRIST

And through him to reconcile to himself all things, whether things on earth or things in heaven, by making peace through his blood, shed on the cross. –COLOSSIANS 1:20

There is power in the blood of Jesus. Those who believe in Jesus believe that He died for us, shedding His blood and suffering to pay for our sins. It is only through His sacrifice that we are reconciled to God. Through His shed blood, our sins are forgiven. His blood is referred to as "precious," and indeed it is (1 Peter 1:19).

It is Christ's blood that removes every guilty stain of sin and allows us to live completely forgiven, free from guilt and condemnation. According to Colossians 1:21–22, "Once you were alienated from God and were enemies in your minds because of your evil behavior. But now he has reconciled you by Christ's physical body through death to present you holy in his sight." No wonder the gospel is called good news.

I encourage you to thank God regularly for sending Jesus. He has done more for us than we may realize. He freely provides every blessing to those who least deserve it, and all He asks is that we believe in Him and let His light shine through us so that others might come to know and believe in Him also.

"Father, I thank You for sending Jesus and for His sacrifice of His blood, which has cleansed me from all sin. Help me always appreciate what You have done for me through Jesus. In His name I pray. Amen."

WHAT HINDERS ANSWERED PRAYER?

And when you stand praying, if you hold anything against anyone, forgive them, so that your Father in heaven may forgive you your sins. —MARK 11:25

Satan gains more ground in a believer's life through unforgiveness than anything else. In Mark 11:22–24, we see that we have the great privilege of going to God and asking for anything in faith, expecting that we will receive it. But immediately after that promise, we read Mark 11:25, which tells us that we must not hold unforgiveness against anyone because it hinders our relationship with God. Therefore, the refusal to forgive people also hinders answered prayer.

If you find it difficult to forgive someone who has offended or hurt you, just think of all the things for which God has forgiven you. This will make it much easier for you to forgive those who have wounded you. I urge you to make the decision today that you will never let bitterness stay in your soul, because it only hurts you and does not change your enemy. Forgive those who have offended you, pray for them, and bless them—and God will be your Vindicator.

Whenever God asks us to do anything, He always gives us the ability to do it. Forgiveness is not a feeling, but a decision you make. As you are obedient to pray for your enemies and bless them, God will heal your emotions. Don't let Satan steal from you any longer through harboring offense in your heart.

"Father, I don't want to hold unforgiveness against anyone. But I need Your help in order to let go of the bitterness I feel because of the pain some people have caused me. Help me stay free from bitterness at all times. Thank You. In Jesus' name. Amen."

HOW DO YOU SEE YOURSELF?

"Pardon me, my lord," Gideon replied, "but how can I save Israel? My clan is the weakest in Manasseh, and I am the least in my family." –JUDGES 6:15

The way we see ourselves determines how far we will be able to go in life and whether or not we will be obedient to what God calls us to do. God called Gideon to save Israel from their enemies, the Midianites, but Gideon was sure that God had the wrong man. He saw himself as small, weak, and incapable. The Lord assured Gideon that He would be with him and strike down the Midianites, but even then, Gideon had doubts and wanted God to give him miraculous signs as proof that he would succeed (Judges 6:17, 36–40).

Fear and doubt prevent us, like Gideon, from doing and being all that God has for us. Millions of people live far below the level at which they could live if they could simply see themselves as God sees them.

God never calls anyone to do anything without giving them the ability and strength they need to do it. He wants to work with and through His people, and our part is to surrender to His will, moving forward in faith that He will never fail us.

Let me ask you: How do you see yourself? The devil wants to make you feel insignificant, but the truth is that you have God's power in you and are capable of far more than you might imagine. I encourage you not to listen to fear and doubt, but instead let God guide you to great things.

"Father, forgive me for all the times I have allowed fear and doubt to hinder me from going forward in Your will. I surrender to You, and with Your help, I will walk by faith and trust You to bring victory. In Jesus' name. Amen."

THE POWER OF UNITY IN FAITH AND PRAYER

They all joined together constantly in prayer, along with the women and Mary the mother of Jesus, and with his brothers. –ACTS 1:14

The Book of Acts tells the story of the early church, and one of its key themes is unity. Many verses in Acts mention that the believers were together, emphasizing the importance of unity in faith and prayer among Christians (2:1, 46; 4:24; 5:12; 15:25). Jesus' early followers lived in an exciting time, when they saw God do great things through their united faith and prayer and by the power of the Holy Spirit.

The apostle Paul, who wrote Acts, also wrote Philippians and mentions the importance of unified faith in Philippians 2:2: "Make my joy complete by being of the same mind, having the same love [toward one another], knit together in spirit, intent on one purpose [and living a life that reflects your faith and spreads the gospel—the good news regarding salvation through faith in Christ]" (AMP).

You do not have to gather a large group of people in order to have unity in faith and prayer. You might consider starting by praying with just one other person. Jesus says, "Where two or three gather in my name, there am I with them" (Matthew 18:20). Start small if you need to, and see how God responds to unity in prayer. When you pray in unity with other believers, no matter how many there are, expect God to do great things.

"Father, I pray that You would connect me with like-minded believers with whom I may join my faith and my prayers. Amen."

STIR UP YOUR FAITH

For the Spirit God gave us does not make us timid, but gives us power, love and self-discipline. —2 TIMOTHY 1:7

The early Christians lived under constant threat of persecution and death due to their commitment to follow Jesus. They lived in times of intense fear and often needed to be encouraged to keep the faith and not give up.

Timothy was facing a time like this in his walk with God when Paul told him to stir up his faith and fan the flame that once burned brightly in him (2 Timothy 1:6). If we keep our faith strong through use, we will be strong when trials and temptations come our way.

Don't wait until you have trouble to get strong, but instead stay strong in the Lord at all times. Enjoy regular fellowship with Him, study His Word, and spend time with other Christians who can build you up in faith instead of with unbelievers who tear you down through their lack of faith.

If faith was once a burning fire in you, but has now become a mere ember, don't delay in stirring yourself up. Remind yourself of what Jesus has done for you and of the opportunities He has given you to serve Him. Remember what a privilege prayer is, and talk with God about anything that concerns you. Ask for what you need and want, and expect Him to do great things for you and through you.

"Father, I want always to burn inwardly with faith and love for You and for Your work on the earth. Anytime I start to weaken in faith, I ask You to strengthen me and remind me to stir myself up by remembering how good and how great You are. In Jesus' name. Amen."

"I AM"

God said to Moses, "I Am who I Am. This is what you are to say to the Israelites: 'I Am has sent me to you.'" –EXODUS 3:14

"I Am" means that God is everything we need in this moment and all we will ever need in the future. He can do anything that needs to be done. He is limitless in His abilities and His resources. He is the answer to all our questions, the solution to all our problems, the worker of every miracle, and the cure for all that afflicts us in spirit, soul, or body. Even if we use the biggest and best words we can think of, God still defies description because He is so great and so powerful.

When God instructed Moses to tell the people that "I Am" had sent him, He was saying, basically, "I have everything you and these people need. There is nothing I cannot do."

In John's Gospel, Jesus refers to Himself as "I am" seven times (6:35; 8:12; 10:9, 11; 11:25; 14:6; 15:5). When we pray in His name, we pray in the name of the great "I Am," the almighty, limitless, eternal God.

Let me encourage you today to allow no limits on the way you think about God. Remember that He is "I Am." He has everything you need today and for every day of your life. He is far beyond the most wonderful thing you could ever imagine, and He loves you more than you will ever know.

"Father, help me to know You and experience You as 'I Am.' You are everything I need. In Jesus' name. Amen."

PERSECUTION

In fact, everyone who wants to live a godly life in Christ Jesus will be persecuted. –2 TIMOTHY 3:12

We have an enemy, Satan, who comes against us in an effort to steal our faith in Jesus and prevent us from passionately serving Him. One way he does this is by bringing persecution from people we know as well as from those we don't. It may even come through friends and family we would expect to love and help us.

We experience rejection, insults, and the loss of friends, and we may even find that family members turn against us due to our faith in Christ. Why? They do this because they are not ready to make the same commitment we have made, and it is easier to find something wrong with us than to face the truth about themselves. When this happens in your life, don't be angry with the people who come against you, but pray for them and ask God to bless them, as Scripture teaches us to do (Matthew 5:43–47).

Those who are persecuted for righteousness' sake are considered blessed, according to Jesus' Sermon on the Mount (Matthew 5:10). He says that we are to rejoice and be glad because our reward will be great in heaven. People may say all kinds of evil things against you because of Jesus, but never forget that they treated Him the same way. Remain obedient to God; resist the devil, and he will flee (James 4:7).

"Father, strengthen me when I am persecuted because of my faith in You. Help me to never give up or compromise in order to gain the favor of other people. Thank You. In Jesus' name. Amen."

GO AHEAD AND DO IT

If you follow my decrees and are careful to obey my commands, I will send you rain in its season, and the ground will yield its crops and the trees their fruit. —LEVITICUS 26:3-4

Do you put off doing things you do not enjoy? Perhaps it's a maintenance appointment for the car, an unpleasant conversation, a mound of paperwork, paying bills, or a housekeeping chore you find especially laborious. When these things must be done, I encourage you to go ahead and do them. Get them over with. Do them early in the day when your energy level is highest, so you can focus on them and finish them.

Life comes with certain responsibilities. I think the best approach to life is to endeavor to enjoy absolutely everything we do, but when we need to do something we don't enjoy, procrastinating accomplishes nothing. The longer you put off doing what needs to be done, the longer you will be tempted to dread doing it, and dread will drain your strength and your enjoyment of the present moment.

What have you delayed doing recently? Do your best to accomplish it today so that next time you think about it, you will not have to say, "I dread that." Instead, you can say, "I did that!"

"Father, help me to do today just one or two things I have been putting off. In Jesus' name. Amen."

ASK AND RECEIVE

Until now you have not asked for anything in my name. Ask and you will receive, and your joy will be complete. –JOHN 16:24

When you ask God for something you need, be sure that you purpose to receive it by faith. Faith is the substance of things we hope for, and it is the evidence of things we do not see (Hebrews 11:1). First, we receive by faith, and then, at the right time, we receive the manifestation of our faith. We may wait a short time or a long time, but at the perfect time, we will see in the natural realm what we have already seen by faith.

I have found in my life that I often prayed and then waited passively to see what would happen. I had asked, but I had not received by faith. I was operating on the wait-and-see plan, and that is not God's plan. He wants us to be filled with hope, which means living with expectancy that what we desire will happen at any moment. When we live with that kind of active, vibrant faith, we will not be disappointed.

I suggest that after you ask God for something, you take a few moments and wait in His presence as you receive it in your heart as done. Tell God you only want His will and His timing, and as you wait, enjoy what you have while you are waiting for what you want.

"Father, teach me not only to ask for what I want and need, but to truly receive it by faith and then wait with expectancy to see Your goodness in my life. In Jesus' name. Amen."

JESUS HEALS THE SICK

Jesus went throughout Galilee, teaching in their synagogues, proclaiming the good news of the kingdom, and healing every disease and sickness among the people. —MATTHEW 4:23

Jesus is our Healer. He may work through some type of medical technology or through a doctor, but I believe all healing comes from Him. He still does miracles, and we should never stop trusting Him for healing and good health. A friend's father had colon cancer and was taking chemotherapy, but he had not been given much hope of surviving. During his treatment, he had a PET scan to determine if the cancer had spread to any other area of his body. Not only had the disease not spread, but the tumor in his colon was completely gone, so they stopped all treatment. The doctor said he had no explanation for this. It was a miracle!

Situations like this are encouraging and compel us to continue trusting God, no matter how difficult a circumstance may be. No one can explain why some people are healed and others are not. But ultimately, we are all healed because there is no sickness in heaven. God is good, and His plan for each of us is perfect. It may not be what we would have chosen, but "all things work together for good to those who love God, to those who are the called according to His purpose" (Romans 8:28 NKJV).

I would rather receive a miracle than have to go to the doctor and take medicine, but if that doesn't happen, I fully intend to continue believing that Jesus is my Healer, and I will continue praying for the sick. There is a great deal in life that we do not understand, but if we never had any unanswered questions, we would have no need for faith.

"Father, I know that You are good, and I believe that Jesus is my Healer. I ask for good health in every area of my body. Thank You. In Jesus' name. Amen."

THE MOST POWERFUL NAME

Then know this, you and all the people of Israel: It is by the name of Jesus Christ of Nazareth, whom you crucified but whom God raised from the dead, that this man stands before you healed. –ACTS 4:10

The best way I know to explain the precious and holy name of Jesus is to say that it represents everything about Him, all that He is. His name is the most powerful name in heaven and on earth. When we believe in Him and when He lives in our hearts as Lord and Savior, we call on the power of His name when we pray.

You may have noticed that many of the prayers in this devotional end with these words: "In Jesus' name. Amen." This is not a religious way to conclude a prayer; it is a privilege, and it demonstrates your faith in His power to answer your prayer according to God's will. Anytime you pray in Jesus' name, you present to God all that Jesus is.

We can pray for miracles such as healing and freedom from oppression in Jesus' name. In fact, we can pray any type of prayer in His name. I believe that when we pray in faith, using Jesus' name, the entire spiritual realm pays attention.

Philippians 2:9–10 says that Jesus' name is "above every name," and that "at the name of Jesus every knee should bow, in heaven and on earth and under the earth."

"Father, I thank You for the power of the name of Your Son, Jesus, because it represents all that He is. In His name, I pray. Amen."

DO NOT WORRY

Can any one of you by worrying add a single hour to your life?

—MATTHEW 6:27

We often tell people not to worry, and when we are worried, they tell us the same thing. But not worrying about a problem we cannot solve is not easy. I've been teaching people not to worry for many years, and I have finally realized that the only way they will ever stop worrying is to fully realize that worry does absolutely no good.

Worry makes people anxious and nervous, and it causes us to be tense and often difficult to get along with. It can even cause a variety of health problems, some of which are serious. Worrying is like rocking in a rocking chair all day—it keeps you busy, but gets you nowhere.

I also think we must realize that we cannot change our situations, but God can. Let us use the energy we spend on worrying to trust God and wait on Him, because what is impossible with human beings is possible with God (Luke 18:27).

"Father, I don't want to waste my time worrying, because I know it doesn't do any good. Help me release my concerns to You so You can take care of me. Thank You. In Jesus' name. Amen."

THE GIFT OF TODAY

Teach us to number our days, that we may gain a heart of wisdom.
—PSALM 90:12

Each day that God gives us is a gift, and we should live it fully. I urge you not to waste one day of your life, for once a day is gone you can never get it back. The best way to make good use of a day is to be thankful, be good to others, use our time wisely, and bear good fruit.

Rejoice in this day. Don't let any opportunity that God places in front of you pass you by. Do as much good as you can, because when you do good you are behaving like Jesus, who went about doing good and curing the people who were oppressed of the devil (Acts 10:38).

We often waste our days searching for ways to make ourselves happy, but the way is right in front of us. All we need to do to increase our joy is to let God use us to increase the joy of others.

"Father, I'm sorry for the days I have wasted, and I pray that I will never waste another one. Help me use this day for good, and let me glorify Your name. Thank You. In Jesus' name. Amen."

FILLED WITH THE HOLY SPIRIT

Do not get drunk on wine, which leads to debauchery. Instead, be filled with the Spirit. –EPHESIANS 5:18

Something amazing happened among the believers in the early church on the day of Pentecost. The Amplified Bible explains vividly what happened: "And suddenly a sound came from heaven like a rushing violent wind, and it filled the whole house where they were sitting. There appeared to them tongues resembling fire, which were being distributed [among them], and they rested on each one of them [as each person received the Holy Spirit]" (Acts 2:2–3).

When the people were filled with the Holy Spirit, they received a spiritual language that their minds could not comprehend (Acts 2:4), known as the gift of tongues. People who witnessed this and were visiting Jerusalem from other countries actually heard the believers speaking in their native languages, even though the believers had never learned those languages. This was a great miracle, but it is only one of many miracles the Holy Spirit can do. The power of God works through the Holy Spirit, and when He fills us, that power flows through us too.

I believe that everyone who trusts Jesus as Savior receives the Holy Spirit. I also believe we need to be filled with the Holy Spirit in an ongoing way, as today's scripture indicates. In its original language, the verb used for *be filled* means to be continually filled. This is God's desire for those of us who walk with Him, and it brings much power and grace to our Christian experience.

"Father, fill me continually with Your Holy Spirit. In Jesus' name. Amen."

HOW TO SUCCEED
IN ALL THINGS

*Except the Lord builds the house, they labor in vain who build it;
except the Lord keeps the city, the watchman wakes but in vain.*

—PSALM 127:1 AMPC

If we want to succeed at what we do, it is vital that we invite
God to be in charge of the project. Whether we are trying
to build a marriage, a business, or a life, our labor will be
in vain unless God is the head of the building committee.

Think about your life today and ask yourself if you are
trying to do things that you have not invited God to be part
of. If so, I can assure you that you are struggling and probably frustrated because things are not working out well.
God is waiting to be invited to help you, and all you need
to do is ask Him. Humble yourself under His hand, and He
will guide and direct you.

*"Father, I am sorry for leaving You out of so many things in my life.
I recognize that I need You and that nothing will prosper without
You. Please help me, guide me, and direct me in all my efforts.
Thank You. In Jesus' name. Amen."*

LOVING OTHERS

And above all these [put on] love and enfold yourselves with the bond of perfectness [which binds everything together completely in ideal harmony]. –COLOSSIANS 3:14 AMPC

My experience has been that I behave more like Jesus if I set my mind in that direction each morning. Before you begin your day, take a little time to think about loving others, plan to be good to everyone, and make a habit of being a blessing everywhere you go. I have spent at least a half hour this morning looking at scriptures about love and thinking of ways I can build up others and add value to their lives. I know that doing this will help me actually follow through and be obedient to God's command to love others.

Love should be the central theme of our lives; however, human nature is selfish and must be disciplined. One of the best things to remember about love is that it is not a mere feeling, but a decision about how we will treat people. Be excited about how you can bless others today, and you will be blessed in the process.

"Father, thank You for loving me. Let Your love flow through me to others. Don't let me miss any opportunity that You give me to add value to another person. Thank You. In Jesus' name. Amen."

ADAPT YOURSELF TO OTHER PEOPLE

Live in harmony with one another; do not be haughty (snobbish, high-minded, exclusive), but readily adjust yourself to [people, things] and give yourself to humble tasks. –ROMANS 12:16 AMPC

If we value peace and desire to walk in it, we need to be willing to adapt ourselves to other people and situations. There are, of course, times when we should stand firm on our convictions and refuse to compromise, but there are also times when keeping the peace is more important. Peace and power go together, and anyone desiring to have power in their life must also have peace.

Peace is what makes life enjoyable. Indeed, truly enjoying life is impossible without it. We often give up our peace for things that are not worthy of the sacrifice—things like winning a useless argument or remaining angry when we feel we have been mistreated. Jesus said that we are to be "makers and maintainers of peace" (Matthew 5:9 AMPC). This means that we must take the initiative in making peace rather than waiting for someone else to do it.

"Father, I choose to dwell in peace. Grant me the grace to adapt and adjust myself to people and situations when I need to. Thank You for Your great mercy. In Jesus' name. Amen."

STOP RUNNING

He makes me lie down in green pastures, he leads me beside quiet waters. —PSALM 23:2

Today's scripture comes from Psalm 23. This is a familiar Bible passage to many people and one that offers much hope and strength.

Simply reading about green pastures and quiet waters can give us a great sense of peace. I don't know anyone who is not longing for more peace right now. Everywhere we look, we see news stories about unrest. We hear about friends or coworkers who have disagreements. We may even find ourselves in a conflict with someone or in some other situation that threatens to steal our peace. Or, as is the case with many people, we may simply lead such a busy, stress-filled life that peace seems out of reach.

To have the peace God longs to give us and to experience His rest we must take time to be still. No one can lie down while they are constantly running—running to work, running to take children somewhere, running to the grocery store, running to care for elderly parents, running to meet a friend for coffee, running to get the house clean. We all have things we must and should take care of, so ask God to show you how to slow down and take time to be still and enjoy peace.

"Father, help me to stop running, to be still, and to enjoy the peace You long to give me. In Jesus' name. Amen."

YOU ARE NOT ALONE

Have not I commanded you? Be strong, vigorous, and very courageous. Be not afraid, neither be dismayed, for the Lord your God is with you wherever you go. —JOSHUA 1:9 AMPC

The Lord wants to remind you today that you are never alone. At times you may feel lonely, or as if no one cares about you, but that is not true. God is never more than one thought away. You can be instantly in His presence by simply remembering and believing His promise to be with you everywhere you go.

Take the time to develop the habit of simply reminding yourself that God is with you in all that you do. The more you think about this, the more of a reality it will become to you. God is omnipresent. He is everywhere all the time, and surely He is with each of us. You are not alone—not now, not ever. God is not only with you, but He loves you unconditionally, and He will guide you throughout your life.

"Father, thank You for being with me. Help me recognize Your presence as a reality in my life. Thank You. In Jesus' name. Amen."

BECOME YOUR OWN BEST ALLY

I praise you because I am fearfully and wonderfully made; your works are wonderful, I know that full well. —PSALM 139:14

For a long time, I was my own worst enemy because all I saw was what I thought was wrong with me. My opinion of myself was based on what other people had said about me and how they had treated me, and the result was self-rejection. God's Word teaches us who we are in Christ and reveals how wonderfully God has created us.

God loves and approves of you, and He is for you, not against you. He desires for you to live in agreement with what His Word says about you. Become a friend to yourself rather than an enemy. Believe in the capabilities God has placed in you. Know that you are special and created for a purpose. Don't be filled with self-doubt and self-criticism, but trust that Christ is in you and is leading you.

When you are in Christ, He is always working in you and changing you into His image. See yourself as God sees you, and stop thinking and saying negative things about yourself. Learning to love and accept yourself changes your life into one that is joyful and exciting.

"Father, help me learn to see myself as You see me. Teach me to be a friend to myself rather than an enemy of myself. Thank You. In Jesus' name. Amen."

THE MERCY OF GOD

Blessed (happy, to be envied, and spiritually prosperous—with life-joy and satisfaction in God's favor and salvation, regardless of their outward conditions) are the merciful, for they shall obtain mercy!

—MATTHEW 5:7 AMPC

If you need an upgrade of joy in your life, one of the best ways to obtain it is to be very merciful to other people, just as God is very merciful to you. God's mercy is abundant and endures forever. It is always available to those who have sinned, but we must receive it by faith in order for it to benefit us. Once we do receive it, we should be prepared to give it to others.

Everything that God gives to us should flow through us to others. We are His ambassadors on the earth, and He is making His appeal to the lost in this world through us (2 Corinthians 5:20). He equips us with many wonderful benefits not only so we may enjoy them, but also so we may share them with others.

Jesus is the light of the world, and His light is in you as a believer in Him, so go out into the world each day and let your light shine (Matthew 5:16).

"Father, I ask that You help me to be merciful to others as You are merciful to me. I ask this in Jesus' name. Amen."

WHAT TO DO WITH BURDENS

Cast your burden on the Lord [releasing the weight of it] and He will sustain you; He will never allow the [consistently] righteous to be moved (made to slip, fall, or fail). —PSALM 55:22 AMPC

The Israelites were commanded to keep one day each week—the seventh day—as a day of complete rest. On that day, they could do no work nor carry any burdens in or out of their homes. This rest was a type and shadow of the true rest that God offers us today (Hebrews 4:9).

The true rest of God is not offered to one race of people for one day a week, but it is offered to all those who believe in Jesus Christ, and it is available for every moment of every day. Sabbath rest includes the absence of burden bearing. Just as we are invited to cast our sin on the Lord, we are also invited to cast our care on Him. Let me encourage you to shut the door to all the burdensome thoughts that come to your mind and to be at peace.

Sadly, burden bearing through worry dishonors God. He wants us to demonstrate our trust in Him by casting our cares and burdens on Him and experiencing His faithfulness in caring for us.

"Father, I am sorry for all the times I carry burdens that You have invited me to cast on You. Grant me the grace to release each burden that tries to enter my soul and steal my peace. Thank You for helping me. In Jesus' name. Amen."

WAIT ON GOD FOR STRENGTH

Wait on the Lord: be of good courage, and he shall strengthen thine heart: wait, I say, on the Lord. –PSALM 27:14 KJV

God promises us His strength if we will wait on it. Anytime you feel weak, timid, or fearful, the best thing to do is to take some time to wait in God's presence and ask Him to strengthen you according to His promise. Don't be in a hurry, but wait and believe that His strength is being poured into you.

Time with God is vitally important to being strong and courageous and to being able to confront life's trials with confidence and assurance. We cannot do it on our own. We all need God's strength, because the strength we have is not enough to meet the challenges we face.

One word from God can change your life forever, and He will speak to you if you get quiet and listen. Twenty-seven years ago, I was diagnosed with breast cancer, and the full weight of fear came against me. In the middle of one particular night, I was lying awake, and I heard God say, "I will take care of you." From that time forward, I was not afraid. Those words carried me through a surgery and into complete healing. Take time to let God speak to you, and His Word will bring you through to victory.

"Father, remind me to take time to wait on You daily, because I need to hear You speak to my heart, encouraging me that I don't need to fear. Thank You. In Jesus' name. Amen."

DON'T COMPROMISE

If anyone, then, knows the good they ought to do and doesn't do it, it is sin for them. —JAMES 4:17

One meaning of *to compromise* is to go a little bit below, or to settle for less than, what you know is right. The temptation to compromise comes to all of us. We often mistakenly think, *A little bit won't matter*, but James clearly says that to know what is right and not do it, is to sin.

If we do what is right, we will be blessed, but if we compromise, we forfeit God's best. I believe you want to do the right thing. When doing so is difficult and temptation is all around you, trust God for His strength to resist the temptation.

Compromising is easy, and many do it, but Jesus says that if we love Him, we will obey Him (John 14:15). I think our level of obedience is equal to our level of love for Jesus. We may love Him a little and still compromise, but if we love Him with all of our heart and soul, we will want to please Him in all things at all times.

"Father, I am sorry for the times I have compromised and settled for less than I know to be Your standard of righteousness. Forgive me, and strengthen me to be able to resist temptation in the future. Thank You. In Jesus' name. Amen."

NO NEGATIVITY TODAY

This is the day that the Lord has made; let us rejoice and be glad in it. —PSALM 118:24 ESV

Have you fallen into a rut of negativity lately? Perhaps you are tired or dealing with a situation that causes prolonged stress, and you feel your joy is at an all-time low. I want to encourage you to take life one day at a time, so just for today, determine to get your joy back by thinking positively about every circumstance in your life.

You can begin to stir up your joy by realizing that any situation could be worse than it is and knowing that you are not alone in your struggle. People everywhere face challenges, and some are dealing with circumstances far worse than anything you or I could even think of.

Next, in everything you face today, ask yourself, "What is one good thing about what I am going through right now?" Or, "Where can I find just a little bit of joy in this situation, just for this day?"

I do understand that some situations are intensely difficult, sad, or emotionally draining. In those cases, simply whispering "God will never leave me or forsake me. He is with me" will help turn negative thoughts to positive ones. Whatever your circumstances are today, decide to think positively about them—and watch your joy increase. Tomorrow is another day, and you can do the same thing all over again.

"Father, I choose today to reject negativity and to think positively about every situation in my life. I cannot do it without You, so I'm asking for Your help. In Jesus' name. Amen."

CHOOSING THE NARROW PATH

By faith Moses, when he had grown up, refused to be known as the son of Pharaoh's daughter. He chose to be mistreated along with the people of God rather than to enjoy the fleeting pleasures of sin.

—HEBREWS 11:24–25

We learn from today's scripture that Moses chose suffering rather than failing to do what he knew God was calling him to do—to lead the Israelites out of bondage in Egypt and into the Promised Land. He chose the narrow path, and on that path, there is no room for us to compromise. It is the path of prompt and complete obedience. Jesus walked that path, and it is the one He wants each of us to walk.

Moses turned down a life of luxury in the palace of Pharaoh and chose to suffer rather than fail to please God. Are you willing to walk away from things you might enjoy in order to be fully obedient to God? God will give you the grace and strength to do it if you are willing.

Jesus said that if we intend to follow Him, we have to deny ourselves and take up our cross (Mark 8:34). He didn't mean to die on a cross as He did, but He did mean that we have to say no to ourselves, if necessary, in order to be obedient to Him.

"Father, if anything stands in the way of my being fully committed to You, please show me what it is and give me the strength to let it go. In Jesus' name. Amen."

GREED CAUSES COMPROMISE

Not given to wine, not combative but gentle and considerate, not quarrelsome but forbearing and peaceable, and not a lover of money [insatiable for wealth and ready to obtain it by questionable means]…not greedy for base gain. —1 TIMOTHY 3:3, 8 AMPC

The apostle Paul teaches that leaders must not be greedy for gain or love money so much that they are willing to compromise in order to get it. The world is watching those who call themselves Christians to see if we live up to what we say we believe, so we must be careful not to compromise to get what we want.

If you want something, ask God for it. If it is the right thing for you, then at the right time and in the right way, He will give it to you. If you compromise your morals or spiritual values in order to secure a promotion at work, get money, or gain certain friends, you will eventually be sorry. If God doesn't want us to have what we want, we should trust that He knows better than we do.

We can usually find ways to make things happen according to our own plan, but we will also find that doing so doesn't fulfill us as we thought it would. In fact, sometimes it makes us downright miserable. Abraham and Sarah didn't want to wait for God's promised child, so they found a way to have a baby through Sarah's handmaid as Abraham's secondary wife. She gave birth to Ishmael, but he caused heartache instead of bringing joy (Genesis 16–18).

I encourage you today to take the peaceful way and wait

on God to give you the desires of your heart instead of trying to obtain them by questionable means.

"Father, You know the things that are in my heart, and I commit to waiting on You to bring them to pass. I trust You. In Jesus' name. Amen."

CANCEL THE PITY PARTIES

Tell the people: "Consecrate yourselves in preparation for tomorrow, when you will eat meat. The Lord heard you when you wailed, 'If only we had meat to eat! We were better off in Egypt!'"

—NUMBERS 11:18

The Israelites often grumbled and complained as they journeyed through the wilderness toward the Promised Land. Throughout Numbers 11, they were unhappy. They even decided they were better off in Egypt—where they were forced into manual labor. They were involved in an all-out pity party.

No doubt the Israelites' travels through the wilderness were inconvenient at times, but instead of thanking God for liberating them from slavery in Egypt and appreciating the manna He sent from heaven to feed them each day, they felt sorry for themselves.

If we want to be strong in the Lord, we must not allow self-pity in our lives. Circumstances will not always be what we want them to be, but we can always find a reason to thank and praise God. God was leading the Israelites to a good land, a land flowing with milk and honey (Leviticus 20:24), but getting there had its challenges.

God is leading you to a good place too. You may be struggling right now as His plan for your life unfolds, but stay positive and confident in God. Don't complain or attend a pity party. Stay focused on God's promises, and appreciate all He does for you along the way.

"Father, I choose to rejoice instead of complain and to be glad instead of feeling sorry for myself. In Jesus' name. Amen."

BE PATIENT WITH YOURSELF

Therefore, my dear friends, as you have always obeyed—not only in my presence, but now much more in my absence—continue to work out your salvation with fear and trembling, for it is God who works in you to will and to act in order to fulfill his good purpose.

—PHILIPPIANS 2:12–13

Our works cannot earn us salvation because it is a gift of God's grace, and we receive it by faith. Nevertheless, today's scripture teaches us to "work out" our salvation. This means that we are to cooperate with the Holy Spirit's sanctifying work as He brings out of us what God deposits in us at the new birth.

When we are born again and Jesus comes to live in our hearts, He brings all the good qualities that He is. But simply having His good qualities by faith is not enough. We also need to show them to the world, and this requires a lifetime of cooperation with God while He works in and through us to fulfill His good will.

Be patient with yourself during this process. As you seek to be all God wants you to be and to be conformed into the image of Jesus, you will experience many victories, but you will also make mistakes. Those mistakes don't disqualify you; they simply remind you that you are human and that you need Jesus at all times. Mistakes remind us to lean and rely on Him, and they help us remain humble and have compassion on others who make mistakes.

God has done a great work in you, and He is in the

process of doing a great work through you, so enjoy your journey.

"Father, thank You for being patient with me during my journey of spiritual growth. Help me be patient with myself so I can enjoy the process. In Jesus' name. Amen."

NO OVERNIGHT SUCCESSES

The Lord your God will drive out those nations before you, little by little. You will not be allowed to eliminate them all at once, or the wild animals will multiply around you. –DEUTERONOMY 7:22

Microwave ovens enable us to heat or cook things much faster than we can prepare them in conventional ovens. They are convenient, but we also know that not everything can be microwaved. We have developed so many ways to do things faster that we have grown weary of waiting on things to develop little by little. Many things carry the claim that they are "instant" these days, but we cannot have instant spiritual maturity.

Transformation takes time and requires us to continue doing the right thing over and over until it becomes part of who we are. We didn't do something wrong one time and get our lives into a mess, and we cannot make one right decision and have everything fixed overnight.

We are to continue to do right and "not become weary in doing good, for at the proper time we will reap a harvest if we do not give up" (Galatians 6:9). Jesus said that if we "continue" in His Word, we will "know the truth" and it would make us free (John 8:31–32 KJV). In order to keep God first in our lives, we have to rearrange our priorities and be willing to let go of the things that waste our time without producing good fruit. We inherit God's promises through "faith and patience" (Hebrews 6:12). Rejoice in the progress you make in your spiritual life, and don't become discouraged about how far you have to go.

"Father, I know that Your timing is perfect, and I want to slow down and be happy with the progress I am making instead of being frustrated that I have not arrived at my destination. Help me. In Jesus' name. Amen."

GOD IS WORKING

And we also thank God continually because, when you received the word of God, which you heard from us, you accepted it not as a human word, but as it actually is, the word of God, which is indeed at work in you who believe. —1 THESSALONIANS 2:13

As long as we continue to believe, God continues to work in us and for us. Sometimes, when I get discouraged because I don't feel that God is doing anything in my life or about my problems, I remember that as long as I keep believing, He keeps working. I even say aloud, "I'm believing, and God is working!" This always makes me feel better and reminds me that God is helping me even if I don't see the results yet.

God is also working in your life, even when you don't see anything happening, and He is present with you even when you don't feel He is near. Don't determine what God is or is not doing based on how you feel and what you see; make your determinations based on His Word and His promises to you. Keep believing, and be assured that He is working.

Very soon, He will unveil what He has been doing, and you will be pleasantly surprised and overjoyed. Expect something good to happen any moment!

"Father, I will continue doing my part, which is to believe, and I know that You will continue working in my life. Help me be patient when it seems You are taking a long time. I trust that Your way is best. In Jesus' name. Amen."

JESUS LOVES SINNERS

Now the tax collectors and sinners were all gathering around to hear Jesus. But the Pharisees and the teachers of the law muttered, "This man welcomes sinners and eats with them." –LUKE 15:1-2

We need to be very careful about our attitude toward sinners. We should not have a "religious attitude" that ignores or belittles them because they are not living in accordance with God's Word. Remember, at one time all of us were in the same condition that they are in now. There is no one who has not sinned, and there is no one who cannot be justified through faith in Christ (Romans 3:23–24).

Show love to sinners without agreeing with their sinful lifestyle. If they never interact with Christians, how will they see Jesus? People whose lifestyles don't agree with God's Word don't need to become our best friends or people with whom we spend excessive amounts of time, but neither should we treat them as though we are better than they are.

Jesus welcomed sinners without agreeing with their sinful ways. He spoke the truth to them in love, and love is what most people are hungry for. If we show love to people, we can draw them to Christ.

Ask the Lord to send sinners into your path so you can show them Christ's love and pray for them. We should always have empathy and mercy for sinners and never judge them, because we don't know what their lives have been like and why they make the choices they make.

Always keep in mind that "mercy triumphs over judgment" (James 2:13).

"Father, help me not to have judgmental attitudes toward sinners, but to love them and pray for them. In Jesus' name. Amen."

EMOTIONAL STABILITY

Like a city whose walls are broken through is a person who lacks self-control. –PROVERBS 25:28

Emotions, high or low, can get us into trouble if we allow them to control us. Instead of making decisions based on emotions, we should make our decisions according to God's Word and His Holy Spirit. God desires for us to live carefully and to be stable, dependable, and reliable. He wants us not to be easily shaken, but to be in control of our emotions. We all have emotions, and while it is true that sometimes we can't help how we feel, we can have feelings without allowing them to have us. We can manage and live beyond our emotions. We can feel them and still make decisions to do God's will even when our emotions don't agree with those choices.

I am often asked how I feel about the traveling I need to do in my ministry. I respond by telling people that long ago I stopped asking myself how I feel about it; I just do it. I am sure Jesus did not feel like going to the cross, suffering, and dying for us, but He did it in obedience to His Father's will.

God's Word teaches us to build our house on the rock (Matthew 7:24–25), which means living by His Word, not according to our thoughts, emotions, or desires. The person who does this will remain strong through the storms of life. If we rely on our emotions, we make ourselves vulnerable to deception, because our feelings change constantly.

Live by God's Word and His wisdom, not by emotions, and you will have a great and enjoyable life.

"Father, I want to be stable in all seasons of life and not allow my emotions to control my behavior. Please help me. In Jesus' name. Amen."

COMPLETE SURRENDER

Father, if you are willing, take this cup from me; yet not my will, but yours be done. –LUKE 22:42

When we surrender to God, we yield to Him and submit ourselves to His power. When we surrender completely to God, we give Him all that we are, but we should also give Him all that we are not.

We don't mind giving God our talents or intelligence or some of our money, but are we willing to also give Him our weaknesses, inabilities, failures, poor reputation, and other aspects of ourselves that we view as less favorable? When God calls us, He invites us to come to Him as we are and let Him make us what He wants us to be. But we rarely encounter people who are willing to offer their weaknesses to God and believe that He can show His strength through them also. It's always important to remember what the Lord said to the apostle Paul: "My strength is made perfect in weakness," for when we are weak in ourselves, then we can be truly strong in Him (2 Corinthians 12:9–10 NKJV).

Many people are frustrated and completely worn-out from trying to be something they are not and trying to give God things they do not have. He wants the real you—the good and the bad. Once you release everything to Him, then He can make something beautiful out of it all.

"Father, I want to surrender all of myself to You. Take my strengths and my weaknesses, so I can truly be strong in You. Help me believe that You want me just the way I am. Thank You. In Jesus' name. Amen."

YOUR REPUTATION

But made himself of no reputation, and took upon him the form of a servant, and was made in the likeness of men. —PHILIPPIANS 2:7 KJV

Jesus was not concerned about His reputation with people, and we should not be concerned about ours either. It is our reputation in heaven that is important, not our reputation on earth. No one wants to have a bad reputation, and if we do, it should not be due to wrong behavior on our part. God doesn't want us to give the world a reason to criticize us, but many people will do so anyway.

Our job is to live before God in godly ways and let Him take care of our reputation. He promises to give us favor (Psalm 30:5), and I believe He will, once we let go of trying to please people in order to have them like us.

The apostle Paul said that had he tried to be popular with people, he would not have become a "servant of Christ" (Galatians 1:10). I wonder how much we may give up in an effort to please people instead of God. Even if we do please people, they may accept us only as long as we continue to do exactly as they desire. Often, they are the first ones to desert us when we need something and helping us would be inconvenient for them. But God will never leave us or forsake us.

"Father, please help me care more about my reputation with You than I care about my reputation with the world. Thank You. In Jesus' name. Amen."

HOW TO RECEIVE HELP
FROM GOD

Our God, will you not judge them? For we have no power to face this vast army that is attacking us. We do not know what to do, but our eyes are on you. —2 CHRONICLES 20:12

Today's scripture shows God's people coming to Him and admitting that they are helpless. Because of this, they received direction and help from God and experienced a great victory.

Paul reminded Timothy that we bring nothing into the world and that we will take nothing out of it (1 Timothy 6:7). We need to ponder this truth. We come into the world with nothing—not even clothes. Everything we have is a gift of God's goodness. We make a huge mistake when we start thinking our blessings are the results of something good that we have done.

Every good gift comes from above (James 1:17), and we can never earn God's grace and favor. He gives them as a gift, and we should receive them with humble hearts, knowing that we don't deserve them. Several times a day, it is good to remind yourself that you are nothing and can do nothing without God (John 15:5).

"Father, I admit that I need Your help because I am helpless without You. Keep me humble, and help me to never forget that every good thing I have is a gift from You, not the result of anything I have done. In Jesus' name. Amen."

AGREE WITH GOD

Do two walk together unless they have agreed to do so? –AMOS 3:3

Two people cannot take a walk together unless they agree to do so. Otherwise, one will go in one direction and the other in the opposite direction. Then, instead of walking together, they will pull against each other. There is power in unity. One can put a thousand to flight and two ten thousand (Deuteronomy 32:30). We are much stronger together than we are individually.

Jesus says that when two people agree in prayer, He is in their midst (Matthew 18:19–20). Living in agreement with people is good, but living in agreement with God is even more important. For example, do you agree with what God says about your past? He says to forget your past, because He is doing a new thing (Isaiah 43:18–19). Do you agree with that? Or are you still dragging your past with you, letting it hound you and make you feel guilty?

Do you agree with God concerning your future? He said through the prophet Jeremiah that He has a good plan for you. He has "plans to prosper you and not to harm you, plans to give you hope and a future" (Jeremiah 29:11). Or are you believing Satan's lie that it is too late for you, and that because of your mistakes you will always live a second-rate life?

God loves you very much, and I urge you to live in agreement with everything He says in His Word. This is the only truth that exists, and anything that disagrees with it is a lie.

"*Father, I want to live in agreement with You. Help me believe what You say about me more than I believe what people say or the lies of the devil. In Jesus' name. Amen.*"

YOU ARE SPECIAL

For you created my inmost being; you knit me together in my mother's womb. I praise you because I am fearfully and wonderfully made; your works are wonderful, I know that full well.

—PSALM 139:13–14

Everyone wants to be special and feel valued, and you are. God created you with His own hand in your mother's womb. Intricately and carefully, He formed you. God doesn't make mistakes, so you are not a mistake. God wanted you and wants you even now. He loves you and calls you His own (Isaiah 43:1–4).

We are all different, but being unlike someone else doesn't mean there is something wrong with us; it means we are unique. I like being unique, because unique things are more valuable than duplicates or replicas.

God has His eye on you all the time (Psalm 32:8). He is always watching over you and taking care of you, even when you don't recognize His working in your life. When you feel alone, you're not. When you feel worthless, you're not. God loves you so much that He sent His only Son to die for you and pay for your sins (John 3:16). When you wonder whether or not you have a purpose in life, the answer is yes. You are not an accident. God has a good plan for you!

"Father, I want to believe that I am special. Help me receive this truth by faith and value myself as You value me. In Jesus' name. Amen."

GRIEF AND LONELINESS

Be strong and courageous. Do not be afraid or terrified because of them, for the Lord your God goes with you; he will never leave you nor forsake you. —DEUTERONOMY 31:6

Grief and loneliness are major problems in our society today. Millions of people suffer from them for a variety of reasons, including feeling that no one understands them; being shy or extremely timid, which prevents them from making friends easily; and enduring abuse. Circumstances such as divorce, single parenthood, death of a spouse, and losing friends to death, or any kind of loss, sickness, pain, or suffering also contribute to feelings of loneliness and grief. In addition, people who go through changes such as retirement or having their children leave home can feel lonely and need to grieve.

When we feel alone, we feel deserted. But we are never truly alone, because God has promised to never leave us.

When you feel lonely, one of the best remedies for it is to look at what you have left, not merely what you have lost. Fix your eyes on what you cannot yet see by looking at your future with hope. And don't just look with your natural eyes; look with your spiritual eyes too. Remembering that you are not the only one who feels alone can also help. Reach out to someone else who is lonely or grieving, and as you minister to and comfort them, you will be comforted too.

God is the "God of all comfort" (2 Corinthians 1:3), and the Holy Spirit, the Comforter, lives inside of you (John

14:16–17). When you are hurting, the first thing to do is ask God to comfort you, and He will.

"Father, when I am lonely or grieving over a loss in my life, I ask You to comfort me. You know how I feel, and You can heal my emotional wound and make me whole again. Thank You. In Jesus' name. Amen."

THE POWER OF AN ATTITUDE

Let this same attitude and purpose and [humble] mind be in you which was in Christ Jesus. —PHILIPPIANS 2:5 AMPC

Guideline number one regarding attitude is to maintain the right attitude when the going gets rough. As soon as you sense your attitude losing altitude, make an adjustment. Maintaining the right attitude is easier than regaining it once it has been lost. It is the devil who wants us to have a bad attitude, and we should "withstand him; be firm in faith [against his onset]" (1 Peter 5:9 AMPC).

Indicators of a bad attitude include grumbling and complaining, self-pity, pride, criticism, judgment, impatience, lack of gratitude, unkindness, being downcast, harshness, and unforgiveness. There are certainly many others, but this list gives us a few things to ponder.

Your attitude belongs to you. No one can make you have a bad attitude if you don't want one. Attitude is powerful because it can make a troubled life good and a good life sour. No matter how good people's lives are, they won't enjoy it if they are ungrateful and greedy. In the same way, no matter how challenging people's lives are, they will have joy if they decide to be thankful for what they do have and purpose not to complain. Let's desire and regularly pray to have the same attitude that Jesus had, as today's scripture encourages us to do. His attitude was always positive!

"Father, I want always to have a good attitude in every situation, and I need Your help in order to do so. Please help me. Thank You. In Jesus' name. Amen."

PASSION FOR GOD

And now, Israel, what does the Lord your God ask of you but to fear the Lord your God, to walk in obedience to him, to love him, to serve the Lord your God with all your heart and with all your soul, and to observe the Lord's commands and decrees that I am giving you today for your own good? –DEUTERONOMY 10:12–13

Today's scripture makes clear what God wanted from His people, the Israelites, after He delivered them from bondage in Egypt. When I think of loving God with all my heart and soul, the word *passion* comes to mind. We hear people say they are passionate about their jobs, passionate about their spouses, passionate about sports teams, passionate about hobbies, and passionate about various causes. Why would we not be passionate about God and the things that matter? He is far better than any job, spouse, sports team, hobby, or cause in the world.

God is looking for people who are passionate about Him and the things that matter to Him. He is looking for those who will pursue Him wholeheartedly and value Him above all else. He doesn't want us to have a mediocre love for Him, but to love Him passionately.

The way we express our love for God is through obedience to His teachings (John 14:15), so one way we demonstrate our passion for Him is by loving others as He commands us to do (John 13:34–35). Another way we show our passion for Him is to help people in need (1 John 3:17–18).

I urge you not to allow yourself to be more passionate about anything in this world than you are about God. He is passionate about you.

"Father, stir in me a passion for You and for the things that matter to You. In Jesus' name. Amen."

RIGHT THINKING

"For who has understood the mind of the Lord so as to instruct him?" But we have the mind of Christ. –1 CORINTHIANS 2:16 ESV

What does the Bible mean when it says that we have the mind of Christ? It means that we can think like Jesus did, but very few of us do. In order to be successful in thinking like Christ, we have to be vigilant in practicing it. Satan loves to fill our minds with all kinds of wrong and tormenting thoughts, but we can cast down those wrong thoughts and choose to think in accordance with God's Word. Paul instructed the Romans to renew their minds in order to be transformed (Romans 12:2). This teaches us that godly thinking produces godly living, but ungodly thinking produces ungodly living.

I like to say, "Where the mind goes the man follows." Our thoughts are very important, and we should take time to think about what we are thinking about, instead of simply allowing ourselves to dwell on any thought that occurs to us. When our thoughts don't line up with God's Word, we should cast down ungodly thoughts and instead think about things that agree with God's Word. For example, if you think nobody loves you, start thinking about how much God loves you. Soon, you will begin to feel loved. Learn to think in agreement with God's Word, and you will quickly have a life you can enjoy.

"Father, I realize that many of my thoughts are not in line with Your Word. Help me renew my thinking and learn to think from the mind of Christ that is in me. Thank You. In Jesus' name. Amen."

AN UNSELFISH ATTITUDE

Let each of you esteem and look upon and be concerned for not [merely] his own interests, but also each for the interests of others.

—PHILIPPIANS 2:4 AMPC

My abusive childhood made me afraid that no one would ever take care of me, so I made a vow in my mind that I would never need anyone and that I would take care of myself. I was selfish, but Jesus died so we could be free from living selfish, self-centered lives (2 Corinthians 5:15).

Many people have great lives, yet they are unhappy. The reason they are not happy is that they are selfish. We cannot be selfish and happy at the same time.

In Philippians 4:5, Paul tells the Philippians that since Jesus is coming soon, they should be careful not to be selfish: "Let all men know and perceive and recognize your unselfishness (your considerateness, your forbearing spirit). The Lord is near [He is coming soon]" (AMPC). This verse helps us understand how vitally important it is not to allow ourselves to become selfish.

Experience has taught me that I can fight selfishness with generosity, but I have to be generous on purpose. Our natural inclination is to do what is best for us at all times, but with God's help, we can resist that temptation and be concerned for others as well as for ourselves.

"Father, I love You, and I am grateful for all You have done for me. Help me to be generous as a way of thanking You for Your goodness in my life. In Jesus' name. Amen."

BE LIGHT

So may all your enemies perish, Lord! But may all who love you be like the sun when it rises in its strength. –JUDGES 5:31

In the Bible, light is associated with God and His goodness, while darkness is a symbol of the enemy and his evil works. Consider the following New Testament passages about light.

Jesus refers to Himself as light in John 8:12: "I am the light of the world. Whoever follows me will never walk in darkness, but will have the light of life."

First John 1:5–7 says: "God is light; in him there is no darkness at all. If we claim to have fellowship with him and yet walk in the darkness, we lie and do not live out the truth. But if we walk in the light, as he is in the light, we have fellowship with one another, and the blood of Jesus, his Son, purifies us from all sin."

Jesus teaches about this in Matthew 5:16: "Let your light shine before others, that they may see your good deeds and glorify your Father in heaven."

With these verses in mind, think about today's scripture. What does the sun do when it rises in its strength? It gives light; it shines brightly. Because we love God, we can give light to the world around us, representing God in such a way that people can find their way to Him.

"Father, help me to shine like the sun when it rises in its strength because of my love for You. In Jesus' name. Amen."

A DECEIVED MIND

Watch out that no one deceives you. —MATTHEW 24:4

To be deceived is to believe things that are not true. Even though they are not true, they become reality to us because we believe them. Jesus says that deception will be great in the last days (Matthew 24:3–25). This means that the closer we get to Jesus' return, the more the lies of Satan will increase. We are already at the point of being so flooded with news and social media content that it is difficult to know what to believe and what not to believe. Simply hearing or reading something doesn't make it true. We need a great deal of God's discernment and should pray for it regularly.

Eve was deceived by the lies of Satan. He attacked her mind, just as he attacks ours. She should have believed God's Word to her more than anything else, but she didn't. Her refusal to believe God's Word stole the life God intended her and Adam to enjoy in the Garden. God's Word is the only truth, and if we believe it with our whole heart, we can avoid deception.

Not only can we be deceived by what we see and hear, but we can also deceive ourselves. James said we must be "doers of the Word," and not merely hearers, or we will deceive ourselves "by reasoning contrary to the Truth" (James 1:22 AMPC). Anytime we disobey God, we always seem to have a reason, but reasons do not excuse disobedience.

Be careful of overthinking God's Word, and simply obey it. This will help you protect yourself against deception.

"Father, I pray that I will not be deceived! Help me to be discerning and always to trust and value Your Word above anything else I hear. In Jesus' name. Amen."

ALL YOU NEED

Saul was very angry; this refrain displeased him greatly. "They have credited David with tens of thousands," he thought, "but me with only thousands. What more can he get but the kingdom?"

—1 SAMUEL 18:8

In 1 Samuel 17, King Saul wanted David to succeed against Goliath and even let David wear his armor for the fight (v. 38). But David chose not to wear it. After he killed Goliath, David had an audience with King Saul (v. 57) and then became best friends with Saul's son Jonathan (18:3). Soon, Saul appointed David to a high government position (18:5), and David ultimately became very popular.

We might think that Saul would have a positive attitude toward David. Instead, he became so jealous and suspicious of David that he wanted to kill him and viewed David as his enemy for the rest of his life (18:11, 29; 19:10, 15; 20:33).

The reason Saul hated David so intensely was that he saw David as a threat to his power and authority. Anyone can hold their position or their influence too tightly and seek their identity and value in it. Remember that positions come and go, but God's love for you remains constant. Find your worth and value in His love for you, not in any role you play in life or in any position you hold. People's acceptance and approval will ebb and flow, but God will always love you and always accept you unconditionally.

"Father, no matter what position I may hold in the world or how much influence I have, help me always to find my identity, worth, and value in You alone. You are all I need! In Jesus' name. Amen."

BELIEVING GOD

Did I not tell you that if you believe, you will see the glory of God?
—JOHN 11:40

Today's scripture is part of the story of Jesus' raising His friend Lazarus from the dead (John 11:1–44). It mentions God's glory, which is the manifestation of His excellence. Jesus knew that Lazarus was sick, but He waited until he had died before responding to calls for His help. He intended to do a great miracle, but to do so, He needed Lazarus's family and friends to keep believing, no matter how bad the situation looked.

When Jesus arrived to heal Lazarus, people said it was too late. Do you feel like it is too late for you? Has a certain situation become so bad that you wonder if God can do anything about it? I encourage you to keep believing. Even if God doesn't fix your current circumstances, He can bring something good out of them.

By the time Jesus reached Lazarus's tomb, Lazarus had been dead for four days, and He was told that the deceased body had already begun to smell. But Jesus told the people nearby to roll away the stone. I think it is very interesting that He wanted the people to roll away the stone when doing so would have been easy for Him in the process of raising Lazarus. However, He wanted the people to act on their faith so He could perform the miracle.

God wants us to believe, and He will work on our behalf.

Keep believing, no matter how long you have to wait, and don't be moved only by what you see.

"Father, I want to believe Your Word at all times. Even if You don't give me what I want, I trust that You will give me something even better. Thank You. In Jesus' name. Amen."

A JUDGMENTAL, CRITICAL, AND SUSPICIOUS MIND

Do not judge, or you too will be judged. For in the same way you judge others, you will be judged, and with the measure you use, it will be measured to you. —MATTHEW 7:1-2

Satan loves to put judgmental, critical, suspicious thoughts about other people into our minds. If you do have an opinion about someone, unless it is encouraging, keep it to yourself. Instead of gossiping, pray. How often do you give your opinion when no one has asked for it? I think we all do this to some degree, but at one time, I had a big problem with it. Thankfully, God has helped me to change, and I find that I am much happier now that I tend to withhold my opinion unless someone wants it.

Because we have God's Spirit, we can recognize sinful behavior. Paul told the Galatians to try to bring the sinner to repentance and restoration, but to do so in an attitude of humility and gentleness and to "watch yourselves, or you also may be tempted" (Galatians 6:1). I would never approach anyone about their sin unless I had prayed diligently and truly felt the Lord wanted me to speak with them.

Finding fault with others can cause us to ignore our own problems. I have known people who were very sinful, yet they were very judgmental and critical of others. I finally realized that they viewed and spoke about others so negatively because that kept them from having to face the truth about themselves.

Pray for people to see truth, and be very careful about forming and sharing hasty or premature opinions.

"Father, I don't want to judge people harshly or criticize them. Rather, I want to pray for them. Please help me to believe the best about others, but also to discern when You do want me to see something and deal with it. In Jesus' name. Amen."

THE POWER OF HOPE

May the God of hope fill you with all joy and peace in believing [through the experience of your faith] that by the power of the Holy Spirit you will abound in hope and overflow with confidence in His promises. —ROMANS 15:13 AMP

When you begin to feel downcast or lack peace, ask yourself what you are believing. As long as we believe and trust that all things are possible with God, the hope in our hearts will keep us joyful and peaceful. Hope means to expect something good to happen. So let me ask you: What are you expecting?

We don't always get what we want when we ask God for something, but we can be sure that we will get what is best for us. James writes that we need to view various types of trials and difficulty with joy, knowing that they will eventually work good, godly qualities into our character (James 1:1–4).

When you encounter a problem, it is a great time to remember all the other problems you have had and to think about how God took care of them. Trust Him to do it again.

Keeping your joy is very important, because your joy is your strength (Nehemiah 8:10). Don't let the devil fill you with fear, doubt, and unbelief. Stay full of hope and faith.

"Father, I want to be stable in all situations and never to stop trusting You. Strengthen my faith, and help me always believe Your promises. In Jesus' name. Amen."

THINGS CAN CHANGE

Jabez was more honorable than his brothers. His mother had named him Jabez, saying, "I gave birth to him in pain." Jabez cried out to the God of Israel, "Oh, that you would bless me and enlarge my territory! Let your hand be with me, and keep me from harm so that I will be free from pain." And God granted his request.

—1 CHRONICLES 4:9–10

The fact that his name means "sorrow" and "pain" may indicate that Jabez did not have a very good start in life. But according to today's scripture, he lived honorably, and he prayed an amazing, heartfelt prayer.

The lesson I see in Jabez's story is that our future is not limited by our past or present circumstances. No matter how things started out for you or how they may be right now, they do not have to stay that way.

Bold, faith-filled prayers and a positive attitude can change the course of your life and give you a future that is better than your past and your present. In response to your prayers, God may lead you to make some changes in the way you think, speak, act, work, or relate to others. He may lead you to stop doing certain things and start doing others because He knows those adjustments will get you where you need to go in life.

When you pray bold, life-changing prayers, expect God to answer. But don't expect Him to supernaturally place you on a whole new path to your destiny. Expect that He will lead you to change certain aspects of the way you currently live. As He leads you, follow Him in obedience—and watch things change.

"Father, I pray that You will give me bold prayers that will change my present and my future. As You lead me, help me to obey. In Jesus' name. Amen."

LOVE YOUR ENEMIES

But to you who are listening I say: Love your enemies, do good to those who hate you, bless those who curse you, pray for those who mistreat you. —LUKE 6:27-28

The world we live in is full of people who are filled with hatred, anger, resentment, strife, and bitterness. Most of them have been unjustly treated in some way and have refused to forgive their enemies. Holding on to past offenses only makes them more miserable, but they hold on anyway.

If you are at odds with anyone, I highly recommend that you do yourself a favor and quickly forgive that person. God's Word teaches us the way to peace, and one of those ways is to love our enemies, do good to them, and pray for them. We may not feel like doing so or think it is fair, but if we will obey God, He will be our Vindicator and bring His justice into our lives.

Forgiving people who have hurt you is not a feeling; it is a decision. This decision is easier to make if we believe the best about people. For example, instead of believing they hurt you on purpose, you could believe they were not even aware they wounded you. Another thing that helps is to realize that hurting people hurt people. Stop speaking negatively about those who have hurt you, and begin to pray for them regularly. Soon, your feelings toward them will change.

"Father, I choose to forgive anyone who has hurt me, but I need Your help to do it. Let me remember that You always forgive me and that I should always be ready to quickly forgive others. Amen."

GIVE FROM WHAT GOD'S GIVEN YOU

Each of you must bring a gift in proportion to the way the Lord your God has blessed you. –DEUTERONOMY 16:17

When you think about what the Lord has blessed you with, what comes to mind? Has He given you talents and abilities? Has He given you resources and relationships? Has He given you the ability to make a living? Has He given you health and strength? Has He given you a purpose for your life? Has He given you food to eat and air to breathe and a roof above your head?

Each of us is created as a unique individual, and God gives us everything we need to carry out His good plan for our lives. More importantly, He has given all of us the gift of salvation through His Son. It is not a gift we can earn or deserve. He offers it to us freely because He loves us.

When we consider all that God has given us in light of today's scripture, we need to think about what we can give to others. What can you share with someone else today? How can you help someone in need, wanting nothing in return? Whatever God has given you, give some of it to someone else and give generously. When you do, you'll find that you've lost nothing. In fact, you'll gain even more than you give away.

"Father, help me to see the opportunities to give that are all around me and to give generously. In Jesus' name. Amen."

GOD'S GUIDANCE

I will instruct you and teach you in the way you should go; I will counsel you with my loving eye on you. —PSALM 32:8

God promises to guide and counsel us, but we must turn to Him in order to receive His help. All of God's ways may not make sense to our reasoning, but His ways always work. If you have tried your way and things in your life are not working well, then I highly recommend that you try God's ways. In a relationship with God, stubbornness is not attractive. He wants us to be pliable and moldable in His loving hands, always ready to do as He suggests or asks.

God works at His pace, not ours. It may seem slow, but His timing is perfect. The fact that we think that now is the right time for something doesn't make it true. God always knows best, and He always does the best thing for us if we are willing to wait on Him and not turn to our own ways to try to get Him to answer more quickly.

Have you ever been in a hurry and tried doing your own thing instead of waiting on God? I think we all have, but hopefully we have learned from our experience that waiting on God is always best. I would rather wait longer and end up with the right thing than push my own plan and end up with the wrong thing.

"Father, You have promised to guide and counsel me, and that is what I want. Help me be patient and wait on You for the guidance I need. In Jesus' name. Amen."

WHAT ARE YOU DOING FOR THE LORD?

Then he said to his disciples, "The harvest is plentiful but the workers are few. Ask the Lord of the harvest, therefore, to send out workers into his harvest field." –MATTHEW 9:37-38

Each of us should ask the Lord daily what we can do to serve Him. He works through people. We are His hands, feet, and mouth on the earth. Many people think if they simply go to church once a week, they are serving God. But what God wants is a church—a group of people—who serve Him daily.

When we come into contact with people each day, we can "preach" a sermon through godly behavior, showing love to people, and helping them. We are God's representatives and should live carefully, making sure that we represent Him properly. There are many simple ways to serve God, and if all of us do our part, the Kingdom of God will grow.

Ask God what He wants you to do each day. In addition, pray for other people He wants to use, as today's scripture suggests. God may want you to give something to someone, show kindness, teach His Word, help the poor, volunteer at church or a local shelter, or visit a nursing home. Ask Him to open doors for you to serve Him, and when He does, walk through them boldly, knowing that He will enable you to do what He asks you to do.

"Father, I offer myself to You, to serve You in any way You want me to. Open the right doors for me, and let me help Your kingdom grow. In Jesus' name. Amen."

CHOOSE YOUR ATTITUDE

But many of the older priests and Levites and family heads, who had seen the former temple, wept aloud when they saw the foundation of this temple being laid, while many others shouted for joy. —EZRA 3:12

The scene depicted in Ezra 3:10–12 clearly shows that people can experience the same thing yet respond to it totally differently, based on their attitude.

The rebuilding of the temple in Jerusalem after it had been destroyed was very important to God and to His people. When the foundation of the temple was complete, many of the priests and worship leaders rejoiced and led the people of Israel in praising God. At the same time, there was a group of older people who wept because this temple was not as great as the previous temple. This group looked back with sorrow and regret, stuck in the past. The other group looked ahead to the future with joy and praise.

This story emphasizes to me that we have the freedom and the power to choose how we respond to the circumstances of our lives. We have many opportunities to be sad over things that have been lost. Each of those opportunities is also a chance to be happy in the current situation. The choice is ours.

Let me encourage you today to decide right now that when you must choose between a sad, negative attitude and a happy, positive attitude, you will choose to be optimistic.

The simple act of being positive will help and strengthen you, whatever your circumstances may be.

"Father, help me to look forward to the future with joy instead of wallowing in the past and mourning over what has been lost. In Jesus' name. Amen."

STAND FIRM

But not a hair of your head will perish. Stand firm, and you will win life. —LUKE 21:18-19

We all want to be successful and to be winners in life. God says that the way to do so is to stand firm. Life is not all easy. It includes hard times and challenges we would rather not have to deal with. You may be going through something very difficult right now, but God promises that not even one hair of your head will be harmed.

The trial you are facing will come to an end, and God will work good out of what you have gone through if you trust Him to do so. God is your strength through every difficulty in life. Don't try to struggle through your problems on your own; ask Him to help you with anything that troubles you. He loves you and wants to hear your prayers and requests.

Stand firm in faith, and don't give up or go weak in your mind. Think good thoughts based on Scripture, and be thankful for all that God has done, is doing, and will do in your life. Being thankful increases your joy and moves the hand of God.

"Father, help me stand firm at all times, never giving up. I need Your strength to help me in my life moment by moment. I love You, and I am thankful for Your love for me. In Jesus' name. Amen."

ONLY JESUS

Salvation is found in no one else, for there is no other name under heaven given to mankind by which we must be saved. –ACTS 4:12

Jesus says that in the last days, many false prophets will arise and great deception will cover the earth. Some will even claim to be the Messiah but are not. Jesus is the only name by which we may be saved; there is no other.

False religions and cults often include some truth—and a little error—in their teachings. As Jesus says, "A little leaven leavens the whole lump" (Galatians 5:9 NKJV), meaning that it doesn't take much of a bad thing to ruin a good thing. Don't be fooled into thinking you need anything except faith in Jesus in order to be saved. It is Jesus only, not Jesus plus anything else.

Our works of righteousness do not save us. We are saved by the righteousness that is found in Jesus (Philippians 3:9). Everyone has sinned, and we all come short of the glory of God, but we all are made right with Him through His grace (Romans 3:23–24). We receive His grace through placing our faith in Him alone for salvation. Don't let anyone deceive you by telling you there is another way, because Jesus said, "I am the way, the truth, and the life. No one comes to the Father except through Me" (John 14:6 NKJV).

"Father, I believe that Jesus is the only way to salvation. I ask You to help me not to ever be deceived into believing there is any other way. In Jesus' name. Amen."

HIGHER OBEDIENCE

"The multitude of your sacrifices—what are they to me?" says the Lord. "I have more than enough of burnt offerings, of rams and the fat of fattened animals; I have no pleasure in the blood of bulls and lambs and goats." –ISAIAH 1:11

In today's scripture, God says that His people have obeyed Him with their actions, while indicating that what He really wants is obedience from the heart. True obedience to God is not about legalistically obeying His teachings, but about obeying with a good attitude and pure motives, out of love for Him.

The enemy tries to trap people in legalism, telling them that they must obey God in order for Him to accept them. This is a lie! God loves and accepts us unconditionally, all the time, no matter what. We don't have to do anything to earn His love, but we do have a chance to obey Him as a way of responding to His great love.

We should obey God all the time, whether we want to do it or not, and we are better off when we obey with a good attitude. I want to encourage you today to come up higher in your obedience and to make sure your heart is right toward God in everything you do. Ask Him to give you pure motives, an open heart to hear His voice and know what He would have you do, prompt obedience rooted in love, and the desire to honor Him in your life. A lifestyle of pure-hearted obedience to God always brings blessings.

"Father, help me to obey You not only with my actions but in my heart. In Jesus' name. Amen."

THE HOLY SPIRIT

But the Helper, the Holy Spirit, whom the Father will send in my name, he will teach you all things and bring to your remembrance all that I have said to you. —JOHN 14:26 ESV

Understanding the ministry of the Holy Spirit is very important. He lives in you as a believer in Jesus, and He is your Helper. He wants to help you with everything in your life, but He waits to be invited before getting involved. He also reminds us of truths and lessons God's Word teaches us and brings Scripture verses or passages to our remembrance when we need them to encourage us or give us direction.

The Holy Spirit frequently speaks to us or answers our questions by reminding us of a scripture that speaks to our situation. He is the Spirit of truth, and He teaches us all truth (John 16:13). We can depend on Him to guide us, and our part is to follow His leading.

The Holy Spirit is also our Comforter (John 14:16–17 AMP). What a blessing to have a Comforter living within us, one who can help us navigate the conditions of the world in which we currently live. I think we would be overwhelmed by life's situations if we didn't have Him to help and comfort us. Learn as much about the Holy Spirit as you can, speak with Him often, and thank God regularly for sending His Holy Spirit to be with us until Jesus returns to take us to our heavenly home.

"Father, thank You for the Holy Spirit. I want to follow His guidance and to receive His help and comfort. Help me learn more about Him and enjoy rich fellowship with Him. Amen."

DON'T DREAD

The Lord is my helper; I will not be afraid. —HEBREWS 13:6

Dread is a close relative of fear. It anticipates the future with fear and apprehension. We are tempted to dread many things. We may dread simple daily chores such as getting up in the morning, driving to work in traffic, going to the grocery store, or doing the laundry. But we can just as easily believe we can fulfill these responsibilities with a good attitude, trusting God to give us the grace we need for each one.

Dread not only steals joy; it also steals much-needed energy. We hear people say often, "I dread doing this or that," but this is useless. They must do the task anyway, so why dread it? If we consistently verbalize our dread, our words will defeat us. We will do what we must, but we will be miserable while doing it. If you have given in to the temptation to dread things in the past, now is an opportune time to decide that you will have a happy attitude instead.

We can and should all be thankful that we have something to do, that food is available for us to purchase, and that God gives us the ability and strength to take care of our possessions. Turn the table on the enemy (the devil) by finding the good in everything. Be positive, and think of what you do have, not what you don't have. Make today a happy day by refusing to dread anything.

"Father, help me not to dread the tasks I have to do. Thank You that I am able to do them and that I can ask for Your help, knowing that You are with me in everything I do. In Jesus' name. Amen."

TRADE WORRY FOR TRUST

Do not let your hearts be troubled. You believe in God; believe also in me. —JOHN 14:1

I don't know what you may be dealing with today, but if it tempts you to worry, I encourage you to trade the worry for trust in God. Worry is a useless waste of energy because it never solves our problems. It does do something—such as making us tired, tense, and often grouchy—but it accomplishes nothing good.

God invites us to trust Him, and when we do, He goes to work on our problems. This may sound strange, but you can go ahead and enjoy your life while God works on your problems. If He shows you something you should do, then obey Him and do it. But if there is nothing for you to do, then just rest in Him and enjoy the day He has given to you.

Casting our care on God requires humility. As long as we worry, we think we can do something to solve our problems. But when we come to the end of our self-effort and humble ourselves under God's mighty hand (1 Peter 5:6), He will lift us up and do for us what we could never do for ourselves.

"Father, I am sorry for all the time I have wasted worrying. I know that I cannot solve my own problems, and I ask You to help me not to worry but to trade the worry for trust in You. Thank You. In Jesus' name. Amen."

NO MORE HATE

So I hated life, because the work that is done under the sun was grievous to me. —ECCLESIASTES 2:17

We can learn an important lesson about the words from today's scripture. The writer says that he "hated life." Have you ever heard anyone say that? Have you ever felt that way? To hear that someone hates life is very sad.

Though the phrase *I hate* is common, it is one we would be wise to eliminate from our speech. *Hate* is a strong word and a destructive force. Remember, words are powerful. To hate something fills us with negativity toward that thing, and the negativity can easily seep into our thoughts and words, poisoning other situations as well.

We all face problems and encounter circumstances we do not like. They may be merely unpleasant, or they may be terribly unjust or even tragic. Our negative feelings toward these things may cause us to say, "I hate this!" But by God's grace, we can endure them, and we may even learn valuable lessons from them.

When you face a challenging situation or simply have a bad day, resist saying "I hate." Instead, remind yourself to think and say by faith that you can do all things through Christ, who gives you strength (Philippians 4:13); that God's grace is sufficient for you (2 Corinthians 12:9); and that you are more than a conqueror through Christ because He loves you (Romans 8:37).

"Father, help me to face challenges in Your strength and with a positive attitude. In Jesus' name. Amen."

THE SHOES OF PEACE

Put on the full armor of God...with your feet fitted with the readiness that comes from the gospel of peace. –EPHESIANS 6:13, 15

The devil is our enemy, and he looks to gain entrance into our lives in any possible way. But God has given us armor that we can put on and wear to protect ourselves from evil attacks. The pieces of armor are the belt of truth, the breastplate of righteousness, the shoes of peace, the shield of faith, the helmet of salvation, and the sword of the Spirit, which is the Word of God (Ephesians 6:10–17).

Have you put on your shoes of peace today? In other words, have you decided to walk in peace today, no matter what happens—even the situations that catch you by surprise? You can be ready for anything as long as you remain at peace, trusting God to help you.

Jesus left us a legacy of His peace, a peace that passes all understanding (John 14:27; Philippians 4:7). God is honored when we remain peaceful in the midst of a raging storm of threatening circumstances. It shows that we trust Him to take care of us. Peace is one of the most beautiful qualities we can possess, so be sure to wear your shoes of peace each day, trusting God with all your heart.

"Father, thank You for the shoes of peace. Remind me to put them on daily and trust You to handle the things I can't. In Jesus' name. Amen."

THE PAIN OF REJECTION

As you come to him, a living stone rejected by men but in the sight of God chosen and precious. —1 PETER 2:4 ESV

People who have experienced the pain of being rejected usually try very hard to avoid rejection in the future. But if they are not careful, they may become people-pleasers and end up living their lives to make others happy, while losing the life they are meant to enjoy.

Jesus experienced rejection from His family, His disciples, the religious leaders of His day, and others. But God chose Him, and He was precious to God. The same is true for us. We don't need to fear the rejection of other people, because we have God's acceptance (1 Peter 2:9). He has chosen us and picked us out for Himself. In the Old Testament, Joseph's brothers hated him so much that they sold him to slave traders, but God was with him and gave him great favor everywhere he went (Acts 7:9–10).

Set your mind to please God, and don't be concerned about who rejects you. Because God is for you, it doesn't matter who is against you (Romans 8:31). God is on your side, and He will lift you up and bless your life.

"Thank You, Father, that You accept me, even when people may reject me. Help me always to please You and not care about my popularity with other people. In Jesus' name. Amen."

A POSITIVE ATTITUDE TOWARD DISCIPLINE

You will say, "How I hated discipline! How my heart spurned correction!" —PROVERBS 5:12

The way to grow stronger in any area of life is to discipline ourselves to do what we need to do to gain the strength we desire. Many people dislike the idea of discipline, but there's no doubt that it is the key to success in most endeavors.

The person described in today's scripture had a negative attitude toward discipline. If I had to guess, I would say this person who hated discipline did not enjoy a very successful life. If we have the kind of attitude reflected in Proverbs 5:12, we make disciplining ourselves unpleasant and difficult, and we struggle to do it. A bad attitude toward discipline is self-defeating because it often causes people to stop disciplining themselves in any way.

In contrast, a positive attitude toward discipline makes our efforts to discipline ourselves more effective, and it can even help us enjoy the process. Thinking optimistically about discipline helps us focus more on the result we desire than on the work we need to invest to reach our goals.

Discipline is our friend, not our enemy. It helps us be who we want to be, do what we want to do, and have what we want to enjoy. Make sure your attitude toward discipline is positive, so you can reap the benefits that discipline will bring to your life.

"Father, help me develop a positive attitude about the discipline I need so I can become stronger in the areas in which I need to gain strength. In Jesus' name. Amen."

THE FORGIVENESS OF SIN

Blessed is the one whose transgressions are forgiven, whose sins are covered. Blessed is the one whose sin the Lord does not count against them and in whose spirit is no deceit. –PSALM 32:1–2

Are you feeling guilty or condemned about your sins today? You can admit your sins, repent of them, and receive God's gift of complete forgiveness.

Jesus paid for our sins; He took our punishment and removed the guilt our sins deserved. He promises not only to forgive us but also to remember our sins no more, removing them as far as the east is from the west (Hebrews 10:17; Psalm 103:12).

For a couple of weeks, I have been thinking about the forgiveness that is promised to us. The more I think about it, the more amazed I am at this wonderful gift God makes available to us. It is sad that so many people ask and ask for this forgiveness, yet fail to receive it by faith. They believe their feelings, such as guilt and condemnation, more than they believe God's Word, which is a big mistake.

After you have sincerely repented for any sin, continuing to feel guilty is unnecessary and self-defeating. When Jesus forgives our iniquities and removes them, there is no longer anything to feel guilty about. Satan is the accuser of God's children (Revelation 12:9–10). He accuses us falsely, and we should not listen to his lies. Tell the enemy that your sins are forgiven and that God no longer remembers them. If you persist in speaking this truth, soon your feelings will change.

"Father, thank You so much for the forgiveness of my sins. Your kindness and mercy are beyond comprehension. Jesus, thank You for taking the punishment I deserved and setting me free from guilt. In Jesus' name. Amen."

THE NEED TO KNOW

For with much wisdom comes much sorrow; the more knowledge, the more grief. —ECCLESIASTES 1:18

Have you ever worked to find out a piece of information and, once you succeeded, wished you hadn't discovered it? Being nosy is not a good trait, because the more we know, the more grief we may feel, according to Solomon in today's scripture.

For example, I found out that people were saying unkind things about me, and I really wished that no one had told me about them. It is amazing how happy we can be not knowing certain things, especially things that make us sad or cause us to worry.

Sometimes people say, "I can't give you that information. It is on a need-to-know basis only." Perhaps God wants to work with us this way. He will let us know what we truly need to know, but we would be wise to leave the rest of it alone. Learn to be happy not knowing, and trust God to inform you of things you need to know when the time is right.

"Father, help me to be satisfied to know what I need to know. And help me never to waste my time trying to find out things I don't need to know. Thank You. In Jesus' name. Amen."

SAY WHAT GOD SAYS

But the Lord said to me, "Do not say, 'I am too young.' You must go to everyone I send you to and say whatever I command you."

—JEREMIAH 1:7

Jeremiah made the mistake of telling God he was too young to be a prophet after God had clearly assigned this important role to him (Jeremiah 1:4–6). In today's scripture God corrects Jeremiah. This is one of many biblical examples that teach us to discipline ourselves regarding what we say, especially what we say to God, and to make sure that what we say agrees with His will.

God has a great plan for your life, perhaps a plan you have never thought about or a plan that will seem too big or too challenging for you. But you can be sure that if God thinks you are able to do it and He calls you to do it, then you most definitely can do it. You may need certain skills, training, experience, or relationships to prepare you to answer God's call. If so, He will arrange those things for you.

Let me ask you: What do you believe God is calling you to do? Begin today to agree with what God says about you and your abilities. As He leads you, take a step of obedience to demonstrate that you believe His call, that you trust Him, and that you are confident He will give you everything you need to fulfill His great plan for your life.

"Father, help me to say what You say about me and to believe I can do everything You call me to do. In Jesus' name. Amen."

TALK LESS, LISTEN MORE

Do not be quick with your mouth, do not be hasty in your heart to utter anything before God. God is in heaven and you are on earth, so let your words be few. –ECCLESIASTES 5:2

Throughout Scripture, especially in Proverbs, the Bible's book of wisdom, we read about the folly of talking too much and the wisdom of holding our tongues (Proverbs 10:19; 17:28; 21:23; Matthew 12:36). Sadly, this is often not the case. We speak many words that should be left unsaid, but once they leave our mouth, we cannot get them back. Some may be harmless, but others cause trouble.

In anger, we may speak words that deeply hurt another person. Even after we apologize, the damage is done, and the person who is wounded does not easily forget it. We may commit to do something without thinking it through, and then when the time comes to do it, we have a begrudging attitude or we don't do it at all. These things are not pleasing to God, and they are harmful to relationships.

According to James 3:8, no one can tame the tongue, so we should make our speech a matter of regular prayer. Ask God to let the words of your mouth and the meditation of your heart be acceptable in His sight (Psalm 19:14). Our words are containers for power, so let's make sure they are positive and life-giving.

"Father, I ask You to help me think before I speak and let my words be few. I repent for any verbal commitments I have made and not kept. Thank You for helping me. In Jesus' name. Amen."

A NEW "WANT-TO"

I will give them an undivided heart and put a new spirit in them;
I will remove from them their heart of stone and give them a heart
of flesh. —EZEKIEL 11:19

To be born again means that we accept Jesus as the perfect sacrifice for our sins and receive Him as Lord and Savior. At this time of spiritual new birth, He gives us a new heart and a new spirit. Ezekiel refers to this as "a heart of flesh," and it replaces our old "heart of stone." This new heart is sensitive and responsive to the Lord and eager to please Him.

When God puts a new heart and a new spirit within us, I say that He gives us a new "want-to." This is why, after we become Christians, we find ourselves wanting to do things we have never done before and not wanting to do things we enjoyed before we knew the Lord. We may not live differently overnight after our salvation experience, but over a period of time, our desires and motivations do change. A new heart gives us fresh, godly desires, and a new spirit gives us the ability to accomplish them.

Getting a new heart and new spirit is not a onetime occurrence. As long as we walk with God, He continually renews our desires and our ability to respond to Him. Maybe you sense a fresh, new desire right now. Ask God to show you what He is leading you to do with it, and follow Him in obedience.

"Father, thank You for giving me a new heart and a new 'want-to.'
In Jesus' name. Amen."

CHOOSE TO LOVE

Now I introduce and commend to you our sister Phoebe…that you may receive her in the Lord [with love and hospitality], as God's people ought to receive one another. And that you may help her in whatever matter she may require assistance from you.

—ROMANS 16:1–2 AMP

The amplification of Romans 16:2 indicates that to receive someone "in the Lord" is to extend "love and hospitality" to that person. This is the way Paul asked the believers in Rome to receive Phoebe. At the end of Romans 16:2, he also told them to help her however she needed help.

Love is not something that automatically happens because we are Christians. We must purposefully choose to love others.

Love is not simply a warm feeling toward someone. It goes beyond feelings, and we demonstrate it through the way we treat people. Love is also a decision. Colossians 3:14 tells us to "put on love," which means that loving people is a choice we make. We do it intentionally, whether we feel like it or not.

One way Paul wanted the Roman believers to express love to Phoebe was to help her, but helping people is only one way to show people we love them. Other ways include forgiving them when they hurt us and sincerely wanting the very best for them and praying for them to have it. We can also show love by respecting people, protecting them, and standing up for them if others speak negatively about them.

I hope that today you will choose to love people and express your love in practical ways.

"Father, help me choose to love—intentionally—everyone who comes across my path. In Jesus' name. Amen."

PATIENCE, PLEASE

The end of a matter is better than its beginning, and patience is better than pride. –ECCLESIASTES 7:8

Patient people are happy people because they are able to fully enjoy the present without trying to rush into the future. Those who possess patience are satisfied to know things as they unfold in their proper timing. Being patient eliminates a lot of stress from our lives, while being anxious adds stress.

Good things almost always take time to develop. Things that arise quickly are often fragile and don't last long, but those that develop slowly are more solid and enduring. In our greedy quest for more and more, we often sacrifice quality for quantity. Producing a quality product or doing a quality job takes time and patience, whereas something that looks good but won't last long can be done quickly.

The only way we can enjoy every moment that God gives us is to be patient. Don't rush through the moments in your life, because if you do, you will miss some very important things. Sometimes missing a small detail can cause a big problem. Rushing through a project is often useless, because it ends up taking more time than we planned. Then, we have to fix the problems that hurry created. As the saying goes, "Haste makes waste."

"Father, help me learn to live in the moment and thoroughly enjoy it rather than rushing through life and being impatient. In Jesus' name. Amen."

KEEP TRUSTING GOD

Those who know your name trust in you, for you, Lord, have never forsaken those who seek you. —PSALM 9:10

You may remember the story of King Jehoshaphat and the great battle he faced against Moab and Ammon, enemies of God's people who had an enormous army. The story is in 2 Chronicles 20. The situation looked impossible, but Jehoshaphat led his people to humble themselves, seek the Lord, trust Him to fight for them, and praise and worship God. Some people, however, seemed to need encouragement to keep going (v. 20). So he told them to have faith and then appointed a specific group of people to sing and continue worshipping God (v. 21).

Are you in a place where you need encouragement to keep trusting and to keep worshipping God? Are you discouraged? Have you been praying and asking God to do something for so long that you now wonder if He will ever do it? I want to encourage you as Jehoshaphat encouraged God's people. Keep trusting God. Keep worshipping. When the people did this, God began to move supernaturally to bring them a miraculous victory.

In addition, keep praying, and stay in God's Word. Keep your heart and mind encouraged by meditating on scriptures that give you hope and remind you of God's power and goodness. God always wins, and as long as you continue to trust Him, you win too.

"Father, no matter how my situation looks right now, give me grace and strength to keep trusting You. In Jesus' name. Amen."

CREATED IN THE IMAGE OF GOD

So God created mankind in his own image, in the image of God he created them; male and female he created them. —GENESIS 1:27

Believing we are created in the image of God is very important. It gives us a sense of worth and value, which we all need in order to live happy, fulfilling lives. This is one reason I think the theory of evolution is dangerous. It teaches that human beings evolved from apes, and I fail to see how that image assigns true value to us. If all I am is an animal, then why not act like one?

The world is filled with insecure people who look for value in all the wrong places. If they only knew that they are created in the image of God, with His own hand—carefully, intricately, and for a purpose—they would find security in knowing He loves them and that they belong to Him.

In addition to being created in the image of God, when we are born again (receive Jesus as our Lord and Savior) we receive a new nature, His nature. God equips us to be all that He wants us to be, and all we need to do is believe it and act accordingly. You have infinite worth and value, and you are greatly loved.

"Father, thank You for creating me in Your image. What a great privilege it is to have the ability to emulate You and display Your nature to the world. I am Your ambassador, and I pray You will help me represent You well. In Jesus' name. Amen."

STAND STRONG FOR RIGHTEOUSNESS

And Nebuchadnezzar said to them, "Is it true, Shadrach, Meshach and Abednego, that you do not serve my gods or worship the image of gold I have set up?" –DANIEL 3:14

King Nebuchadnezzar of Babylon wanted three young Hebrew men—Shadrach, Meshach, and Abednego—to worship his gods and a golden image he had set up. They refused, because to do so would be disobedient to God. Nebuchadnezzar became so angry that he threatened to throw them into a fiery furnace and kill them.

They were not intimidated. In fact, they said, "If we are thrown into the blazing furnace, the God we serve is able to deliver us from it, and he will deliver us from Your Majesty's hand. But even if he does not, we want you to know, Your Majesty, that we will not serve your gods or worship the image of gold you have set up" (Daniel 3:17–18).

Because they did not back down, Nebuchadnezzar did throw the young men into the furnace, and God did deliver them, just as they had said. The three young men stood strong for righteousness in the face of a terrible threat. Many times, people cower in the face of threats and intimidation. They are afraid of the consequences they will face if they obey God and stand up for what is right.

I encourage you to live with a reverential fear and respect of the Lord, determined to honor Him at all times and to trust Him in every situation. Refuse to compromise, don't

be intimidated, and stand strong for righteousness, knowing that God never fails.

*"Father, help me to stand strong for righteousness and remain loyal
to You in every situation. In Jesus' name. Amen."*

DO YOU WANT TO LOVE LIFE?

Whoever would love life and see good days must keep their tongue from evil and their lips from deceitful speech. They must turn from evil and do good; they must seek peace and pursue it. —1 PETER 3:10-11

In today's scripture, Peter offers simple, succinct advice to anyone who wants to enjoy life. We could summarize his advice by saying: Speak well and speak truth, do good, and seek peace intentionally. I want to focus today's devotion on the importance of our words.

We can enjoy life even under difficult circumstances if we keep our tongue from evil. We may think we do not speak evil because we do not say things that are blatantly horrible or mean or frightening. But to keep from speaking evil, we also need to refrain from speaking negatively, complaining, spewing anger, and gossiping. When 1 Peter 3:10 says we should keep our lips from speaking deceit, it means more than simply not telling harmful lies. It means that we should not use our words to spin a story or a situation to make it appear one way when it really happened another way.

Our words have a tremendous impact on us and on the people around us. We can use them to encourage—or to discourage—ourselves and others. Our words can make us stronger or weaker, and they can impact others similarly.

I encourage you to pay attention to the words you speak

today, knowing that they are very important in determining whether you love life and enjoy good days or not.

"Father, help me to use my words in positive, truthful ways, so I may love life and see good days. In Jesus' name. Amen."

NEVER ALONE

God is with you in everything you do. –GENESIS 21:22

How awesome is it to think that God is with you in everything you do? Thinking about what this really means is amazing. We are never alone, never without help, never without someone to talk to, and never without guidance.

Loneliness is a widespread problem in our society. We can even be with people and still feel lonely if we feel misunderstood or unaccepted, but God understands us and accepts us because we are in Christ. Thinking about this makes me feel safe and cared for. Hopefully it makes you feel that way too.

Immanuel is one of Christ's names, and it means "God with us." We are God's home, and He is our home. If we abide in Him, we can ask what we will and He will do it, and when we abide in Him, we will bear much good fruit (John 15:7–8). As you go about your day today, think and whisper to yourself, "God is with me."

"Father, I am amazed to know that You are with me in whatever I do. Help me keep this wonderful truth in mind and enjoy good fellowship with You all throughout this day and night. In Jesus' name. Amen."

STOP DILUTING YOUR JOY

I say these things while I am still in the world, so that My joy may be made full and complete and perfect in them [that they may experience My delight fulfilled in them, that My enjoyment may be perfected in their own souls, that they may have My gladness within them, filling their hearts]. —JOHN 17:13 AMPC

We have joy, but we will not experience it fully unless we stop doing things that dilute or hinder it. The devil tries to make us joyless, but we do not have to let him succeed. Here are five simple ways to keep your joy today.

First, remember that your thoughts are very important. Don't worry, fret, or be anxious about the future. Instead of reasoning, which leads to confusion, trust God.

Second, don't become entangled or meddle in other people's business. We all have enough to attend to, and we should not waste our time in situations that do not concern us. Learn to pick your battles, and don't make a big deal out of little things.

Third, learn to forgive quickly for your own sake. And when you sin, be quick to repent and don't waste time feeling guilty about something God has forgiven and forgotten.

Fourth, be positive in your thoughts, words, and attitudes—and your joy will overflow.

Finally, live one day at a time. God gives us grace for each day, but not until that day comes, so go ahead and enjoy today fully.

"Father, I'm sorry for the joyless days I have spent because of wrong thoughts and attitudes. Forgive me, and teach me how to experience full joy in You. Thank You. In Jesus' name. Amen."

HOPE AGAIN

There I will give her back her vineyards, and will make the Valley of Achor a door of hope. There she will respond as in the days of her youth, as in the day she came up out of Egypt. –HOSEA 2:15

Hosea's prophecy focuses on God's desire to restore unfaithful Israel to Himself. In today's scripture, the Valley of Achor represents a place of trouble. God is saying in this verse that He will turn Israel's trouble into hope. He will do the same for you and me.

As I have said many times, hope is the confident expectation that something good will happen. It leaves no room for the idea that something bad might happen. We develop and maintain hope through the way we think. If we think about possibilities instead of problems, hope takes root and grows in our minds.

What situation has been a Valley of Achor in your life? What was—or is—your place of trouble? Did that circumstance make you reluctant to hope again? Did you face disappointment or pain there to the point that you now live with very little hope because you do not want to be hurt or disappointed again?

Let me encourage you to be willing to hope again. Choose to believe that God will do something good in your situation and in your life. Gather your strength and determine that you will trust Him and that you will begin to live at a whole new level of hope.

"Father, no matter how I have been disappointed or how much trouble I have been through, help me to hope again. Amen."

GROWING IN SPIRITUAL MATURITY

You, therefore, must be perfect [growing into complete maturity of godliness in mind and character, having reached the proper height of virtue and integrity], as your heavenly Father is perfect.

—MATTHEW 5:48 AMPC

We can have a perfect heart toward God and not demonstrate perfect behavior. People with a perfect heart want to be all God wants them to be, and they cooperate with the work of the Holy Spirit in their lives as He changes them. They love God's Word and desire to be obedient to Him. They love Jesus with all their heart, soul, mind, and strength, and when they do sin, it saddens them and they repent immediately.

God has begun a good work in us and promised to complete it (Philippians 1:6). He works in us gradually as we continue in His Word and in fellowship with Him. He changes us little by little.

As God works in you, celebrate your progress and don't let yourself be overly concerned about how far you still have to go. The good news is that you are on your way. Each day you grow spiritually, even though you may not see the changes that are taking place.

Be patient with God's work in you, and be patient with yourself. There are no overnight successes. If at first you don't succeed at something, you are normal. The key is to never give up. Keep pressing toward victory, letting go of what lies behind you.

"Father, thank You for the work You are doing in me. I love You very much and I want to be all You want me to be. I trust that You are working in me each day, and I celebrate my progress. In Jesus' name. Amen."

GUIDED BY GOD'S WORD

Your word is a lamp for my feet, a light on my path. —PSALM 119:105

People who don't have knowledge of God's Word walk in darkness and have no proper guidance in their lives. They may have a plan for their lives and be working that plan. It may even appear to benefit them, but they are rarely peaceful and filled with joy.

God's Word gives us a plan for our lives—a plan that will bring not only success but also peace and joy. However, we must follow the plan God gives us, or it will be useless. God teaches us to meditate on His Word day and night and to be "careful to do everything written in it"; then we will be "prosperous and successful" (Joshua 1:8).

God's Word not only gives us knowledge; it also gives us strength to do what God instructs us to do. When you spend time studying God's Word or in prayer and fellowship with God, you receive strength spiritually and physically. God enables us to do whatever we need to do in life as we put Him first in all things.

Apart from Him we can do nothing (John 15:5), but through Him, we can do all things (Philippians 4:13).

"Father, strengthen me through Your Word and through my time with You. I need You, and I look to Your Word to give me light and direction in my daily life. In Jesus' name. Amen."

HOW IS YOUR HEART HEALTH?

But the Lord said to Samuel, "Do not consider his appearance or his height, for I have rejected him. The Lord does not look at the things people look at. People look at the outward appearance, but the Lord looks at the heart." –1 SAMUEL 16:7

It is important to examine our hearts and make sure that everything inside of us is in line with God's will. We spend a great deal of time on our appearance, and experience stress over what people think of us, but what is inside of us—the hidden person of the heart—is more important to God than the outside.

Even though David did not appear to be the right choice for a future king, God chose him because David had a heart after God (1 Samuel 13:14; Acts 13:22). Paul told the Corinthians that God chooses the weak and "foolish things of the world to confound the wise" (1 Corinthians 1:27 KJV), so human beings cannot take glory for themselves.

God has chosen you for a special purpose. I urge you to follow His guidance and do all He asks you to do with your whole heart. He may choose you to encourage others, or to be in business and make money to support the spread of the gospel, or to be a helper or a great orator.

It doesn't matter what God guides us to do as long as we do it. God isn't looking for natural talent; He is searching for those whose hearts are right toward Him.

"Father, I want You to use me according to Your plan for my life. Help me surrender fully to Your will. If anything in me is not pleasing to You, please show me what it is. In Jesus' name. Amen."

CARE WITHOUT FEELING CONDEMNED

What shall we say, then? Shall we go on sinning so that grace may increase? By no means! We are those who have died to sin; how can we live in it any longer? –ROMANS 6:1-2

As true Christians, we cannot sin and then ignore it. We cannot fail to care that we have disobeyed God. We know that sin offends Him and separates us from Him, so we will not disregard our sinful behavior. However, there is a difference between caring about the fact that we sin and feeling condemned because of it.

I want you to understand today that feelings of guilt and condemnation will steal your joy and your inner strength, and they will hinder you from fulfilling God's purpose for your life. God does not want you to obsess over every mistake you make or to beat yourself up when you sin. According to Romans 3:23, everyone sins. So you will sin at times.

Learning to deal with your sin appropriately is most important. Jesus shed His blood on the cross as payment in full for all of your sin—past, present, and future. He makes total forgiveness possible, and all you have to do is repent of your sin and receive His forgiveness. He wants you free and strong, and He knows that forgiveness will help you live that way, so don't wallow in guilt and condemnation when you sin. Simply repent, accept His forgiveness, and keep moving forward with Him.

"Father, I want to remain sensitive, to care about the fact that I sin sometimes, and to be quick to repent. But because of Jesus' work on the cross, I will no longer feel condemned. Amen."

NO REGRETS

Until the day Samuel died, he did not go to see Saul again, though Samuel mourned for him. And the Lord regretted that he had made Saul king over Israel. —1 SAMUEL 15:35

The story of Saul is sad because God trusted him with the great honor of being Israel's first king and he failed miserably. He had several problems, but the biggest was disobedience. He was also a people-pleaser instead of a God-pleaser, and he was jealous of anyone he feared might get ahead of him. In short, his heart was not right.

It saddens me to read that God regretted making Saul king. I don't ever want the Lord to say He regrets anything He entrusts to me, and I'm sure you feel the same way. Each day, we must do what we believe pleases God and never allow the fear of other people to cause us to sin. When we stand before God at the end of our lives on earth, I am sure we want to hear, "Well done, good and faithful servant! You have been faithful with a few things; I will put you in charge of many things. Come and share your master's happiness" (Matthew 25:23).

At the end of my life, I don't want to have any regrets. I don't want to give God a reason to have regrets either. Let's commit to do everything we do in the most excellent way we can do it, always behaving in ways we believe will glorify God.

"Father, I am sorry if I have given You reason to regret anything concerning me. Help me live for You and always put a smile on Your face with my behavior and my choices. In Jesus' name. Amen."

STAND FIRM

Therefore, my dear brothers and sisters, stand firm. Let nothing move you. Always give yourselves fully to the work of the Lord, because you know that your labor in the Lord is not in vain.

—1 CORINTHIANS 15:58

Many believers feel called to do certain things to serve God or to help other people. They may be called to ministry as a profession, or they may also be called to honor God and help others in various other professions or in ways that do not involve a career. They try to do what they believe they should do but find that the right opportunities never come along for them. Doors that need to open for them seem to stay shut.

I believe one reason this happens to people is that they are able but not stable. In other words, they have the skills and gifts they need, but they do not have the maturity, character, or emotional stability that will be required to do what they feel called to do.

In today's scripture, Paul urges the Corinthians to "stand firm" and to "let nothing move" them. This means they are to be strong and to remain committed to what they know is right and to refuse to allow difficulties or perplexities to make them doubt their calling or stray from what they need to do.

If you are eager to serve God and others but feel you keep running into roadblocks, you should ask God to help you stand firm and to let nothing move you. He wants you to fulfill His call on your life and to enjoy doing it.

"Father, help me stand firm and not allow anything to move me as I seek to serve You and help other people. In Jesus' name. Amen."

JUDGE NOT

Why do you look at the speck of sawdust in your brother's eye and pay no attention to the plank in your own eye? –MATTHEW 7:3

Our society is in desperate need of genuine love, but we will never reach that ideal until we stop judging one another. We should pray for people instead of judging them, while also keeping an attentive eye on ourselves. Many times, our faults are greater than those we judge in other people. God is merciful, and He expects us to let the mercy He gives each of us to flow through us to others who need it.

We are not blind to people's sin and faults, but the fact is that they are God's servants, and He has not given us the ministry of criticism or faultfinding. There is a time to confront those whose behavior is immoral, but we should do so with a humble attitude, remembering that we ourselves have our own shortcomings.

Do certain people frustrate or irritate you on a regular basis? Perhaps God has placed them in your life as a test, just to see how you will treat them. If we let those who irritate us help us practice love, kindness, and mercy, they can become a help and benefit to us. Only when we are tested do we grow spiritually.

"Father, when You send people into my life who are difficult for me to deal with, help me treat them the way You would. Help me look at myself before I criticize anyone else. In Jesus' name. Amen."

SEEK GOD'S STRENGTH

Seek the Lord and his strength; seek his presence continually!

—1 CHRONICLES 16:11 ESV

The apostle James writes, "You do not have, because you do not ask" (James 4:2 ESV). It is sad to think about how often we struggle in our own effort and strength to get a job done or to endure a difficult time. As we struggle, we wonder where God's strength is, but we forget that we have not asked for it. John said, "Ask, and you will receive, that your joy may be full" (John 16:24 NKJV).

Many are the days I have spent with a headache and then realized about six p.m. that I had not once asked Jesus to heal me. There is so much more available to us than we take advantage of because we simply fail to ask for it. We cannot assume that God will help us; He wants us to ask. Asking is polite; assuming is rude and often the fruit of pride.

Ask God each and every morning to strengthen you for whatever you know you have to do and for the unexpected things that may arise. Don't ask only for the strength to get through them, but ask for the strength to behave as Jesus would in the same situation.

We are God's representatives on earth, so let's do our best to represent Him well.

"Father, forgive me for assuming and presuming on Your help and Your goodness. I pray that You would remind me to ask You to help me in everything I do. In Jesus' name. Amen."

DEAL WITH LIFE ONE DAY AT A TIME

Therefore do not worry about tomorrow, for tomorrow will worry about itself. Each day has enough trouble of its own. —MATTHEW 6:34

I don't know about you, but I definitely need God's strength in order not to worry, especially about areas in which I feel weak. Maybe you also need help to keep from worrying in certain areas of your life, such as with your children, your money, or what people think of you. No matter how you struggle with worry, you can overcome it, but only with God's strength. You cannot do it on your own.

Worry is useless. It does no good at all. I know this, but it doesn't always keep me from worrying. Sometimes I get my Bible and look at today's scripture and a few others on worry. Then I read and reread them until the worry begins to fade away. What we focus on is what becomes largest in our minds, and worrying is focusing on a problem we cannot solve. But if we cast our care and anxiety on God, He will take care of us (1 Peter 5:7).

My husband Dave's formula for peace is always to do what he can do and then cast his care on God. Because of this, he enjoys a peaceful and joy-filled life. Our daughter Laura is a lot like her dad, and she says in times of difficulty, "It is what it is, and I will deal with it one day at a time."

"Father, thank You for granting me strength not to worry about anything. Let me take life one day at a time, trusting You every moment. Thank You. In Jesus' name. Amen."

THE POWER OF BEING THANKFUL

Always giving thanks to God the Father for everything, in the name of our Lord Jesus Christ. —EPHESIANS 5:20

I know a man whose goal is to be the most thankful person on earth. What a wonderful aspiration! I think everyone should have this as one of their goals in life. I've been thinking a lot lately about being thankful. The Bible instructs us hundreds of times in different ways to be thankful and say so and to give thanks at all times, in all circumstances (Psalm 107:1–2; Ephesians 5:20; 1 Thessalonians 5:18). Does this mean that we thank God for our problems? No, but it does mean to thank God in the midst of them.

If we thank God for what we do have, we won't notice what we don't have so much. If we complain about what we already have, why should God give us more? We would only complain about that too. One reason there is power in being thankful is that it keeps our eyes off ourselves and on the Lord or others. There may be multiple people in our lives who have repeatedly done kind things for us for which we have never thanked them.

Have you ever thanked the people who haul your trash away, or the crew who keeps your office building clean? What about your parents? Have you thanked them for the time, effort, and money they spent raising you? And, above all, what about the Lord? Do you thank Him multiple times a day for all His goodness in your life? Let's join together in being more thankful than ever, and we will see a new power and strength added to our lives.

"Father, thank You for Your goodness to me. I'm sorry for all the times I have not even noticed how much You do for me. I'm also sorry that I haven't been more thankful toward the people You have placed in my life to help me and do things for me. I want to be the most thankful person in the world! In Jesus' name. Amen."

Do you have a real relationship with Jesus?

God loves you! He created you to be a special, unique, one-of-a-kind individual, and He has a specific purpose and plan for your life. And through a personal relationship with your Creator—God—you can discover a way of life that will truly satisfy your soul.

No matter who you are, what you've done, or where you are in your life right now, God's love and grace are greater than your sin—your mistakes. Jesus willingly gave His life so you can receive forgiveness from God and have new life in Him. He's just waiting for you to invite Him to be your Savior and Lord.

If you are ready to commit your life to Jesus and follow Him, all you have to do is ask Him to forgive your sins and give you a fresh start in the life you are meant to live. Begin by praying this prayer . . .

Lord Jesus, thank You for giving Your life for me and forgiving me of my sins so I can have a personal relationship with You. I am sincerely sorry for the mistakes I've made, and I know I need You to help me live right.

*Your Word says in Romans 10:9, "If you declare
with your mouth, 'Jesus is Lord,' and believe in your
heart that God raised him from the dead, you will be
saved" (NIV). I believe You are the Son of God
and confess You as my Savior and Lord. Take me just
as I am, and work in my heart, making me the person
You want me to be. I want to live for You, Jesus,
and I am so grateful that You are giving me
a fresh start in my new life with You today.
I love You, Jesus!*

It's so amazing to know that God loves us so much! He wants to have a deep, intimate relationship with us that grows every day as we spend time with Him in prayer and Bible study. And we want to encourage you in your new life in Christ.

Please visit joycemeyer.org/salvation to request Joyce's book *A New Way of Living*, which is our gift to you. We also have other free resources online to help you make progress in pursuing everything God has for you.

Congratulations on your fresh start in your life in Christ! We hope to hear from you soon.

ABOUT THE AUTHOR

Joyce Meyer is one of the world's leading practical Bible teachers. A *New York Times* bestselling author, Joyce's books have helped millions of people find hope and restoration through Jesus Christ. Joyce's programs, *Enjoying Everyday Life* and *Everyday Answers with Joyce Meyer,* air around the world on television, radio, and the Internet. Through Joyce Meyer Ministries, Joyce teaches internationally on a number of topics with a particular focus on how the Word of God applies to our everyday lives. Her candid communication style allows her to share openly and practically about her experiences so others can apply what she has learned to their lives.

Joyce has authored more than one hundred books, which have been translated into more than one hundred languages, and over 65 million of her books have been distributed worldwide. Bestsellers include *Power Thoughts*; *The Confident Woman*; *Look Great, Feel Great*; *Starting Your Day Right*; *Ending Your Day Right*; *Approval Addiction*; *How to Hear from God*; *Beauty for Ashes*; and *Battlefield of the Mind*.

Joyce's passion to help hurting people is foundational to the vision of Hand of Hope, the missions arm of Joyce Meyer Ministries. Hand of Hope provides worldwide humanitarian outreaches such as feeding programs, medical care, orphanages, disaster response, human trafficking intervention and rehabilitation, and much more—always sharing the love and gospel of Christ.

JOYCE MEYER MINISTRIES

U.S. & FOREIGN OFFICE ADDRESSES

Joyce Meyer Ministries
P.O. Box 655
Fenton, MO 63026
USA
(636) 349-0303

Joyce Meyer Ministries—Canada
P.O. Box 7700
Vancouver, BC V6B 4E2
Canada
(800) 868-1002

Joyce Meyer Ministries—Australia
Locked Bag 77
Mansfield Delivery Centre
Queensland 4122
Australia
(07) 3349 1200

Joyce Meyer Ministries—England
P.O. Box 1549
Windsor SL4 1GT
United Kingdom
01753 831102

Joyce Meyer Ministries—South Africa
P.O. Box 5
Cape Town 8000
South Africa
(27) 21-701-1056

Joyce Meyer Ministries—Francophonie
29 avenue Maurice Chevalier
77330 Ozoir la Ferriere
France

Joyce Meyer Ministries—Germany
Postfach 761001
22060 Hamburg
Germany
+49 (0)40 / 88 88 4 11 11

Joyce Meyer Ministries—Netherlands
Lorenzlaan 14
7002 HB Doetinchem
+31 657 555 9789

Joyce Meyer Ministries—Russia
P.O. Box 789
Moscow 101000
Russia
+7 (495) 727-14-68

OTHER BOOKS BY JOYCE MEYER

JOYCE MEYER SPANISH TITLES

La Dosis de Aprobación
(The Approval Fix)
Efesios: Comentario Bíblico
(Ephesians: Biblical Commentary)
Empezando Tu Día Bien
(Starting Your Day Right)
Hágalo con Miedo (Do It Afraid)
Hazte un Favor a Ti Mismo…
Perdona (Do Yourself a Favor…
Forgive)
Madre Segura de Sí Misma
(The Confident Mom)
Momentos de Quietud con Dios
(Quiet Times with God Devotional)
Pensamientos de Poder
(Power Thoughts)
Sanidad para el Alma de una Mujer
(Healing the Soul of a Woman)
Santiago: Comentario Bíblico (James:
Biblical Commentary)
Sobrecarga (Overload)*
Sus Batallas Son del Señor
(Your Battles Belong to the Lord)
Termina Bien Tu Día
(Ending Your Day Right)
Usted Puede Comenzar de Nuevo
(You Can Begin Again)
Viva Valientemente
(Living Courageously)

BOOKS BY DAVE MEYER

Life Lines

* Study Guide available for these titles